TREATING
ANXIETY DISORDERS

THE JOSSEY-BASS LIBRARY OF CURRENT CLINICAL TECHNIQUE

IRVIN D. YALOM, GENERAL EDITOR

NOW AVAILABLE

Treating Alcoholism
Stephanie Brown, Editor

Treating Schizophrenia
Sophia Vinogradov, Editor

Treating Women Molested in Childhood
Catherine Classen, Editor

Treating Depression
Ira D. Glick, Editor

Treating Eating Disorders
Joellen Werne, Editor

Treating Dissociative Identity Disorder
James L. Spira, Editor

Treating Couples
Hilda Kessler, Editor

Treating Adolescents
Hans Steiner, Editor

Treating the Elderly
Javaid I. Sheikh, Editor

Treating Sexual Disorders
Randolph S. Charlton, Editor

Treating Difficult Personality Disorders
Michael Rosenbluth, Editor

Treating Anxiety Disorders
Walton T. Roth, Editor

Treating the Psychological Consequences of HIV
Michael F. O'Connor, Editor

FORTHCOMING

Treating Children
Hans Steiner, Editor

TREATING ANXIETY DISORDERS

**A VOLUME IN THE JOSSEY-BASS
LIBRARY OF CURRENT CLINICAL TECHNIQUE**

Walton T. Roth, EDITOR

Irvin D. Yalom, GENERAL EDITOR

Jossey-Bass Publishers • San Francisco

Substantial discounts on bulk quantities of Jossey-Bass books are available to corporations, professional associations, and other organizations. For details and discount information, contact the special sales department at Jossey-Bass Inc., Publishers (415) 433–1740; Fax (800) 605–2665.

For sales outside the United States, please contact your local Simon & Schuster International Office.

Jossey-Bass Web address: http://www.josseybass.com

Manufactured in the United States of America on Lyons Falls Turin Book. This paper is acid-free and 100 percent totally chlorine-free.

Library of Congress Cataloging-in-Publication Data

Treating anxiety disorders/Walton T. Roth, editor; Irvin D. Yalom, general editor—1st ed.
    p.   cm.—(The Jossey-Bass library of current clinical technique)
Includes bibliographical references and index.
ISBN 0-7879-0316-7 (alk. paper)
1. Anxiety—Treatment. I. Roth, Walton T. II. Yalom, Irvin D., date. III. Series.
[DNLM: 1. Anxiety Disorders—therapy. WM 172 T7836 1997]
RC531.T67 1997
616.85'22306—dc20
DNLM/DLC
for Library of Congress
96-28708
CIP

FIRST EDITION
PB Printing 10 9 8 7 6 5 4 3 2

CONTENTS

FOREWORD

At a recent meeting of clinical practitioners, a senior practitioner declared that more change had occurred in his practice of psychotherapy in the past year than in the twenty preceding years. Nodding assent, the others all agreed.

And was that a good thing for their practice? A resounding "No!" Again, unanimous concurrence—too much interference from managed care; too much bureaucracy; too much paper work; too many limits set on fees, length, and format of therapy; too much competition from new psychotherapy professions.

Were these changes a good or a bad thing for the general public? Less unanimity on this question. Some pointed to recent positive developments. Psychotherapy was becoming more mainstream, more available, and more acceptable to larger segments of the American public. It was being subjected to closer scrutiny and accountability—uncomfortable for the practitioner but, if done properly, of potential benefit to the quality and efficiency of behavioral health care delivery.

But without dissent this discussion group agreed—and every aggregate of therapists would concur—that astounding changes are looming for our profession: changes in the reasons that clients request therapy; changes in the perception and practice of mental health care; changes in therapeutic theory and technique; and changes in the training, certification, and supervision of professional therapists.

From the perspective of the clientele, several important currents are apparent. A major development is the de-stigmatization of psychotherapy. No longer is psychotherapy invariably a hush-hush affair, laced with shame and conducted in offices with separate entrance and exit doors to prevent the uncomfortable possibility of clients meeting one another.

Today such shame and secrecy have been exploded. Television talk shows—Oprah, Geraldo, Donahue—have normalized psychopathology and psychotherapy by presenting a continuous public parade of dysfunctional human situations: hardly a day passes without television fare of confessions and audience interactions with deadbeat fathers, sex addicts, adult children of alcoholics, battering husbands and abused wives, drug dealers and substance abusers, food bingers and purgers, thieving children, abusing parents, victimized children suing parents.

The implications of such de-stigmatization have not been lost on professionals who no longer concentrate their efforts on the increasingly elusive analytically suitable neurotic patient. Clinics everywhere are dealing with a far broader spectrum of problem areas and must be prepared to offer help to substance abusers and their families, to patients with a wide variety of eating disorders, adult survivors of incest, victims and perpetrators of domestic abuse. No longer do trauma victims or substance abusers furtively seek counseling. Public awareness of the noxious long-term effects of trauma has been so sensitized that there is an increasing call for public counseling facilities and a growing demand, as well, for adequate counseling provisions in health care plans.

The mental health profession is changing as well. No longer is there such automatic adoration of lengthy "depth" psychotherapy where "deep" or "profound" is equated with a focus on the earliest years of the patient's life. The contemporary field is more pluralistic: many diverse approaches have proven therapeutically effective and the therapist of today is more apt to tailor the therapy to fit the particular clinical needs of each patient.

In past years there was an unproductive emphasis on territoriality and on the maintaining of hierarchy and status—with the more prestigious professions like psychiatry and doctoral-level psychology expending considerable energy toward excluding master's level therapists. But those battles belong more to the psychotherapists of yesterday; today there is a significant shift toward a more collaborative interdisciplinary climate.

Managed care and cost containment is driving some of these changes. The role of the psychiatrist has been particularly affected as cost efficiency has decreed that psychiatrists will less frequently deliver psychotherapy personally but, instead, limit their activities to supervision and to psychopharmacological treatment.

In its efforts to contain costs, managed care has asked therapists to deliver a briefer, focused therapy. But gradually managed care is realizing that the bulk of mental health treatment cost is consumed by inpatient care and that outpatient treatment, even long-term therapy, is not only salubrious for the patient but far less costly. Another looming change is that the field is turning more frequently toward the group therapies. How much longer can we ignore the many comparative research studies demonstrating that the group therapy format is equally or more effective than higher cost individual therapies?

Some of these cost-driven edicts may prove to be good for the patients; but many of the changes that issue from medical model mimicry—for example, efforts at extreme brevity and overly precise treatment plans and goals that are inappropriate to the therapy endeavor and provide only the illusion of efficiency—can hamper the therapeutic work. Consequently, it is of paramount importance that therapists gain control of their field and that managed care administrators not be permitted to dictate how psychotherapy or, for that matter, any other form of health care be conducted. That is one of the goals of this series of texts: to provide mental health professionals with such a deep grounding in theory and such a clear vision of effective therapeutic technique that they will be empowered to fight confidently for the highest standards of patient care.

The Jossey-Bass Library of Current Clinical Technique is directed and dedicated to the front-line therapist—to master's and doctoral-level clinicians who personally provide the great bulk of mental health care. The purpose of this entire series is to offer state-of-the-art instruction in treatment techniques for the most commonly encountered clinical conditions. Each volume offers a focused theoretical background as a foundation for practice and then dedicates itself to the practical task of what to do for the patient—how to assess, diagnose, and treat.

I have selected volume editors who are either nationally recognized experts or are rising young stars. In either case, they possess a comprehensive view of their specialty field and have selected leading therapists of a variety of persuasions to describe their therapeutic approaches.

Although all the contributors have incorporated the most recent and relevant clinical research in their chapters, the emphasis in these volumes is on the practical technique of therapy. We shall offer specific therapeutic guidelines, and augment concrete suggestions with the liberal use of clinical vignettes and detailed case histories. Our intention is not to impress or to awe the reader, and not to add footnotes to arcane academic debates. Instead, each chapter is designed to communicate guidelines of immediate pragmatic value to the practicing clinician. In fact, the general editor, the volume editors, and the chapter contributors have all accepted our assignments for that very reason: a rare opportunity to make a significant, immediate, and concrete contribution to the lives of our patients.

Irvin D. Yalom, M.D.
Professor Emeritus of Psychiatry
Stanford University

INTRODUCTION

Walton T. Roth

Anxiety as a human problem has existed as long as there have been humans, so it is hard to believe that anything new can be said about it. Yet from the perspective of treatment professionals, in the last few decades much has changed. Some of you may have done clinical work long enough to realize that such diagnoses as panic disorder and social phobia were not made until about fifteen years ago.

The third edition of the American Psychiatric Association's *Diagnostic and Statistical Manual of Mental Disorders* (*DSM-III*), published in 1980, signaled (and subsequently caused) a profound change in thinking about anxiety disorders. Before that, labeling abrupt episodes of anxiety, excessive shyness, persistent worrying, and fears of spiders (for example) as distinct mental disorders would have seemed like the height of naïveté, a throwback to a pseudoscientific psychiatry of the nineteenth century. This opinion was based on two influential, but opposing, theoretical beliefs—psychoanalysis and learning theory—that had deemphasized or outright rejected classification as a way of understanding deviant behavior.

The founder of psychoanalysis did not always hold this opinion. In fact, a paper Sigmund Freud published in the *Neurologisches Zentralblatt* in 1895 (entitled in English translation "On the Grounds for Detaching a Particular Syndrome from Neurasthenia under the Description 'Anxiety Neurosis'") was an attempt to classify what would now be called anxiety disorders. The paper contained a detailed, vivid, and very modern description of the symptoms of panic attacks. At that point in his thinking, Freud attributed the anxiety of this syndrome to a purely organic cause, namely dammed-up sexual energy that erupted suddenly in the form of multiple somatic anxiety symptoms. But once Freud elaborated the fundamental theories of psychoanalysis, he lost most of his interest in what he came to consider the superficial grouping of symptoms and signs of disease just because they co-occurred in a number of individuals.

Freud taught us to go beyond mere symptoms and understand the "dynamics" of neuroses as a meaningful constellation of drives and defenses in an individual. Although he never completely gave up certain kinds of classification—such as associating personality types with oral, anal, and phallic stages of childhood development—these classifications were peripheral to psychoanalysis as a therapy. Freud did remain a biologist at heart, with a great affinity for what is now called sociobiology; but many of his followers discarded these ideas as relics of German reactions to Charles Darwin and Darwin's predecessors.

Learning theory was given its initial scientific formulations by Freud's Russian contemporary, Ivan Pavlov. At first it was restricted to university psychology departments. Animal learning experiments, such as the ones conducted by B. F. Skinner in the 1950s and 1960s on operant conditioning in pigeons, exemplify this approach. For a long time, little attempt was made to apply either classical or operant conditioning to clinical problems, although towards the end of his life Pavlov made some theoretical excursions into psychiatry. Part of the resistance in the United States came from the ascendancy of psychoanalytically inspired therapies, but another barrier was the doctrine of Behaviorism, which had rejected the introspective data that Freudian and neo-Freudian talking therapies were based on. Many therapists and potential clients regarded radical rejection of the mind as contrary to common sense for humans therapies, however suitable such a theoretical position might be for the psychology of other species.

In the 1960s, learning theory, together with its behaviorist philosophy, suddenly escaped from the laboratory and entered clinics and hospitals under the name of "behavior modification." Learning theory principles were applied to clinical problems as diverse as schizophrenia (called "schizophrenic behavior") on the one hand, and specific phobias on the other. The essence of the new approach was analysis of the reinforcement contingencies that maintained an undesirable behavior, followed by modification of these contingencies to cause that behavior to be extinguished. In the case of phobias, the connection between the phobic object and the emotional response of fear had to be broken. One way to do that was to have the client imagine phobic objects while maintaining a state of relaxation, a method called "systematic desensitization."

In this way the connection was made between the phobic object—fear could be replaced by phobic object—and relaxation. The psychoanalytic need to uncover the origins of the phobia and its symbolic meaning were rejected as irrelevant, as was traditional medical diagnosis based on specific clusters of symptoms, a common course of illness, or need for a specific treatment. With respect to the irrelevance of diagnosis, however, behavior therapy and psychoanalysis remained in agreement. To the new clinical learning theorists, classifying the infinite variety of behavior deviations into disease entities made no more sense than did classifying the infinite variety of unconscious conflicts into disease entities for most psychoanalytic therapists.

THE RETURN OF THE MEDICAL MODEL

This consensus began to fail in the late 1970s, when new drugs became available to treat schizophrenia, depression, and anxiety disorders. The most powerful rationale for prescribing a drug or any other treatment is that it is specific to a disease, and psychiatrists and pharmaceutical companies began to think that the time was ripe for a medical model of classification in psychiatry.

The medical model assumes that a disease can be defined in terms of its etiology, course, and response to specific treatments. For example, tuberculosis is caused by a specific group of bacilli; when untreated it usually runs a chronic, fluctuating course; and it can be treated with specific antibacterial agents. The usefulness of the medical model in psychiatry had an important historical precedent, since in the last century many delusional and hallucinating patients in mental hospitals were suffering from central nervous system syphilis. Once the cause of their illness was discovered and treatments such as penicillin were developed, these patients could be diagnosed and treated successfully. Psychiatry had hoped for three-quarters of a century to repeat this success with another group of patients. Schizophrenics were of particular interest, although it has only been in the last decade that organic causes of some cases of schizophrenia were tentatively identified. Less consensus existed and exists about depression. Until this recent revolution, anxiety disorders were usually considered exempt from the medical model.

The Impact of Klein and Upjohn

Much of the initial success in medicalizing anxiety can be attributed to one psychiatrist, Donald Klein, and one pharmaceutical firm, the Upjohn Company. They were looking for treatments for a newly defined anxiety syndrome, panic disorder. Because this kind of unexpected panic attack seemed to have no triggering stimulus, from the beginning it was considered more biological than learned. Klein presented evidence that panic was different from other kinds of anxiety because it could be blocked effectively by tricyclic antidepressants, but not by benzodiazepines. Surprisingly, however, the Upjohn Company demonstrated in an international multicenter trial that a benzodiazepine, alprazolam (Xanax), could treat panic, and with documentation submitted to the U.S. Food and Drug Administration the company got recognition for panic disorder as a specific indication for Xanax treatment. In addition to clinical trials, Upjohn generously supported for several years a variety of research in panic disorder, which firmly established it on the scientific map.

These developments reinforced the value of the just-developed third edition of the *Diagnostic and Statistical Manual*, whose categories were more empirically based and more reliably diagnosed than those of previous editions. Pharmaceutical firms continue their search for drugs that can be shown to be effective for specific anxiety diagnoses, concentrating particularly on panic disorder, social phobia, generalized anxiety disorder, and obsessive-compulsive disorder.

Surprisingly, an increasing number of behavior therapists in the last few years have chosen to operate within this medical model at least as far as diagnostic categories are concerned. Chapter One is an example of this point of view. I think the main reason is that psychological therapies have been developed that are as effective as or more effective than drug therapies for groups of patients classified by the *DSM* as having a specific diagnosis. As Chapters Eight and Nine in this book explain, panic disorder and social phobia are now indications for specific psychological therapies, just as they have been taken as indications for specific psychotherapeutic drugs. By emphasizing the diversity of anxiety symptoms, the *DSM* diagnostic distinctions stimulated behavior therapists to develop specific ways of treating classes of symptoms such as agoraphobic avoidance, panic attacks, and worry.

Accepting a disease model does not automatically mean that psychological factors are secondary. The tendency to catastrophize bodily sensations in panic disorder can be considered as specific an etiology as the tubercle bacillus. At the very least, *DSM* classification is useful in comparing the outcomes of different treatments in different centers. It provides a reliable way of defining who can and should be treated, a way that is reproducible in different clinics. National and private health insurance can be convinced to pay for psychological treatment more readily if the treatment is for a specific disease with a known course.

A Multidimensional Model

Some think the diagnostic pendulum has swung too far. Wouldn't a diagnostic system where a client is placed on a multidimensional scale of degree of depression, unrealistic thinking, obsessionality, panic attacks, free-floating anxiety, shyness, and so on, be more valid? Such a scale might represent more accurately what in a categorical system based on the medical model is called "co-morbidity," the presence of multiple diagnoses in the same person. Most clients with panic disorder qualify for one or more additional diagnoses: depression, substance abuse, social phobia, and specific phobia, to list frequent examples.

My colleagues and I became sensitized to this issue when we studied people who have difficulty speaking in front of others. Some of them seemed to have symptoms of panic disorder, social phobia, and specific phobia at the same time. When talking in front of others, their anxiety could quickly and unpredictably escalate. Their thoughts centered on failing in the eyes of others, thoughts not restricted to the speaking situation; yet their anxiety rose to its highest levels and caused the greatest disruptions just before or during speaking. Rather than saying these speech phobics had three diseases, they might be better characterized along dimensions of panic, social anxiety, and phobic situations. Such people may generally react with anxiety more than the average person, may lack the biological or psychological means to dampen this anxiety, and may have learned by painful experience to avoid public speaking. The first two characteristics might depend on biological differences that lie on one or two continua, and the third might result from a sociocultural environment where expressing one's opinion in a formal talk is necessary for work success.

BEHAVIORISTS REDISCOVER THOUGHT

Another surprising development in behavior therapy has been the acquisition of a hyphenated name, namely cognitive-behavior therapy, as if the lineage of this therapy could be traced to two equally important parents. Historically, however, *cognitive-behavior* is an oxymoron since the behavioral point of view firmly rejected giving importance to thoughts or mind. Yet in the clinic the mind could not be ignored. Clients believe they have minds, and a therapy that ignores that cannot be totally plausible. It is only common sense to try to modify the clients' self-defeating attitudes and false opinions; Chapter Three outlines some ways that that can be accomplished.

The scientific reasonableness of considering cognitions became more apparent with the success of "cognitive psychology," a new branch of experimental psychology that constructed models of mental operations that captured features of memory, attention, and other kinds of information processing. Adding *cognitive* to *behavior* especially made sense in explaining panic attacks that seemed to come out of the blue. Only by looking at the clients' selective attention to bodily sensations and their belief in the dire consequences of these sensations could a credible psychological theory of panic be formulated.

Changing Beliefs

The version of history that I am presenting here is only a sketch; the work of many individuals and influences have converged to create the treatments presented in this book. Even in the days before behaviorists discovered cognition, Albert Ellis promoted a rational-emotive psychotherapy that directed his clients' attention to their irrational self-defeating beliefs and taught them how to change those beliefs. Furthermore, it would be arrogant to claim that psychology has a monopoly on methods of changing people's beliefs. Cognitive-behavioral change had been the province of salesmanship, proselytizing, and politics for a long time before mental health professionals came on the scene. In America in the 1930s, salesmen and executives were taught how to overcome their fears of public speaking in Dale Carnegie seminars, using techniques identical to what is now called exposure therapy.

Mary Baker Eddy (1821–1910), the originator of Christian Science, made the relationship between mental attitudes and somatic concerns the cornerstone of her religion, which teaches its followers that positive thoughts are more real and more divine than negative ones. Religion and culture sometimes are able to motivate people so strongly that psychological therapists can only wonder. As some of us try to develop ways to get flying phobics, who come to us for help in overcoming their fears of highly improbable air catastrophes, at least to where they are able to enter an airplane, we regard with a certain awe the commanders of Japanese kamikaze pilots who got their men to enter airplanes to fly to certain death. As we try to get agoraphobics to board a bus while thinking they might die from a panic attack, we are sorry that we cannot motivate them with the assurance of certain Islamic leaders who guarantee suicide bombers instant passage to paradise when they die.

BIOLOGY VERSUS PSYCHOLOGY

Today one of the main polarities in the treatment of anxiety disorders is whether to treat with medication or not. Chapter Seven lists the many medicines that are in such use. Ostensibly, the issue is whether biological factors or psychological factors are more important in specific anxiety disorders. But professional rivalries around this issue fuel the controversy. Economic changes also have contributed to the conflict; the professions have not always been aligned as they are now. In the 1950s and 1960s, a group of medical doctors had a near monopoly on psychoanalysis in the United States, and they were known for their disdain of any drug treatment of anxiety. Now, in the 1990s, psychoanalytic institutes enroll primarily nonphysicians.

Some physicians, wanting to maintain their incomes, feel forced by health maintenance organizations and insurance companies to see such greater numbers of patients for so little time that only brief evaluation and prescription of drugs is feasible. A hopeful development is that some HMOs and insurance companies have realized that at least cognitive-behavior therapies make economic sense. They are hiring psychologists, social workers, and nurses to treat conditions like panic disorder, which without therapy can lead to repeated emergency room visits and expensive but futile medical workups. The psychoanalytic perspective also has a contribution to make, as Chapter Six explains.

The truth of the matter is that both psychological and biological perspectives on anxiety disorders have partial validity but neither alone is complete. Genetic studies might be able to prove that innate differences contribute to the development of anxiety disorders, but it is likely that genes will remain predisposing factors rather than sufficient causes. Experiments showing that patients with panic attacks react with more anxiety to lactate infusions or to breathing CO_2 than control subjects do not prove the existence of a biological disorder. A person who has experienced panic attacks is bound to be more afraid when given an agent expected to produce anxiety, especially when the agent mimics the body sensations that accompany panic attacks. On the other hand, the psychological theory that catastrophic thoughts about bodily sensations are a cause of panic attacks can be faulted for confusing cause and effect. For someone who has experienced a severe panic attack, the fear of an impending health collapse is a natural learned response. Of course, some people with panic attacks deny such thoughts, and the search for them by an overly zealous therapist in the face of client denial has an uncomfortable resemblance to early psychoanalysis.

Furthermore, proving that an anxiety disorder has a biological component does not entail that the best treatment is necessarily pharmacological, or, conversely, that the best treatment for psychologically caused anxiety is necessarily psychological. Some therapies, such as those described in Chapters Four and Five, do not even fit into this dichotomy since they are equally psychological and biological: clients are taught a psychological process to directly modify biological responses. Which is the best therapy for a given problem is an empirical question. Well-designed outcome studies, not polemics, will decide these issues.

I have no doubt that exposure and certain cognitive-behavior therapies are here to stay. The intermediate-term effectiveness of psychological treatment packages for panic disorders such as the one described in Chapter Eight is well established, although the relative usefulness of specific components is uncertain. As mentioned in Chapter Two, long-term follow-ups of agoraphobia successfully treated with exposure have demonstrated sustained improvement. Existing drug treatment for these conditions, though effective to a certain degree, requires continued taking of the drug with the inconvenience and risks that that entails. But the fact that drugs work at all keeps the hope alive that more perfect drugs can be discovered. In certain cases, combining drugs with cognitive-behavior therapy may be advantageous, at least in the case of imipramine and exposure in agoraphobia, as explained in Chapter Seven. Not every potential client is willing to embark on an exposure program, at least without the reassurance of medication. Upon hearing what therapy consists of, phobics often excuse themselves and disappear. Handling patients like these is more the art of therapy than its science.

Medication and Exposure

Frank Wilhelm and I know from our own research that medication and exposure are not compatible in every circumstance. We tested twenty-eight women who were afraid of flying. Their fear was severe enough and their need to fly strong enough that they had turned to us for help. Our experiment was this: they agreed to take two thirty-mile flights between San Jose and San Francisco. On the first flight fourteen of the women were given 1 mg of alprazolam before the flight, and fourteen a placebo pill. All were given oral and written instructions about the value of exposure to flying for overcoming their phobia.

On the first flight, the alprazolam group was significantly less anxious than the placebo group and was optimistic that their anxiety would be even less on the next flight. On the second flight, neither group was given or allowed to take medication. Contrary to their own expectations, the group that had taken alprazolam on the first flight was significantly more anxious than the group who had taken the placebo. While the placebo group showed a significant decrease in anxiety from the first to the second flight, showing that exposure had worked to reduce anxiety, the alprazolam group showed a significant increase. We concluded that alprazolam was preventing exposure from working and that we should recommend to our clients not to take a benzodiazepine (or drink alcohol) if they wanted the maximum benefit from exposure.

OVERVIEW OF THE CONTENTS

This book provides a comprehensive, up-to-date overview of how mental health professionals treat anxiety. In general, the contributors to the volume have come to peace with the historical controversies outlined above, and they accept both behavioral and cognitive approaches and the usefulness of a diagnostic classification. Nor do they reject biological perspectives. This book contains vivid descriptions of what anxiety patients are like and explains in considerable detail a wide variety of therapies for anxiety disorders other than obsessive-compulsive disorder (which is too large a topic to include here). The chapters are oriented toward practicing therapists, although students, nontherapists, and anxious potential clients can find valuable information in them. Of course, reading a book does not suffice to prepare a therapist. Personal supervision by someone experienced with a therapy provides crucial corrections to the novice's misapprehensions. Attending seminars can be helpful as well. Practicing professionally, of course, means that you have met the licensing requirements of your state.

Chapter One, "Diagnostic Evaluation," by Silvia Schneider and Martina Ruhmland, explains the use of classification and dimensional assessment in clinical work with anxious patients. Here you will find the *DSM-IV* definitions of the anxiety disorders and some of the critical questions for screening patients who might have an anxiety disorder. The chapter then describes formal evaluation by structured diagnostic interviews, clinical questionnaires, and medical testing for medical diseases that can result in abnormal anxiety levels. In preparation for therapy, the therapists analyze the client's problem areas and observe the client's response to hyperventilation.

Chapters Two and Three introduce two of the main psychological treatment modalities for treating anxiety: exposure and cognitive therapy. In Chapter Two, "Techniques of Exposure," by Brunna Tuschen and Wolfgang Fiegenbaum, we learn that the *art* of exposure therapy is to find ways to motivate clients to do what they must do to get over their fears, namely, confront the frightening situations repeatedly. Simply telling clients to expose themselves to anxiety rarely suffices. Instead, clients must be prepared by the construction of an individualized rationale that is compatible with their beliefs, will not be refuted by a single failure experience, and explains logically how change can take place. Tuschen and Fiegenbaum give a number of examples of successful treatment, including the case of Monica, a thirty-six-year-old whose fear of spiders had prevented her from living a satisfactory life as a wife and mother, and the case of Robert, a thirty-two-year-old with a five-year history of panic attacks who had had many unnecessary medical examinations in the stubborn belief that he was suffering from undiagnosed heart disease.

Chapter Three, "Techniques of Cognitive Therapy," by Stefan G. Hofmann and Patricia Marten DiBartolo, explains that anxiety has three components—cognitions, behavior, and physiology—and that in treating humans the first component offers considerable therapeutic leverage. Changing thinking changes emotional reactions. Anxious clients harbor irrational thoughts they should learn to recognize, monitor, and challenge. Old maladaptive beliefs—such as that a racing heart is a sign of an impending heart attack—need to be put to empirical test. In that way, rational thoughts can replace irrational ones.

Chapters Four and Five present two methods for changing the physiological component of anxiety directly. Paul Lehrer and

Richard Carr, in "Progressive Relaxation," teach us how to instruct clients to relax muscles according to a procedure developed early in the twentieth century by Edmund Jacobson, a physician and psychologist. Clients learn to relax not only when lying or sitting in a quiet place but also when engaged in activities. This method has the advantage that it can be practiced without any special biofeedback equipment. Chapter Five, "Autogenic Training," by Wolfgang Linden and Joseph W. Lenz, presents a second equipment-free physiological approach to stress management. It was developed by Johann Schultz, a physician who was pursuing an interest in the therapeutic use of self-hypnosis at about the same time that Jacobson developed his method. Autogenic training addresses more physiological systems than just the muscular, particularly the cardiovascular and respiratory systems.

Chapter Six, "Psychodynamic Therapies," by Richard Almond, explores ideas originated by Freud about the role of unconscious mental activity in anxiety disorders. Almond distinguishes between different kinds of anxiety: traumatic, disintegration, separation, and conflictual or neurotic anxiety. In psychoanalysis or psychoanalytically oriented psychotherapy, the *transference* reactions of the client to the therapist offer important insights into the thoughts behind the client's fears. One of the advantages of psychodynamic therapies is that more than any other therapy they protect the autonomy of the client from imposition of the therapist's goals.

Chapter Seven, "The Role of Medication," by Matig R. Mavissakalian and Martin T. Ryan, is a concise summary of the different drugs being used to treat anxiety. This is a topic that no therapist can ignore, since many of the clients who come to us for psychological treatment are taking medication or have taken it recently. The number and variety of therapeutic drugs available have expanded tremendously in the last decade; these drugs now include benzodiazepines, tricyclic antidepressants, selective serotonin re-uptake inhibitors, monamine oxidase inhibitors, and beta-blockers. An important question for therapists is how well psychological and pharmacological therapies mix. The authors attempt to give some answers to this knotty and still inadequately researched question.

Chapters Eight and Nine give details of two treatment programs, one for panic disorder and the other for social phobia. "A Cognitive-Behavioral Treatment Package for Panic Disorder with Agoraphobia," by Frank Wilhelm and Jürgen Margraf, describes a fifteen-session, individual treatment. The package is based on a treatment manual written by Margraf and Silvia Schneider for a research study that demonstrated the efficacy of this treatment. It combines exposure to external and internal feared stimuli and cognitive restructuring in the context of a clearly articulated rationale based on the concept of the vicious circle and the effects of nonspecific stressors. Here you can read what therapists actually say when they introduce the client to the different elements of the therapy.

Chapter Nine, "A Cognitive-Behavioral Treatment Package for Social Anxiety," by Karin Gruber and Richard G. Heimberg, describes a twelve-session group treatment based on a manual written by Heimberg. Like the one of Wilhelm and Margraf, this package emphasizes systematic exposure and cognitive restructuring. Participants learn to identify individual thoughts automatically occurring in social interactions and to categorize the cognitive distortions in these thoughts, such as all-or-nothing thinking, jumping to conclusions, magnification/minimization, and disqualifying the positive. They are then taught to challenge their distorted ideas by considering questions such as "How certain are you that your thought will come true?" or "What is the worst that could happen?" Transcripts of dialogues between Karin and actual clients convey how this therapy is actually practiced.

ACKNOWLEDGMENTS

This book is the product of many people. First, I want to thank the authors, who were asked to write in a style, and in some cases a language, that was different from their usual academic one. They were asked to be personal and direct as they are when they deal with their clients. Second, I want to thank Alan Rinzler and the Jossey-Bass editors whose advice was critical in making our book more user-friendly. Third, I want to acknowledge the group of faculty members, residents in psychiatry, and graduate students in psychology who have created a stimulating, questioning atmosphere for our research and clinical activities in the area of anxiety. Particular thanks are due to C. Barr Taylor and W. Stewart Agras, who helped me get started in what was for me, in 1984, a new area of endeavor.

NOTES

P. xiii, *The third edition of the American Psychiatric Association's* Diagnostic and Statistical Manual of Mental Disorders . . . , *published in 1980:* American Psychiatric Association. (1980). *Diagnostic and statistical manual of mental disorders (3rd ed.).* Washington, DC: Author.

P. xiii, *In fact, a paper Sigmund Freud published in the* Neurologisches Zentralblatt *in 1895:* Freud, S. (1962). On the grounds for detaching a particular syndrome from neurasthenia under the description 'anxiety neurosis'. In J. Strachey (Ed. and Trans.), *The standard edition of the complete psychological works of Sigmund Freud* (Vol. 3, pp. 90–115). London: Hogarth Press. (Original work published 1895)

P. xvi, *Klein presented evidence that panic was different . . . , but not by benzodiazepines:* Klein, D. F. (1980). Anxiety reconceptualized. *Comprehensive Psychiatry, 21,* 411–427.

P. xvii, *Some think the diagnostic pendulum has swung too far:* Andrews, G. (1996). Comorbidity in neurotic disorders: The similarities are more important than the differences. In R. M. Rapee (Ed.), *Current controversies in the anxiety disorders* (pp. 3–20). New York: Guilford Press.

P. xviii, *My colleagues and I became sensitized to this issue when we studied people who have difficulty speaking in front of others:* Hofmann, S. G., Newman, M. G., Ehlers, A., & Roth, W. T. (1995). Psychophysiological differences between subgroups of social phobia. *Journal of Abnormal Psychology, 104,* 224–231.

P. xxii, *We tested twenty-eight women who were afraid of flying:* Wilhelm, F., & Roth, W. T. (1996). *Acute and delayed effects of alprazolam on flight phobics during exposure.* Unpublished manuscript.

P. xxiii, *Here you will find the* DSM-IV *definitions of the anxiety disorders:* American Psychiatric Association. (1994). *Diagnostic and statistical manual of mental disorders (4th ed.).* Washington, DC: Author.

TREATING
ANXIETY DISORDERS

I

DIAGNOSTIC EVALUATION

Silvia Schneider and Martina Ruhmland

A forty-five-year-old man with symptoms of dizziness, heart pounding, sweating, and hot flashes in certain situations seeks psychological treatment. He says that these symptoms, together with a feeling of intense fear, typically strike in supermarkets, shopping malls, buses, and restaurants. But sometimes they come out of the blue, without warning, in other places. The client worries about what other people think of him and is afraid that they find him ridiculous. He also reports feelings of hopelessness, poor appetite, and difficulty in doing his daily work. During the last few weeks, he has had recurrent thoughts about death and suicide. He is very upset about what is happening to him and asks for immediate treatment.

This man came to us with obvious symptoms of both anxiety and depression. Based on these symptoms, we developed an initial hypothesis about the nature of his problems: his complaints suggested that he suffered from panic attacks, agoraphobia, social phobia, and major depression. However, it was unclear exactly what kind of disorder he had. Avoidance of supermarkets, shopping malls, buses, and restaurants occurs in social phobia as well as agoraphobia. Did the client really suffer from panic attacks?

For treatment planning, it was essential to clarify whether his central problem was agoraphobia or social phobia, since their treatments are quite different (see Chapters Eight and Nine, respectively). If several diagnoses are valid, the therapist has to decide what the primary diagnosis is, and which problems are consequences of this diagnosis or of other diagnoses.

Some clinicians question the value of diagnostic evaluation and treat all anxiety problems the same way. This has been especially true for therapists with a Rogerian or psychoanalytic background. But this is not the case for cognitive-behavioral therapists, for whom the goal of the diagnostic evaluation of anxiety disorders is to suggest the proper treatment. Diagnosis is not an end in itself but something that leads to a treatment plan. Diagnoses based on the fourth edition of the *Diagnostic and Statistical Manual of Mental Disorders* can be used to develop specific cognitive-behavioral treatment plans.

Furthermore, diagnosis can be used to introduce the client to therapy. Having a framework that clarifies and differentiates a previously undifferentiated set of difficulties helps the client to recognize that problems can reduced to manageable proportions and that change is possible. Diagnostic evaluation can emphasize the possibility of change by showing the client what may be attainable, rather than remaining resigned to continuing unhappiness.

It is also important, however, that treatment goals be realistic. For example, it would be unrealistic to expect that after successful therapy a social phobic would never again experience social unease; a more realistic goal is that a social phobic would be able to socialize with other people in a satisfying way most of the time.

This chapter describes how anxiety disorders are classified and diagnosed. We place special emphasis on diagnostic procedures and tests that are relevant to treatment, and how therapeutic rationales can be introduced during a diagnostic evaluation.

CLASSIFICATION OF ANXIETY DISORDERS

Our understanding of the nature and treatment of anxiety disorders has expanded immensely since the introduction of the third edition of the *DSM*. *DSM-III* departed radically from its predecessors in several ways. Its atheoretical and descriptive approach and its specificity were major changes that resulted in a more reliable and valid classification of anxiety and other mental disorders. A better diagnostic system stimulated more specific and detailed treatment research. *DSM-III* distinguished for the first time among several phobic disorders (depending on the content of the phobia); the diagnosis "anxiety neurosis" was divided into panic disorder and generalized anxiety disorder, and the diagnosis "posttraumatic stress disorder" was introduced. However, improved understanding of anxiety has not raised substantial challenges to the new classification of anxiety disorders. In this respect, *DSM-III-R* and the current *DSM-IV* are very similar to *DSM-III*.

Before going on to describe the diagnostic procedure in detail, we present a short characterization of the main anxiety disorders listed in *DSM-IV*. Alongside the essential features of the different disorders, we briefly discuss the differential diagnosis of each disorder. Then we give an example of a question useful in screening for the respective disorder. An affirmative answer indicates that follow-up questions should be asked to rule in or rule out that diagnosis. A diagnosis cannot be made on the basis of a yes answer to a single question, since all anxiety disorder diagnoses require that multiple criteria be fulfilled simultaneously.

Panic Disorder Without Agoraphobia

The essential feature of panic disorder is the presence of recurrent unexpected panic attacks. The person:

1. Worries about having another panic attack, or

2. Worries about the implications of the attack or its consequences, or

3. Shows a significant change in behavior related to the attacks

A panic attack is defined as a discrete period of intense fear or discomfort that is accompanied by a variety of somatic and cognitive symptoms and the sense of imminent danger. The attack has a sudden onset and rapidly builds to a peak. Common symptoms are palpitations; pounding heart or accelerated heart rate; sweating; trembling or shaking; shortness of breath; feeling dizzy, unsteady, or faint; nausea or abdominal distress; derealization (feelings of unreality) or depersonalization (being detached from oneself); fear of losing control or going crazy; and fear of dying. Clients seeking help for panic attacks usually report having had episodes of intense fear, coming "out of the blue." They thought they were going to die, have a heart attack, lose control, or "go crazy."

Differential diagnosis may be difficult because panic attacks, in the sense of sudden increases of fear, can occur in any anxiety disorder and in other psychiatric disorders. It is important to explore very carefully to what extent the attacks were "unexpected" or came "out of the blue." The client should be asked whether panic attacks occur while alone at home, or in situations where he or she does not expect them. If the panic attacks never occur when the client is alone or only in situations where they are expected, then a diagnosis of a phobia may be more appropriate.

Do you ever experience sudden unexpected panic attacks that come out of the blue without there being any real danger?

Panic Disorder with Agoraphobia

Some clients with recurrent panic attacks begin to avoid places where they have had a panic attack, places from which escape in the event of having a panic attack might be difficult or embarrassing, or places in which help may not be available. Typical situations are being in a crowd, being in a line of people at a department store, traveling in a bus or an airplane, or being on a bridge or in an elevator. If at least some of the panic attacks are situationally predisposed and if the client shows avoidant behavior, panic disorder with agoraphobia is diagnosed.

Do you fear or avoid special situations or places, for example, department stores, driving in a car, crowds of people, bridges, high towers, or elevators, because you're afraid of getting a panic attack?

Agoraphobia Without a History of Panic Attacks

The essential features of agoraphobia without a history of panic attacks are similar to those of panic disorder with agoraphobia, except that the focus of fear is on the occurrence of incapacitating or extremely embarrassing paniclike symptoms, or limited symptom attacks rather than full panic attacks.

Specific Phobia

The essential feature of specific phobia is an intense, unreasonable, and persistent fear and avoidance of clearly discernible, circumscribed objects or situations. Exposure to the feared object provokes an immediate anxiety response that may take the form of a panic attack. Most frequent are fears of heights, enclosed places, flying, seeing blood or an injury, receiving an injection, or fear of animals (spiders, snakes, dogs, rats). In phobic people, these very common fears are so intense that their everyday life is affected, and there is marked distress about having the phobia.

Although specific phobics sometimes experience panic attacks in specific situations and may avoid situations similar to those avoided by agoraphobics, the two disorders are distinct. To clarify the diagnosis, it is helpful to find out whether the client is afraid of the panic symptoms themselves and whether panic attacks occur in multiple agoraphobic situations. Individuals with specific phobia are typically afraid of features of the feared situation rather than panic symptoms themselves. Furthermore, if several agoraphobic situations (not specific situations such as presence of blood, injuries, or animals) are feared or avoided, the diagnosis of agoraphobia is appropriate.

> *Are there any objects, situations, or animals that you are afraid of and try to avoid, such as dogs, spiders, the sight of blood or injuries, enclosed places, heights, or airplanes?*

Social Phobia

The essential feature of social phobia is a persistent, excessive, or unreasonable fear and avoidance of social or performance situations in which the person is exposed to others. People with social phobia fear being judged by others as anxious, weak, or stupid. They are concerned about being embarrassed and humiliated. Social phobias may be circumscribed (for example, fear of speaking in public) or generalized, the latter meaning that the fears are present in most social situations. Typically, marked anticipatory anxiety occurs in advance of upcoming social or public situations. Exposure to the feared situation provokes an immediate anxiety response that may take the form of a panic attack.

Like specific phobics, social phobics may experience panic attacks in the feared situations and may avoid the same situations as agoraphobics. To distinguish social phobia from agoraphobia, the clinician should find out whether the client is afraid of the panic symptoms themselves and whether his panic attacks occur in several agoraphobic situations. Individuals with specific phobia are typically afraid of characteristics of the feared situation instead of panic symptoms. Furthermore, if several agoraphobic situations are feared or avoided, the client should be asked what she fears about each situation. For example, social phobics are afraid of being embarrassed or humiliated in a restaurant or supermarket, while agoraphobics commonly fear having a heart attack in the same places.

Do you avoid situations in which you could be noticed by other people and in which you are afraid of doing something humiliating or embarrassing? Situations such as speaking or eating in front of others, parties, dates, or discussions or conversations with other people?

Obsessive-Compulsive Disorder

Obsessions are recurrent and persistent thoughts, impulses, or images that are experienced as intrusive (becoming contaminated by shaking hands, or harming a loved one). The person with obsession usually attempts to ignore or suppress such thoughts or impulses, or to neutralize them with some other thought or action (that is, a compulsion).

Compulsions are repetitive behaviors or mental acts (for example, counting, repeating words silently) that a person feels driven to perform in response to an obsession, or according to rules that must be applied rigidly. Compulsions are aimed at preventing or reducing distress or preventing some dreaded event or situation. However, they are not connected in a realistic way with what they are designed to neutralize or prevent (frequent hand washing in order to prevent contracting AIDS, thinking "good thoughts" in order to prevent a spouse from having a car accident) or are clearly excessive. When attempting to resist a compulsion, the sufferer typically experiences mounting anxiety or disgust. The most common compulsions involve cleaning, checking, and repeating actions.

Sometimes it is hard to distinguish obsessions from excessive worries, which are characteristic of generalized anxiety disorder. Worries typically represent excessive concerns about real-life circumstances and are experienced most of the time as appropriate. On the other hand, the content of obsessions is more likely to be unrealistic, and the obsessions experienced as inappropriate.

For example, people with obsessions might worry about touching something carrying germs, while people with generalized anxiety disorder might worry about finances or losing their jobs.

People with obsessive-compulsive disorder avoid situations similar to those which phobics avoid (restaurants, car driving, dogs). To distinguish the diagnoses, it is important to ask the client why he avoids these situations: what is the content of his fear? People with obsessive-compulsive disorder avoid restaurants because they are afraid of contaminated food. In contrast, social phobics avoid restaurants because they are afraid of being embarrassed or humiliated in the restaurant.

A further problem is the differential diagnosis of obsessive-compulsive disorder from hypochondriasis. Hypochondriacal concerns are common in clients with illness-related obsessions. The best way to distinguish the two diagnoses is to check for the presence or absence of compulsions. For people who show somatic obsessions and checking rituals, the diagnosis of obsessive-compulsive is most likely appropriate. A diagnosis of hypochondriasis should be considered if clients are preoccupied with their own health and excessively seek information about illness.

> *Obsessions: Are you often disturbed by thoughts, impulses, or images that keep coming back and that you cannot get rid of, although they are unreasonable or ridiculous?*

> *Compulsions: Do you have to repeat particular behaviors, although you think they're exaggerated or unreasonable things such as washing your hands several times, counting objects, checking several times to see if electrical lights or appliances are turned off, or feeling driven to repeat specific words?*

Posttraumatic Stress Disorder

This is a long-lasting disorder that follows exposure to an extreme traumatic event (for example, sexual assault or other violent crime, torture, natural or man-made disasters). The person's response to the stressor is one of intense fear, helplessness, or horror. Besides intense fear and avoidance of stimuli associated with the trauma, typical symptoms are persistent reexperiencing of the traumatic event (e.g., intrusive recollections or distressing dreams), numbing of general responsiveness, and persistent symptoms of increased arousal.

Posttraumatic stress disorder must be distinguished from adjustment disorder. Adjustment disorder is an appropriate diagnosis (1) when the response to an extreme stressor does not meet all the criteria for posttraumatic stress disorder (for example, symptoms of intense fear and helplessness after a rape, but no symptoms of avoidance of stimuli associated with the trauma) and for situations in which the symptom pattern of posttraumatic stress disorder occurs in response to a stressor that is not extreme (being fired, failing an examination).

Have you ever had an extremely traumatic event in your life?
For example, have you experienced anything that involved actual
or threatened death, serious injury, or sexual abuse? Have you
ever witnessed such an event? Have you suffered from
physical or mental complaints after this event?

Acute Stress Disorder

The essential features are the development of characteristic anxiety, dissociative, and other symptoms within one month of exposure to an extreme traumatic stressor (see the preceding diagnosis). If these symptoms persist for more than four weeks, the diagnosis of posttraumatic stress disorder is made.

Generalized Anxiety Disorder

This diagnosis is given to people with excessive anxiety and worries. People with generalized anxiety disorder often worry about ordinary life circumstances, such as job responsibilities, finances, and the health of family members. The intensity, duration, or frequency of the anxiety and worry is far out of proportion to the actual likelihood or impact of the feared event. Typical symptoms are restlessness, irritability, difficulty in concentrating, and being easily fatigued.

When another Axis I disorder (for example, panic disorder or bulimia nervosa) is present, an additional diagnosis of generalized anxiety disorder should be made only if the focus of anxiety and worry is unrelated to the other disorder (that is, the excessive worry is not limited to panic attacks, or in the case of bulimia to episodes of binge eating and their consequences).

Are you often worried, or do you suffer from permanent fears that you think are far out of proportion to the actual likelihood or impact of the feared event?

Anxiety Disorder Due to a General Medical Condition or Substance-Induced Anxiety Disorder

These diagnoses apply when prominent symptoms of anxiety are present that are judged to be a direct physiological consequence of a general medical condition (anxiety disorder due to a general medical condition) or of a drug abuse, medication, or toxin exposure (substance-induced anxiety disorder).

DIAGNOSTIC PROCEDURES

Before we describe in detail our way of assessing anxiety disorders, we would like to make a few general remarks about how the therapist should act. Clients need to feel safe before they can disclose important and often distressing information. Therefore, the atmosphere needs to be a warm and trusting one, precluding censure. The therapist should be empathic and clearly committed to helping clients overcome their problems. Clients must receive an introduction to each diagnostic procedure, in which are explained its nature, goals, duration, and benefit to the client.

First Contact

The goal of first contact is to obtain an overview of the major complaints of the client and to initiate a positive therapist-client relationship. The first session can be started with questions such as "What is it that you need help for?" or "You told me on the phone that you're afraid of contact with people. Tell me more about your anxiety." In the course of the first session, further questions may be appropriate: "What are the symptoms you experience most often?" "What do you think about the symptoms?" "How does your anxiety interfere with your life?"

To build up a positive therapeutic relationship, therapists should show that they are familiar with the client's problems. An agoraphobic who talks about his anxiety in supermarkets, shopping malls, or elevators feels understood when the therapist replies, "I can imagine that these situations must be very frightening for you, since they're ones in which you can't get immediate help." Or a client with obsessions about germs feels understood if the therapist asks her, "How do you feel in this room? Can I do anything to make you feel more comfortable here?"

At the end of the first session, the therapist should give information about treatment: how long the typical treatment course runs, how many treatment sessions to expect, how long each session will last, and where treatment will take place.

Let me give you some information about treatment. The first step will be a thorough diagnostic assessment, because I need to know in detail what your problems are and what the important factors are that cause and maintain your symptoms. The diagnostic assessment will include a diagnostic interview, some questionnaires, a diary for you to monitor your complaints, and a careful medical workup.

After analyzing the diagnostic information, I'll be able to provide a treatment plan and tell you ways you might conquer your fears.

Structured Diagnostic Interviews

Before treatment planning is initiated, it is important to assess the presenting complaint; screen for related and unrelated complaints; and assign primary and secondary diagnoses, both psychological and medical. For comprehensive evaluation, semi-structured or fully structured interviews are very helpful. Several structured interviews have been developed over the last few years. One that specializes in the differential diagnosis of anxiety disorders is the Anxiety Disorders Interview Schedule for *DSM-IV.* It is a structured interview for the assessment of current anxiety disorders designed for differential diagnosis according to *DSM-IV.* A special advantage of the ADIS is that it provides data beyond basic information. Such data permit a functional analysis of anxiety that can be used for treatment planning, including information regarding history of the problem, situational and cognitive factors influencing anxiety, and ratings of an array of individual symptoms. Besides the ADIS for current episodes, there is a lifetime version for assessment of both current and lifetime diagnoses.

The ADIS-IV is organized as follows: it starts with an introduction (which includes questions soliciting demographic information), a brief description of the presenting problem when it began, how it has varied over time, and what effects it has had on several areas of life. After this introductory section, the assessment of specific mental disorders begins. Each section starts with screening questions for current, and then past, occurrences of the essential features of the specific mental disorder. If these questions are answered affirmatively by the client, then a detailed inquiry for *DSM-IV* criteria is made. If these questions are answered negatively, the examiner skips to the next section.

Many clinicians say they object to structured interviews because they anticipate resistance from the client; but often clinicians have their own resistances. Practitioners have told us: "It's naïve to believe the answers you get by asking clients directly about their problems," "Clients won't accept all that questioning," or "Structured interviews aren't empathic enough to make the client feel understood." We disagree. Our experience is that clients react very positively to structured interviews if they are properly prepared. When this is the case, clients take the direct and specialized questions as evidence that the clinician is familiar with their problems, because some of the questions are bound to be relevant. A good interview will end up helping build a positive therapeutic relationship. When the structured interview takes place in a therapeutic setting, clients should be told that topics that were not addressed completely during the interview can be discussed in later sessions.

Organic Differential Diagnosis

Before psychological treatment is undertaken, a physician should investigate potential organic causes or complications of anxiety. Many clients have had extensive medical workups before seeking psychological or psychiatric treatment. If this is not the case, the client should be referred to a primary care physician or specialist for an examination to rule out the numerous organic syndromes that may be associated with panic attacks or other kinds of anxiety. A comprehensive discussion of the relevant differential diagnosis that a physician should consider appeared first in Jacob and Rapport (1984). A modified version of this discussion is outlined in Table 1.1.

In our experience with hundreds of anxiety clients, the existence of a serious organic illness is exceptional. Nevertheless, in every single case a somatic differential diagnosis should be carried out, even if this is stressful for some clients. We think it is imperative to exclude organic causes because of the implications of overlooking a serious illness. Bear in mind, however, that the existence of an organic condition does not preclude behavioral treatment. This is particularly true for such diagnoses as mitral

Table 1.1
Differential Diagnosis of Panic Disorder
(*Based on Margraf & Schneider, 1990*)

Main Symptom	Condition Suspected	Differentiating Symptoms	Confirming Test
Palpitations	Paroxysmal atrial tachycardia, ventricular extrasystoles	Sudden onset of rapid heart rate	24-hr. EKG monitoring, event recording
	Mitral-valve prolapse	Systolic click or late systolic murmur	Echocardiogram
Dizziness	Orthostatic hypotension	Worse upon standing	Blood pressure and pulse, standing vs. sitting or lying
	Anemia	Worse with exertion	Blood count
	Benign positional vertigo, Cupulolithiasis	Triggered by rotation of head	Barany maneuver, otoneurological examination
Dyspnea, hyperventilation	Congestive heart failure	Rapid shallow breathing	Chest x-ray, EKG
	Pneumonia, pleuritis	Fever	Chest x-ray
	Asthma	Wheezing on expiration	Pulmonary function tests
	Chronic obstructive pulmonary disease	Associated with smoking	Pulmonary function tests
	Alcohol withdrawal	History of alcohol use	
Tremor, sweating, pallor, dizziness	Reactive hypoglycemia	Symptoms 2–4 hours after meal	5-hr. glucose tolerance test
	Insulin-secreting tumors	Symptoms after physical exercise, in the morning	Fasting blood glucose and blood insulin levels

Table 1.1
Differential Diagnosis of Panic Disorder *(continued)*

Main Symptom	Condition Suspected	Differentiating Symptoms	Confirming Test
Nausea, abdominal pain	Pregnancy	Menstrual history	Gynecological evaluation
	Gastritis, stomach ulcer	Heartburn, bloated feeling	Gastric endoscopy
	Enteritis	Diarrhea, fever, anorexia	Colonic endoscopy
Hot and cold flashes	Carcinoid syndrome	Diarrhea, asthma	5-HIAA in 24-hr. urine
	Menopause	Female sex, appropriate age	Estrogen level
Chest pain	Angina pectoris	Precipitated by physical exercise, emotions, or heavy meals	EKG, exercise EKG
	Myocardial infarction	Prolonged severe pain	EKG, cardiac enzymes
	Costal chondritis	Tender spots in costochondral junctions	Normal cardiologic evaluation
	Pleuritis, pneumonia	Fever	Chest x-ray
Feelings of unreality	Temporal lobe epilepsy	Micropsia, macropsia, perceptual distortions, hallucinations	EEG
	Psychedelic use or "flashback"	History of use	
Weakness	Multiple sclerosis	Age < 40, fluc-tuating neuro-logic symptoms	Neurologic evaluation
	Transient ischemic attacks	Temporary neurologic deficiency symptoms	Neurologic evaluation

(continued)

Table 1.1
Differential Diagnosis of Panic Disorder *(continued)*

Main Symptom	Condition Suspected	Differentiating Symptoms	Confirming Test
Miscellaneous	Hyperthyroidism	Rapid heart rate, warm, sweaty hands	Thyroid function tests
	Hypothyroidism	Voice changes	Thyroid function tests
	Hyperpara-thyroidism	Varied psychiatric symptoms	Blood calcium and phosphate level
	Hypopara-thyroidism	Tetany, increased sensitivity to hyperventilation	Blood calcium and phosphate level
	Pheochromo-cytoma	High blood pressure	Catecholamines in 24-hr. urine
	Acute intermittent porphyria	History of barbiturate intake	Urine porphibilinogen during attack

Source: Adapted from Jacob, R. G., & Rapport, M. D. (1984). Panic disorder: Medical and psychological parameters. In S. M. Turner (Ed.), *Behavioral theories and treatment of anxiety.* New York: Plenum Press; and Margraf, J., & Schneider, S. (1990). *Panik: Angstanfälle und ihre Behandlung* (pp. 187–237). Heidelberg: Springer-Verlag.

value prolapse or hypoglycemia, whose contributions to the client's anxiety may be minimal if indeed they play any role, and whose treatment may not lead to any improvement in anxiety. Hyperthyroidism, on the other hand, can contribute substantially to anxiety, and medical treatment may successfully eliminate it.

Problem Analysis

After the diagnostic interview and medical workup have been completed, an analysis of each of the client's problem areas should be undertaken. Most therapists insist that a thorough analysis of each problem area is essential for designing effective, personalized treatment. Here are the questions to be answered in this context:

1. What problems does the client suffer from?
2. How do the problems express themselves in the cognitive-emotional, physiological, and behavioral realms?
3. Does a problem have organic causes or complications?
4. What factors maintain a problem?
5. What psychological and possibly physiological mechanisms have contributed to the development of the problem?
6. What is the relevance of diagnoses other than anxiety disorder?

The first question is closely related to psychological diagnosis, since diagnosis is a framework for conceptualizing problems. But is a diagnostic framework useful for treatment? For example, the diagnosis agoraphobia does not tell us anything concrete about the circumstances that elicit the client's anxiety, which knowledge is presumably important for treatment. One client is afraid of being on bridges but has no difficulty waiting in a line in a department store; another can go anywhere but to many destinations only if accompanied by his wife. Because of differences between individuals, we usually assume that lack of attention to the client's individual characteristics should lead to poorer outcome results.

The second question asks for a more precise description of each problem. What cognitions and emotional reactions does the client have in a certain type of feared situation? What somatic symptoms and behaviors are elicited? For example, a client with a diagnosis of panic disorder with agoraphobia reports that the attacks occur in situations where no medical help would be available. The attacks are triggered by cognitions such as "What would happen if the symptoms occurred right now?" or "No doctors are available here." Physiologically, palpitations, sweating and trembling, and feeling dizzy occur. At the height of the anxiety, fear of having a heart attack and dying is prominent. Behaviorally, the client immediately tries to get to a hospital emergency room. The client's emotion is overwhelming anxiety.

The fourth question refers to maintaining factors, which may be separate from initiating factors. When her panic attacks occurred for the first time, one of our clients sought help with a doctor who gave her medicine. She quickly learned that her anxiety was reduced by taking the medicine and by immediately leaving the anxiety-provoking situation. Consequently, she began to avoid places with a greater likelihood of the occurrence of a panic attack or where escape in case of a panic attack would be difficult. In general, the therapist has to find out how the problem behavior is maintained. It is useful first to look at the time course of external and internal events that precede or follow an episode of psychological distress. Then the therapist formulates hypotheses based on principles of learning about individual patterns of reinforcement.

In answering the fifth question, the therapist tries to discover stress factors that may have contributed to the development of the problem or the disorder. Often the original contributing factors are no longer in play when the client comes to psychotherapy and so are not relevant for therapy. Nevertheless, many clients are relieved to understand how their problem got started.

The last question reminds the therapist to be sure that the client's presenting problem is really the one to be treated first and, if so, what other problems may become prominent when the first one is resolved. Depression is a good example of a disorder that may take precedence over anxiety disorders, particularly if suicidal thoughts are present. For the differential diagnosis of other psychological problems or disorders, structured diagnostic interviews (such as ADIS) should be used.

The problem analysis outlined here acquaints the therapist with the idiosyncratic phenomenology and history of a client's problems. Therapists need to adjust their explanations and treatment rationales on the basis of the client's information base and cognitive-emotional characteristics. They must try to see the world through the eyes of their client and give the client a new, therapeutically beneficial perspective.

Clinical Questionnaires

Questionnaires should not be neglected as a way of gathering information. After you have established the diagnosis, you need more details about the individual expression of anxiety in your particular client. For this purpose, clinical questionnaires can save time and effort for both therapist and client. Table 1.2 lists questionnaires that in our experience have proved useful.

The Fear Questionnaire and the Fear Survey Schedule offer an overview of phobias. The Mobility Inventory was developed

Table 1.2
Clinical Questionnaires for Anxiety Disorders

Anxiety Disorder	Questionnaires
Panic Disorder/ Agoraphobia	Agoraphobic Cognitions Questionnaire (ACQ) Body Sensations Questionnaire (BSQ) Mobility Inventory (MI) Fear Questionnaire (FQ)
Social Phobia	Social Phobia and Anxiety Inventory (SPAI) Social Interaction Self-Statement Test (SISST) Fear Survey Schedule (FSS)
Specific Phobia	Fear Questionnaire (FQ) Fear Survey Schedule (FSS)
Generalized Anxiety Disorder	Worry Domains Questionnaire (WDQ) Penn State Worry Questionnaire (PSWQ) Symptom Checklist 90-R (SCL-90)
Obsessive- Compulsive Disorder	Maudsley Obsessive-Compulsive Inventory (MOCI) Compulsive Activity Checklist (CAC)
Posttraumatic Stress Disorder	PTSD Symptom Scale (PSS) PTSD Diagnostic Scale (PDS) Impact of Event Scale (IES)

specifically for measuring agoraphobic avoidance behavior. With the help of the Mobility Inventory, you can make a ranking list of situations avoided by the client and so begin to plan exposure therapy. Two short scales, the Agoraphobic Cognitions Questionnaire and the Body Sensations Questionnaire, survey typical catastrophic cognitions during a panic attack and the fear of bodily sensations. The Social Phobia and Anxiety Inventory affords a detailed assessment of social phobic situations by asking about anxious feelings in a variety of social situations. Positive and negative cognitions in social phobic situations can be measured by the Social Interaction Self-Statement Test. The Penn State Worry Questionnaire assesses the frequency and intensity of the act of worrying. Since it does not ask about the contents of the worry, it needs to be supplemented by content items such as those found in the Worry Domains Questionnaire. For the assessment of the severity of PTSD symptoms, the PTSD Symptom Scale and the PTSD Diagnostic Scale can be used. The most frequently used self-report measure of severity of posttraumatic symptoms is the Impact of Event Scale. Questionnaire measures of obsessional behavior include the Maudsley Obsessive-Compulsive Inventory and the Compulsive Activity Checklist. General anxiety can be quantified with the Beck Anxiety Inventory. A multidimensional assessment of the general psychopathology is given by the Symptom Checklist (SCL) 90-R.

Diaries

An important way to document anxiety experiences is through standardized diaries, which we ask clients to keep from our first contact with them until the end of therapy. Self-monitoring by diaries is an important complement to clinical interviews and questionnaires. They are another way to document change during therapy. The exact data monitored depends on the specific anxiety disorder, as explained in Table 1.3.

Table 1.3
Diaries for Anxiety Disorders

Anxiety Disorder	*Diaries Data*
Panic Disorder	First signs, trigger
	Maximum of anxiety during panic attack
	Symptoms, cognitions during panic attack
	Situation (where, who accompanied?)
	Behavior (flight, distraction, avoidance)
Phobias	Trigger
	Maximum of anxiety during phobic situation
	Symptoms, cognitions during phobic situation
	Situation (where, who was there)
	Behavior (flight, distraction, avoidance)
Generalized Anxiety Disorder	Average level of anxiety during the day
	Maximum level of anxiety during the day
	Average level of depression
	Percentage of day worried
	Content of worries
Obsessive-Compulsive Disorder	
Obsessions only	Frequency of obsession
	(e.g., tallied with a hand counter)
	Ratings of anxiety and depression
Compulsions	Time spent on rituals
	Ratings of discomfort
	Urge to neutralize
	Ratings of anxiety and depression
Posttraumatic Stress Disorder (Variable)	Frequency of intrusions
	Content of intrusions
	Avoidance of trauma-related stimuli
	Ratings of anxiety and depression

Besides providing a record of anxiety and the context in which it occurs, diaries register the client's everyday activities. Many anxieties come up only in special situations or with special activities. These connections may be overlooked without a thorough self-monitoring procedure. In the case of agoraphobic avoidance, for example, it is crucial that anxiety data be supplemented by activity data. Avoidance behavior can take on such subtle forms that outside observers miss many of the client's self-imposed restrictions, which not even the client is fully aware of.

Exhibits 1.1 and 1.2 are diaries that are used in our institution, for self-monitoring of anxiety attacks and of daily activities.

Before clients use the diaries, first emphasize the importance of self-monitoring and give them instructions so that they are clear about the what, when, how, and why of recording information. Subsequent treatment sessions are built in part on diary material, which contains a description that is not retrospective but contemporaneous in detailing anxious events. Retrospective information can be lost or distorted in failures of memory. To ensure that the client knows how to keep the diary, the therapist goes through a sample entry with the client. The therapist stresses that the client should make an entry as soon as possible after anxiety has occurred, because by the end of the day some episodes may be forgotten and others only partially remembered.

To stress the importance of self-monitoring, discuss the diary with the client at the beginning of each session.

Psychophysiological Tests

Hyperventilation may play a role as a trigger or reinforcement for anxiety. Because anxiety clients often do not notice that they hyperventilate, some therapists routinely conduct a hyperventilation test. This test is a safe diagnostic tool if the clients are physically healthy. A standardized protocol can be described in six points:

1. Instructions. The test is introduced as a diagnostic procedure. Client should be warned that it is possible that the test will

cause a panic attack. While this would be unpleasant, it would also have a positive side by clarifying a potential cause of the disorder.

2. Posture. Client sits upright with one hand on the chest and the other on the abdomen to learn to distinguish between thoracic and abdominal breathing.

3. Hyperventilation. Breathing is paced at about sixty cycles per minute for two minutes. The therapist explains and demonstrates that hyperventilation requires thoracic breathing through the mouth. Client is instructed to breathe out as deeply as possible with each signal given by the therapist (a metronome or a signal prerecorded on a tape is best).

4. Assessment. At the end of hyperventilation, client is asked to rate anxiety on a scale from 1 to 100, fill out a symptom checklist, and rate the similarity of the hyperventilation experience to a naturally occurring panic attack. The symptom checklist contains relevant symptoms for hyperventilation and panic attacks as well as five control items not usually associated with anxiety (see Exhibit 1.3). Persons who also check these symptoms have a tendency to report somatic symptoms indiscriminately.

5. Recovery. If client reacts strongly to hyperventilation, client may need to be instructed to breathe slowly (about eight to twelve cycles per minute) and shallowly for a while.

6. Evaluation. If the effects of hyperventilation are rated as similar to naturally occurring panic attacks, this serves as the starting point for therapy. Evaluation must take into account that the presence of the therapist may greatly reassure some clients; this can attenuate the client's response to the test.

TREATMENT INDICATIONS

We emphasized at the beginning of this chapter that diagnostic assessment leads to a treatment plan. Table 1.4 lists therapeutic approaches to the specific anxiety disorders. Detailed descriptions of the interventions are found in the chapters indicated.

Exhibit 1.1
Anxiety Attack Diary

Diary for self-monitoring of anxiety attacks.

This form is based on the diaries used in Margraf and Schneider (1984). In addition to the diary form, clients receive a list of symptoms. They are instructed to code symptoms by their list numbers on the diary.

The symptoms and codings are (1) shortness of breath; (2) palpitations (heart racing, pounding, or skipping beats); (3) sweating; (4) choking or smothering sensations; (5) faintness; (6) dizziness, lightheadedness, or unsteady feelings; (7) chest pain or discomfort; (8) trembling or shaking; (9) fear of dying; (10) numbness or tingling sensations; (11) fear of going crazy or doing something uncontrolled; (12) hot or cold flashes; (13) nausea or abdominal distress; (14) feelings of unreality or being detached from parts of body or things around; (15) other (if other, specify).

Name: _____   Date: _____

Please enter every anxiety attack (continue on the back if necessary).

	Monday	Tuesday	Wednesday	Thursday	Friday	Saturday	Sunday
Attack #1							
Begin:							
End:							
Anxiety (0–10)							
What happened before?							
Where were you? With whom?							
What were you doing?							
Thoughts?							
Bodily sensations?							
What happened afterwards?							

Attack #2					
Begin:					
End:					
Anxiety (0–10)					
What happened before?					
Where were you? With whom?					
What were you doing?					
Thoughts?					
Bodily sensations?					
What happened afterwards?					
Please note at the end of each day:					
Average anxiety level during day?					
Comments					

Source: Margraf, J., & Schneider, S. (1990). *Panik: Angstanfälle und ihre Behandlung.* Heidelberg: Springer-Verlag. This anxiety attack diary also appeared in Margraf, J. (1990). Behavior therapy. In A. S. Bellack and M. Hersen (Eds.). *Handbook of comparative treatments for adult disorders* (pp. 144–175). New York: Wiley. Reprinted by permission of John Wiley & Sons, Inc.

Exhibit 1.2
Activity Diary

Name:_____ Week No.:_____

Please note every activity you have left your apartment or house for,
immediately after having returned (make notes on the back if necessary).

Event		1	2	3	4
Date					
Time	left				
	returned				
Company	reliable person				
	other person				
	alone				
Kind of activity	work/ training				
	shopping				
	friends, relatives				
	leisure time				
	movement, transport				
	other				
Maximal anxiety (0–10)					
Panic attack	none				
	expected				
	unexpected				

Exhibit 1.3
Symptom Checklist for Hyperventilation Test

Name:_____ Date:_____

Please indicate whether you experienced the following symptoms by circling the appropriate word.

1. Numbness or tingling sensations in parts of your body? yes no
2. Sweating? yes no
3. Dizziness, lightheadedness, or unsteady feelings? yes no
4. Itchiness in parts of your body? yes no
5. Fear of dying? yes no
6. Feeling faint (you don't have to actually faint)? yes no
7. Choking or smothering sensations? yes no
8. Sore throat? yes no
9. Trembling or shaking? yes no
10. Feeling of unreality or being detached? yes no
11. Shortness of breath? yes no
12. Swollen tongue? yes no
13. Palpitations (heart racing, pounding, or skipping beats)? yes no
14. Chest pain, pressure, tightness, or discomfort? yes no
15. Fear of losing control? yes no
16. Burning ears? yes no
17. Nausea or abdominal distress? yes no
18. Hot or cold flashes? yes no
19. Fear of going crazy? yes no
20. Sweet taste in your mouth? yes no

Note: Items 4, 8, 12, 16, and 20 are control items not usually associated with anxiety. They serve to measure a tendency to report somatic symptoms indiscriminately.

Table 1.4
Therapeutic Approaches for Various Anxiety Disorders

Anxiety Disorder	Therapeutic Interventions	Chapter(s)
Panic Disorder	Cognitive reattribution, exposure with internal stimuli	2, 3, 8
Agoraphobia	In-vivo exposure with external stimuli	2, 8
Social Phobia	Exposure, cognitive reattribution, social skills training (group therapy)	3, 9
Specific Phobia	In-vivo exposure	2
Generalized Anxiety Disorder	Anxiety management training, relaxation techniques	4, 5
Obsessive-Compulsive Disorder	In-vivo exposure, response prevention, flooding, tape confrontation	
Posttraumatic Stress Disorder	Exposure, supportive therapy	

The major aim of diagnostic assessment is to establish a diagnosis and treatment plan. Diagnostic information can be gathered by structured interview, questionnaires, diaries, and sometimes psychophysiological tests.

At the end of the diagnostic assessment, the therapist and clients should have adequate information for knowing how to proceed. The results of the diagnostic assessment lead directly to a treatment plan.

The formal diagnostic evaluation may take three to four sessions. But information about the client's anxiety does not stop there; trying to alleviate the client's distress inevitably brings new understandings of what initiated it and is maintaining it.

NOTES

P. 2, *fourth edition of the* Diagnostic and Statistical Manual of Mental Disorders: American Psychiatric Association. (1994). *Diagnostic and statistical manual of mental disorders (4th ed.)*. Washington, DC: Author.

P. 3, *third edition of the* DSM: American Psychiatric Association. (1980). *Diagnostic and statistical manual of mental disorders (3rd ed.)*. Washington, DC: Author.

P. 12, *Anxiety Disorders Interview Schedule for* DSM-IV: Brown, T. A., Di Nardo, P. A., & Barlow, D. H. (1994). *Anxiety disorders interview schedule for DSM-IV (ADIS-IV)*. Albany, NY: Graywind Publications.

P. 12, *lifetime version:* Di Nardo, P. A., Brown, T. A., & Barlow, D. H. (1994). *Anxiety disorders interview schedule for DSM-IV: Lifetime version (ADIS-IV-L)*. Albany, NY: Graywind Publications.

P. 13, *numerous organic syndromes:* McCue, E. C., & McCue, P. A. (1984). Organic and hyperventilatory causes of anxiety type symptoms. *Behavioural Psychotherapy, 12,* 934–941.

P. 13, *Jacob and Rapport (1984):* Jacob, R. G., & Rapport, M. D. (1984). Panic disorder: Medical and psychological parameters. In S. M. Turner (Ed.), *Behavioral theories and treatment of anxiety* (pp. 187–237). New York: Plenum Press.

P. 19, *The Fear Questionnaire:* Marks, I., & Mathews, A. M. (1979). Brief standard self-rating for agoraphobics. *Behaviour Research and Therapy, 8,* 915–924.

P. 19, *the Fear Survey Schedule:* Wolpe, J., & Lang, P. J. (1964). A fear survey schedule for use in behavior therapy. *Behavior Research and Therapy, 2,* 27–30.

P. 19, *The Mobility Inventory:* Chambless, D. L., Caputo, G. C., Jasin, S. E., Gracely, E. J., & Williams, C. (1985). The mobility inventory for agoraphobia. *Behavior Research and Therapy, 23,* 35–44.

P. 20, *the Agoraphobic Cognitions Questionnaire and the Body Sensations Questionnaire:* Chambless, D. L., Caputo, G. C., Bright, P., & Gallagher, R. (1984). Assessment of fear in agoraphobics: The body sensations questionnaire and the agoraphobic cognitions questionnaire. *Journal of Consulting and Clinical Psychology, 52,* 1090–1097.

P. 20, *The Social Phobia and Anxiety Inventory:* Turner, S. M., Beidel, D. C., Dancu, C. V., & Stanley, M. A. (1989). An empirically derived inventory to measure social fears and anxiety: The social phobia and anxiety inventory

(SPAI). *Psychological Assessment: A Journal of Consulting and Clinical Psychology, 1*, 35–40.

P. 20, *the Social Interaction Self-Statement Test:* Dodge, C. S., Hope, D. A., & Heimberg, R. G. (1988). Evaluation of the social interaction self-statement test with social phobic population. *Cognitive Therapy and Research, 12,* 211–222.

P. 20, *The Penn State Worry Questionnaire:* Meyer, T. J., Miller, M. L., Metzger, R. L., & Borkovec, T. D. (1990). Development and validation of the Penn State worry questionnaire. *Behavior Research and Therapy, 28,* 487–495.

P. 20, *the Worry Domains Questionnaire:* Tallis, F., Eysenck, M., & Mathews, A. (1992). A questionnaire for the measurement of nonpathological worry. *Personality and Individual Differences, 13,* 161–168.

P. 20, *the PTSD Symptom Scale:* Foa, E. B., Riggs, D. S., Dancu, C. V., & Rothbaum, B. O. (1993). Reliability and validity of a brief instrument for assessing post-traumatic stress disorder. *Journal of Traumatic Stress, 6,* 459–473.

P. 20, *PTSD Diagnostic Scale:* Foa, E. B. (1995). *PDS™ (posttraumatic stress diagnostic scale™) manual.* Minneapolis: National Computer Systems, Inc.

P. 20, *the Impact of Event Scale:* Horowitz, M., Wilner, N., & Alvarez, W. (1979). Impact of event scale: A measure of subjective distress. *Psychosomatic Medicine, 41,* 209–218.

P. 20, *the Maudsley Obsessive-Compulsive Inventory:* Hodgson, R., & Rachman, S. J. (1977). Obsessional-compulsive complaints. *Behavior Research and Therapy, 15,* 389–395.

P. 20, *the Compulsive Activity Checklist:* Freund, B., Steketee, G. S., & Foa, E. B. (1987). Compulsive activity checklist (CAC): psychometric analysis with obsessive-compulsive disorder. *Behavioral Assessment, 9,* 67–79.

P. 20, *the Beck Anxiety Inventory:* Beck, A. T., & Steer, R. A. (1993). *Beck anxiety inventory.* (Manual). San Antonio, TX: Psychological Corporation.

P. 20, *the Symptom Checklist (SCL) 90-R:* Derogatis, L. R. (1977). *SCL-90 administration, scoring, and procedures manual-I for the r(evised) version.* Baltimore: Johns Hopkins University School of Medicine.

P. 22, *A standardized protocol can be described in six points:* Margraf, J., & Ehlers, A. (1986). Erkennung und Behandlung von akuten Angstanfällen. In J. C. Brengelmann & G. Behringer (Eds.), *Therapieforschung für die Praxis* (pp. 69–98). München: Röttger.

2

TECHNIQUES OF EXPOSURE

Brunna Tuschen and Wolfgang Fiegenbaum

We are two clinical psychologists working at the Department of Psychology, University of Marburg, and in an outpatient setting in Münster. One of our research and therapeutic specializations is exposure therapy with anxiety patients. We use exposure as a way of reaching several therapeutic goals. First, exposure allows our clients to discover whether their cognitive and emotional reactions to their anxiety-evoking situations are realistic. Instead of trying to educate our clients to think more logically or rationally, we help them test for themselves whether their view of the world withstands scrutiny. Clients with panic disorder who are afraid of shopping malls, subways, trains, or tunnels are led to confront their fears in the very situations where the fears occur; after a while this brings about a reevaluation of the dangerousness. Second, exposure promotes psychological and physiological habituation to fear. Our clients usually report a progressive decrease in anxiety during prolonged exposure, accompanied by a reduction in physiological signs of anxiety such as sweating or tremor. Third, exposure gives clients a way to combat emerging new fears and lingering old fears. We instruct clients to take the initiative and act quickly in confronting even minor fears, since running away from them leads to their growing worse.

One of the characteristics of exposure treatment is that when clients are told what it will entail, many find it so terrifying that they immediately think it would be impossible for them and ask if we have other, less daunting remedies. Even when we inform them of the high success rate of this approach, most initially lack sufficient motivation to embark upon such a frightening program. Thus integral to our approach is the use of special communication strategies to convince our clients to weigh fairly the pros and cons of exposure therapy and to get them to make a preliminary commitment to give it a try.

PHASES OF TREATMENT

In our experience, exposure therapy is most effective when all of the following phases are included in the treatment package: assessment, client preparation for therapy, intensive exposure, and self-management. We begin by describing these various phases of exposure therapy.

The Assessment Phase

One goal of this phase is to describe exactly the kind of anxiety disorder the clients are suffering from and to obtain the information needed for carrying out the exposure therapy. In addition, we must determine whether exposure therapy is indicated or not. The assessment phase has these components:

- A first consultation
- *DSM* diagnostic assessment
- Medical examination
- Specific psychological assessments

Chapter One goes into the assessment of anxiety in some detail; here we present mainly a summary.

From the first consultation, we focus more on building up a trusting therapeutic relationship than on diagnosis. To achieve this goal we use a specific therapeutic communication strategy, system adoption, in which the client's cognitive and emotional systems are adopted for communication purposes. This means we anticipate client attitudes, feelings, and hesitations and provide information that encourages clients to talk about their anxieties. A part of this strategy is to interpret the clients' anxieties—in a way compatible with their attitudes, beliefs, and values—as normal, understandable, and reasonable, and to anticipate and verbalize their thoughts and feelings. This serves to "depathologize" their anxieties and make them easy to talk about openly. Furthermore, such a strategy allows us to present ourselves as experts on anxiety disorders, being familiar with unusual feelings and thoughts of anxious clients, which they may mistakenly believe are unique to themselves.

Here is a good example of this process. Martin, a thirty-eight-year-old client with panic disorder, once came to us because he found it difficult to stay in places which he could not quickly and easily leave, such as a car, bus, or train. In such situations he felt overwhelmed by fears of dying and bodily symptoms such as shortness of breath, sweating, and heart pounding. Whenever it was possible, he avoided such situations. His fears and avoidances were incompatible with his self-concept as a man: he wished to be a masterful male who had his life under control. Thus he felt ashamed about his psychological restrictions and was reluctant to talk concretely about his fears. As Martin's therapist, Wolfgang first needed to create an atmosphere in which it was easier for the client to discuss his problems. In addition, he construed Martin's avoidances as reasonable in terms of the client's assumptions and fears by telling him that if Martin were afraid of dying suddenly, the only responsible course of action would be to avoid situations where he couldn't get medical help in time.

After a positive relationship and atmosphere has been established, the client is referred for medical examination. It is important that the client be physically healthy enough to undertake exposure therapy, which can be physiologically stressful. For example, if clients have coronary artery disease, the physician must decide if the disease is so debilitating or unstable that exposure therapy is contraindicated. We then conduct a semistructured interview which diagnoses the client in terms of *DSM-IV.* Usually the semistructured interview provides enough information for a detailed cognitive behavioral analysis, although for atypical anxiety problems additional analysis may be required.

On the basis of all of the psychological assessments (including a battery of self-report tests), we decide whether the client's anxiety complaints are amenable to treatment by exposure. In our experience, exposure therapy is widely applicable. Even if the anxiety disorder has lasted for decades or if the client is older than sixty, exposure therapy can be effective. Severity is no contraindication: we have observed some of the most dramatic improvements in people who had reacted to their anxiety-provoking situations with intense somatic symptoms and extreme avoidance behavior. On the other hand, exposure is not likely to help people whose anxieties are primarily due to social-skills deficits. For them, assertiveness training or training in social problem solving is likely to be more helpful.

Patient Preparation

One goal of the client preparation phase is to work out, together with the clients, a plausible model for explaining the development and maintenance of their fears up to the present time. A second goal is to encourage clients to think through the implications of the model for overcoming these fears in the future. As much as possible, we do not take the position, or allow the client to put us in the position, of being the authority figures who tell clients what they must do. Instead, we promote the clients' active engagement in setting their own goals and in devising ways of attaining them, using principles derived from the explanatory model. Active engagement is the key to motivating people to enter and continue in a therapeutic program as frightening as exposure therapy.

Our system adoption strategy is another means of enhancing motivation. Instead of arguing against the client's assumptions and convictions, we try to combine their core belief systems with our scientifically based models of etiology and therapeutic change. Accordingly, the individual causal models that our clients develop with us should have certain characteristics. First, the model should be compatible with the cognitive-affective system of the client; second, it should not be formulated in such absolute terms that it can be discredited by a few experiences seemingly contrary to it (nonfalsification by exceptions); third, it should imply an appropriate prospect for change; and fourth, it should be plausible to the client. These four characteristics are elaborated in the following paragraphs.

Compatibility. Theories of cognitive consistency suggest that individuals generally strive to organize their cognitions (that is, beliefs, values, and attributions) in a tension-free manner. Information that contradicts clients' central beliefs will result in cognitive dissonance, inducing them either to change their beliefs or to doubt the therapist's explanations. This is particularly true of fundamental, personally meaningful beliefs such as those based on religion, as the following example illustrates.

Arthur, a thirty-two-year-old client, came to us to get help for his panic attacks. He lived in a small town where most of the people he knew were Roman Catholics. Arthur, also a Catholic, believed that his panic attacks were a punishment from God for his repeated unfaithfulness to his wife. Consequently, he had doubts whether psychological treatment would be successful. We encouraged him to consider whether he believed that God was merciful and accordingly might not wish Arthur's life to be destroyed by these attacks. In line with this suggestion, Arthur was able to view the therapy as a challenge to fight against his panic disorder as permitted by God's grace. Through this new interpretation, Arthur became highly motivated to participate in exposure therapy.

Nonfalsification by Exceptions. The models that we develop for explaining the development and maintenance of fears and the models for getting over these fears are to be applied throughout the course of therapy. Thus, it is important that such models not be falsified by a single experience that does not fit the assumptions and predictions of the models. To accomplish this, we avoid formulating assumptions or predictions in absolute terms. For instance, if we firmly predict that the anxieties of a client will decrease within three or four exposure sessions, we will be discredited if it takes more time for the client to improve. Thus, it is better to formulate predictions in probabilistic terms. A psychological prediction, unlike ones in mathematics or physics, is only generally true, and not true of every individual on every occasion. For example, we tell our clients that about 80 percent of our clients are treated successfully by a massed exposure program lasting less than two weeks. At the same time, we let them know that some clients take more than two weeks to reach their therapeutic goals and that some fail to be helped at all by our program. We also tell clients that therapeutic success depends on factors such as how involved they are and how well the therapy fits their goals.

In our experience, it does not pay to try to quell the client's doubts in an authoritarian manner; it is much better to take the client's views seriously and leave open which model is most appropriate for the explanation of the client's problems. Clients must feel free to make up their own minds whether it is worthwhile to test out the therapist's suggestions. At the same time, we as therapists are under less pressure for immediate success since the therapeutic process is construed as quasi-experimental; no firm conclusions can be drawn until a number of tests of the model have been made.

Prospect for Change.   Another characteristic that has a substantial influence on the clients' therapeutic motivation and compliance is the model's implications for how change can be expected to take place. Models that emphasize early developmental circumstances, such as too little attachment in early childhood, as central etiological factors of the psychological disorder lead clients to believe that they are severely disturbed. Accordingly, they may reasonably conclude that change can occur only after years of psychotherapy, if ever. This perspective can leave clients pessimistic and unmotivated to embark on an exposure program. More favorable explanations emphasize causal mechanisms that are directly accessible and can be changed by the client, such as the role of avoidance in perpetuating anxiety.

Plausibility. How plausible the client finds the explanations of etiology and therapy depends in part on the characteristics already described: the more the model corresponds to the client's personal beliefs (compatibility) and the more the model matches the client's experiences (nonfalsification by exceptions), the more plausible it will be. As a consequence, the credibility of the therapist is enhanced.

In addition, clients will find models more convincing if they are actively involved in their construction. A concrete exercise for doing this is the *thought experiment*, illustrated in the following dialogue between Wolfgang, the therapist, and Barbara, a client suffering from panic disorder with agoraphobia.

> *Wolfgang:* I know, you haven't done that yet, but what do you think would happen if you traveled by subway or train, or used elevators? Would you, just as a thought experiment, imagine what would happen to you, if you had to travel by subway for hours?
>
> *Barbara:* That would be horrible. I wouldn't do that!
>
> *Wolfgang:* I understand very well that it would be terribly anxiety-provoking for you, and I'm not sure you would ever do it. But I'd just like you to think about the possibility. What do you think would happen?
>
> *Barbara:* It would be terrible. I'm sure I couldn't handle it! My heart would be racing and I'd be afraid I'd die.
>
> *Wolfgang:* That's possible. I know that you're afraid you couldn't deal with the situation and that you would have strong anxiety reactions. How would you rate the intensity of those anxiety reactions, for instance, on a scale of

0 to 100, where 0 is no anxiety and 100 is maximum
anxiety?

Barbara: Oh, at least 100!

Wolfgang: So your anxiety would hit 100. Okay, let's go on a
little further with our thought experiment. Imagine that
you were forced to ride the subway for a long period of
time, like three, four, or even more hours. What do you
imagine would happen to your anxiety then? Would it
stay the same, decrease, or fluctuate up and down?

Barbara: I think the intensity would stay at the same high
level. . . . *(Barbara became more reflective and Wolfgang
encouraged her to take her time to carefully think about the
situation. After a while she continued.)* I suppose I would
finally get tired and maybe my heart palpitations would
let up a little bit.

Wolfgang: Usually physiological anxiety reactions cannot
remain elevated for too long. It's reasonable to think that
your heart rate might decrease.

Thought experiments give clients an opportunity to explore
the possibility of change step by step. By actively involving
clients, the therapist makes the plausibility of change greater.

Intensive Phase of Exposure Therapy

The basic idea of exposure therapy is to encourage clients to
expose themselves to their particular anxiety-provoking stimuli
until their anxiety decreases. Clients with panic attacks and agoraphobia will be encouraged to confront their fears actively—by
shopping in busy malls, frequenting crowded movie theaters,
walking in unfamiliar places, traveling by bus and subway, and
staying in enclosed spaces—until their worries about losing control, having a heart attack, or going crazy recede and finally disappear. Clients with social phobia need to expose themselves to
social situations like giving talks, participating in group discussions, or going on dates until they become more relaxed and

their dread of humiliation eases. Clients with such compulsions as repetitive hand washing are taught not to allow themselves to perform these rituals and to enter situations in which they fear contamination with germs. In our experience, change in exposure therapy is facilitated by direct confrontation, prolonged and repeated exposure, and response prevention, each of which we now describe in more detail.

Direct Confrontation. Clients should be confronted as directly as possible with the particular stimuli or situations that elicit anxiety. We usually expose clients to the feared stimuli in real-life situations. In our experience, this kind of exposure facilitates a comprehensive activation of anxiety reactions, usually including physiological, behavioral, and cognitive components. However, for some anxiety problems, for example, fear of thunderstorms or blood-injury phobias, the phobic stimuli are not easily available in the natural environment. In such cases, we expose our clients to imagined or to analogous or artificial situations, such as looking at a film portraying the fear situations.

Prolonged and Repeated Exposure. Clients need to remain in the feared situations for prolonged periods of time, until the anxiety clearly abates. They should repeatedly confront these situations. The length of exposure depends on how long it takes the anxiety symptoms to decrease. Exposure sessions can be carried out either in spaced or massed practice. In spaced practice, exposure sessions take place at approximately weekly intervals, whereas in massed practice sessions are scheduled on five to twelve successive days, in sessions lasting eight to ten hours a day. We prefer massed practice because it minimizes anticipatory anxiety and spontaneous recovery of the anxiety symptoms; quicker treatment success can thereby be achieved.

A further question with prolonged exposure is whether clients should begin with the least feared situations and slowly work up to most feared situations (graded exposure), or whether clients should be confronted with the most frightening situations right from the beginning of therapy (ungraded exposure or flooding). The first procedure is the more cautious and finds greater acceptance by both clients and therapists. Nonetheless, clinical trials have shown that exposure treatment that begins immediately with the most feared situations is more successful than the graded form. A plausible explanation for this finding is that when clients are immediately confronted with the most feared situations, they learn rules of behavior that may help them deal with relapses: they learn how to expose themselves in a sustained way to strongly feared stimuli and to suppress avoidance behavior.

A sample of clients who had finished their ungraded confrontation treatment five years before were asked which principles they had learned from their therapeutic experience. Nearly 75 percent said that "putting yourself into the feared situation for as long as necessary for your anxiety to disappear" was the most important rule for mastering their anxieties. This rule leaves little room for avoidance behavior, facilitating the long-term efficacy of exposure therapy.

Response Prevention. The therapist should try to discourage every form of avoidance response, including cognitive avoidance. To counteract avoidance, we focus our clients' attention on the details of their fear-provoking stimuli and the thoughts and feelings they evoke by having the client describe them to us. We do not allow clients to engage us in irrelevant conversation when we accompany them into a feared situation, thus preventing a diversion of attention and reduction of the impact of exposure.

MONICA

A good example of the three main components of exposure therapy is the case of Monica, a thirty-six-year-old who came to us because she was terrified of spiders. If she caught sight of a spider in her house, she became so frightened she could not continue her daily routine. She would immediately close the door of the room where she saw a spider and try to seal any gaps around the door with adhesive tape. For the rest of the day, she would be obsessed by fearful thoughts about spiders. As soon as her husband came home from work, she would insist that he move all the furniture in the room where the spider had been seen until he found and killed it. But even if he eliminated the spider, Monica would begin to worry that other spiders had got into the house. Her excessive fear of spiders had begun to depress her because she felt she could not be a good mother to her five-year-old daughter, Lisanne. She thought that she was a bad example for Lisanne, who might become fearful too.

Monica's husband was a forest ranger, and for several years the family lived in a lodge in a forest. Since spiders were abundant in this location, there was a very high probability that spiders would come into the lodge. The spider phobia occupied more and more of Monica's life, and finally she did not want to live there any longer. She began to think that living in a new house could help her to become more relaxed, especially if it was in the city, where there are fewer spiders. So Monica and her husband decided to build a new house in the city, a decision that made Monica very happy. She made suggestions about how the house should be constructed, for example, that the windows and doors fit in their frames more tightly than those of the old house so that spiders could not get in.

Unfortunately, moving brought new stresses. The move itself was complicated since Monica insisted that every item the family owned, including every book, had to be checked for spiders before it was brought into the new house. Her husband had to look for a new job because in the city he could no longer work as a forest ranger. Lisanne, who had just turned six and started school, became increasingly shy and said she didn't like school. Monica interpreted this as the beginning of a serious disturbance and felt responsible. But worse, despite the new house in the city Monica's spider phobia did not decrease. Needless to say, this was a great disappointment for the family. At that point, Monica realized she needed professional help and came to our clinic.

After a medical check-up, the psychological assessment, and the client preparation phase, Monica began our exposure program, which was ungraded in difficulty and concentrated in time. In this case, Wolfgang was the therapist and Corinna, a doctoral student, assisted him. (It is important for the reader to understand that in Germany, where we conducted this therapy, there are no poisonous spiders outside of zoos. Monica had heard this many times and had long realized that her fear of spiders was completely irrational.) During the first day of therapy, Monica was encouraged to enter a narrow and dark room where several spiders were crawling on the walls. She was asked to move her hands along the walls without regard to where the spiders were. This task was very anxiety-provoking for her, and she began to sob. Wolfgang encouraged her to go on with the task, reminding her it was essential not to leave before her anxiety decreased. After two hours she was able move her hands along the wall or lean against the wall without being very anxious. Wolfgang and Corinna then brought her into a room where twenty spiders were crawling in a bathtub. She was asked to describe their movements and to put her arms into the tub. Her anxiety again increased when she saw some big, black spiders crawling toward her. After an hour in this situation, she became more relaxed and noticed that the spiders ran to escape her hands and arms. She wondered how the spiders might feel, and she sympathized with them a bit. The therapists then encouraged Monica to help the spiders crawl out of the tub into the room. As expected, this again increased Monica's anxiety. Wolfgang and Corinna encouraged Monica to watch out for the spiders. Instead of reassuring her, they voiced her fears that spiders can move so rapidly that you never know where they are and where they will go. After about an hour Monica's anxiety again decreased.

After a short break the next exercise was performed: Wolfgang and Corinna drove to Monica's house with a bag of spiders that they released in the house. On the therapists' recommendation, Monica's husband and daughter had left for three days. Monica cried so loudly that a neighbor hurried over, wondering what was going on. It wasn't easy for the therapists to hear Monica crying like that, but their impulse to tell her to step outside or to comfort her was inhibited by the knowledge that such actions would undermine the therapy. The exposure program went on. Monica finally became tired, at which time her anxiety decreased as well. That evening, Wolfgang went home while Corinna remained overnight, sleeping in the same room with Monica. Corinna encouraged Monica to avoid the behaviors that she normally used to control her anxiety. For example, she was discouraged from turning on the lights and checking for spiders. Monica didn't sleep very well that night, but she was proud that she performed such difficult therapeutic exercises successfully.

The next four days were used to repeat these exercises and some additional ones. For instance, the therapists borrowed a large spider from the biology department of the University of Marburg. Monica's first task was to look at the spider in its glass case and describe it in detail. Then she had to move the glass case several times to different places. Monica was afraid that her hands might tremble so much that she would drop the case, but after a few exercises she was convinced that she could perform the task successfully. After the third day of therapy, Monica planned and initiated her own exposure exercises. The therapists encouraged her to do more and more exercises on her own, later going over together what she had done. In five days of exposure therapy, her spider phobia was successfully treated. One- and five-year follow-ups showed that Monica was able to maintain her therapeutic gains.

STRATEGIES TO ENHANCE MOTIVATION FOR THERAPY

Flooding is the version of exposure in which anxiety-provoking situations are confronted en masse in ungraded order. It is highly effective but liable to result in early drop-outs. Cognitive intervention tailored to the individual client's viewpoint is often able to prevent these drop-outs.

To take an example, here is the strenuous schedule for the first day of therapy for Susan, a twenty-five-year-old agoraphobic afraid of heights, confined places, and crowds:

Sitting in the cramped back seat of the two-door car while Brunna, who had picked her up at 8:00 A.M., drove on a freeway (two hours)

Confinement in a narrow and dark room (one hour)

Traveling by train (two hours)

Having a meal in an overcrowded cafeteria (forty-five minutes)

Climbing up the long narrow stairway to the outlook on the top of the tower of the Cologne Cathedral (ninety minutes)

Taking a ride over the city in a gondola suspended from an aerial cable (one hour)

Walking through large department stores (ninety minutes)

Repeatedly taking the elevator up Cologne's Television Tower and lingering at the outlook on top (one hour)

Having dinner in a restaurant (one hour)

Staying overnight in a hotel

The exposure exercises of the first day of therapy were, as expected, extremely anxiety-provoking for Susan, and at the end of the day she felt exhausted. The following morning Susan expressed strong doubts about continuing with this kind of therapy. Brunna talked to her in a warm and empathetic manner, encouraging her to think about the consequences of a decision to drop out. Brunna started by mentioning the typicality of Susan's reactions. This served to depathologize Susan's exhaustion and her doubts about holding up under all the stress. The discussion went on to clarify the implications of the alternatives. The negative consequences of breaking off therapy became especially salient to Susan. As a result she continued the exposure treatment, which turned out successful.

SELF-MANAGEMENT: THE FINAL PHASE OF TREATMENT

To maintain therapeutic gains, we encourage our clients to become their own therapists. That means that they need to continually expose themselves to feared situations, as they begin doing in the intensive phase of exposure. If the exposure is conducted initially in a massed version, self-initiated exposure homework exercises begin already on the second day of therapy. We prepare our clients for homework by advising them on what kinds of situations they should expose themselves to, how they can avoid distraction, and how long to remain in the feared situation.

To facilitate the change from therapist-guided to client-initiated therapy, it is helpful at first to accompany the client in such situations as driving a car on a freeway, travelling by train or subway, or going to shopping malls. But as soon as the client can complete a task with the therapist physically present, he or she should be encouraged to do the same thing while the therapist waits at the entrance of the shopping mall, restaurant, or subway station. Whenever the client avoids or prematurely leaves a feared situation, you should instruct him or her to repeat the exposure task immediately.

Finally, you can start meeting less frequently with your clients. Therapeutic contacts can take place by phone. During this last phase of therapy, coping with relapse becomes the main topic of the therapeutic sessions. A general strategy is to depathologize relapse by encouraging clients to interpret it as a challenge to practice what they have learned to do in therapy. You may say, for instance, that relapses do not predict long-term therapy failure. What is important for ultimate success is whether clients actively practice the single rule of *exposing themselves to the feared situations until their anxiety decreases.*

Finally, we offer a more comprehensive case example demonstrating our approach in the various treatment phases.

ROBERT

Robert, a thirty-two-year-old computer programmer, had suffered from panic attacks for five years. He was primarily worried about having a heart attack and was, therefore, very sensitive to internal sensations. He often would count his pulse and became anxious if he thought he detected any momentary increase in heart rate. He also worried when he got the impression that his heart was beating too slowly. He exercised often with bicycle riding, jogging, and gymnastics; he monitored his physical condition carefully. He interpreted shortness of breath while riding his bicycle as a sign of heart disease. Chest pain during or after exercise made him so uneasy that he would consult a doctor. On a number of occasions, he called hospital emergency numbers and paramedics were sent to his home for supposed cardiac emergencies. Although none of the medical workups, which included extensive batteries of cardiovascular tests, showed any abnormalities that could explain his symptoms, Robert remained convinced he suffered from a heart problem. Either the doctors had not yet done the right test or they had failed to draw the correct conclusions from the results. This belief was strengthened with every new "heart attack," which to him felt real and life-threatening.

HISTORY

Concerns about physical health were a central theme in Robert's family when he was a child. His father had also suffered from sudden "heart attacks" for which no physical basis could be determined. Robert remembered occasions of coming home from school and seeing his father lying in bed with the doctor examining him. At those times, his mother was frightened that her husband was dying. In addition to those events, which were stressful for the whole family, Robert's mother feared becoming ill herself, although she was in good physical health. She would have depressed moods, during which her thoughts focused on disease and death.

A few months before his first panic attack, Robert was under stress from family and work problems. With respect to his family, he felt he had to decide whether or not he wanted a child because his wife did not want to put off this decision any longer. Robert wanted a child but was afraid of the responsibilities that that would entail. Regarding work, he had been put in charge of a large project for a health insurance company; the project was time-consuming and difficult. He had to become familiar with new technologies and to deal with interpersonal frictions within his team.

Robert's first "heart attack" occurred after a hard day at work. He was exhausted and decided to take a hot shower to relax. After getting out of the shower, he felt dizzy and weak. His heart was beating rapidly, and he began to sweat more and more. The thought came to him that he was having a heart attack and was going to die. He yelled to his wife, who immediately telephoned for emergency help. He was taken to the hospital in an ambulance, where a comprehensive medical examination was performed. None of the results supported a diagnosis of heart disease. Contrary to the doctor's expectation, Robert was not relieved or reassured to learn this, because it did not explain what had just happened to him. It was at this point that Robert became preoccupied with his health and started concentrating his attention on bodily sensations.

COURSE OF ILLNESS

Following this attack, Robert became very anxious whenever he was in situations where emergency medical help would not be summoned immediately or would not arrive quickly. He was worried if his wife left the house before he did, or if she was gone on a weekend. Thus he always tried to be the last to leave the house and to visit friends on weekends when she was gone. When he was trapped in a traffic jam or felt his exits from an unfamiliar place were blocked, he would be overwhelmed with anxiety and the thought that he was going to die. In spite of his fears and avoidances, he struggled to remain active in his job and to drive his car to work. He drove alone, but with great tension. He preferred smaller roads over major highways, since he figured that on smaller roads he could turn off and stop more easily if he began to become incapacitated.

His anxiety symptoms could be triggered by merely reading information articles on heart disease or by reading or hearing about individuals—especially those near his age—who had died from such disorders. Furthermore Robert became aware of the unhealthful aspects of his habits and behavior. He limited his cigarette and alcohol consumption. He worried whether his past cigarette smoking would have long-term effects on his health. When a colleague gave him a newspaper article about the effects of cigarette smoking on the heart, it precipitated a panic attack.

DIAGNOSTIC PHASE

Robert was referred by his primary care physician, who reviewed his numerous diagnostic workups and confirmed that there was no evidence of organic causes for Robert's complaints. We conducted a comprehensive psychological assessment, which confirmed our initial impression that he could be diagnosed as having panic disorder with agoraphobia.

CLIENT PREPARATION FOR THERAPY

First we tried to identify any predisposing factors that might have led to the onset of the disorder. To make it as concrete as possible, we gave Robert a note pad and had him make a diagram of possible factors. Without hesitating to communicate our scientific knowledge about panic disorder, we encouraged Robert to draw his own conclusions.

We asked Robert to think about his family history as a possible origin of his strong health concerns. He understood that his father's illness together with his mother's anxieties of becoming ill could explain why he was so often worried about his physical health. We encouraged him to identify stressors operating at the time his panic attacks began. We then worked out with him that these stressors could have caused Robert's physiological levels to fluctuate, making it easier for him to be aware of his body functions. His family experiences had predisposed him to interpret somatic sensations as signs of illness. Additionally, we used our thought experiment method to have Robert think about body reactions to a hot shower after a hard day at work. He concluded that under such circumstances feelings of dizziness and weakness could occur even in physically healthy people.

We also worked on what maintaining factors might explain why he was not getting over his fears. Robert was asked to think whether constant monitoring of physiological sensations in itself may have led to changes in his physiological reactions, which were in turn perceived as danger signals. Although Robert appreciated intellectually that self-monitoring might influence physical reactions such as an acceleration of heart rate, he was not terribly convinced that psychological factors were responsible in his case. Therefore, we initiated a therapeutic exercise, in which Robert was asked to concentrate on his eye blinks and to monitor how often they occurred. After a short time, Robert started blinking very frequently, which impressed him since he had never had this symptom before. This helped him to accept the possibility that such mechanisms could explain his "heart condition." Finally, we discussed the role of avoidance behavior in the maintenance of his anxieties.

After developing the model of predisposing and maintaining factors of Robert's complaints, which took us about an hour, we went on to discuss its implications for therapeutic change. This took us an additional hour. We kept in mind Robert's skepticism about psychological therapies and agreed with him, for example, that his heart problems might still be due to physical causes that the doctors had failed to diagnose. In that case, we admitted, psychological treatment would fail and there would be no alternative but to turn again to experts in cardiac disease.

We discouraged Robert from making his decision for or against the therapy immediately but told him to take the next three days to weigh the pros and cons and then to decide. After this waiting period, he said he'd like to take the opportunity to test whether psychological processes were really important for his problems. He might even be helped, he said.

EXPOSURE THERAPY

The kind of exposure in which Robert participated was ungraded in difficulty and concentrated in time; it addressed a variety of anxiety stimuli. By means of certain therapeutic exercises—hyperventilation, stair climbing, and deep knee bends—Robert was exposed to the internal bodily sensations he was afraid of. In addition, he was confronted with external cues that had triggered his anxieties: newspaper articles about risk factors for cardiovascular disease, photographs of heart surgery, articles about people who had died of heart disease. He was also exposed to situations where medical assistance would be slow in coming: he was encouraged to remain in his apartment alone after his wife had gone to her office, to stay in a hotel room in an unfamiliar city, and to spend a weekend alone at home.

In preparation for the hyperventilation procedure, we told Robert that many clients with cardiac complaints breathe incorrectly and that their breathing patterns can produce chest pain and other symptoms. Then we proceeded with hyperventilation (as described in Chapter One). Right after the hyperventilation, we asked Robert to compare his internal sensations to those he had previously attributed to heart disease. Robert felt chest pains like those of his "heart attacks" and experienced a slight sense of unreality. At first he thought he might be having a heart attack and became a bit nervous, but then he remembered the eye-blink demonstration and tried to convince himself that his pains might not have such a sinister origin. This helped him to cope with his anxiety and gave him some insight into his mind's influence on his body. We told him that how sensations are interpreted can play a crucial role in maintaining heart symptoms. But we also cautioned that further experiments were needed to assess how much Robert's heart problems were psychologically triggered.

The physical exercises (climbing stairs and deep knee bends) led to a little shortness of breath. Because Robert expected himself to be in superior physical condition, he worried that this might indicate weakness of his heart. We did not argue against this interpretation, except to say that physical condition normally fluctuates and that in any case some shortness of breath during exercise is inevitable. But we also anticipated and verbalized Robert's fear that his sensations might indicate physical causes of his "heart problem" that the doctors had not correctly diagnosed. This remark led to an increase in Robert's concern, and he asked us how often we had seen this in our practice. We replied that none of our clients so far had turned out to have undiagnosed heart problems, but that such information was unlikely to reassure Robert, since he could be the first.

Our rationale for these statements was, on the one hand, to give Robert information that ultimately might reduce his anxieties. This was the first part of our communication, which conveyed to him that the probability was extremely low that the feared event would actually happen. On the other hand—considering Robert's cognitive and emotional system—it was obvious that he would doubt our assertion, since a core belief of his was that doctors had not correctly diagnosed his heart condition. Thus, he was bound to suspect that he would turn out to be the first client in our practice with life-threatening undiagnosed heart disease. But since we anticipated and verbalized this core belief, it was his turn to examine the likelihood of his assumptions. We knew that he had begun to reformulate his thoughts when he mentioned in passing, "You can never be totally sure you're physically healthy, but after all those medical tests there's not much chance I really have heart disease."

We continued our strategy of expressing the negative thoughts that Robert normally had in various situations. The basic reason for this strategy is that the cognitive and emotional system of clients— as well as that of people without psychological disorders—includes opposing ideas and feelings, for example on the issue of physical health. If you as a therapist take a one-sided position, namely that the client is totally healthy, then according to reactance theory opposing currents in the client's mind will become more ascendant, namely doubts about his or her physical health. On the other hand, if you take these doubts seriously, there is a good chance that clients will take the other side of the argument.

Subsequently Robert was exposed to published articles about heart disease. The first, in a health insurance company newsletter, provided information about the symptoms of a heart attack. Robert's anxiety increased rapidly while reading the article. Comparing the symptoms described with his own, he found both similarities and differences. We asked Robert to rate his anxiety on a scale of 0 to 100, where 0 indicated no anxiety and 100 maximal anxiety. Robert rated his anxiety at 85. We encouraged him to read the article several times and to rate his anxiety after each reading. After the third time, Robert's anxiety decreased to 45, and after the fourth reading to 25. He then read the article once more while we were out of the room. Immediately after we left, Robert's anxiety rose to 75. But

after a few minutes it decreased to 20 and remained low during subsequent readings.

After repeated readings, Robert became more detached and critical towards the article. As an educated person, he found that many
of its assertions were vague and unscientific. Thus, he was able to
evaluate coolly a topic that was emotionally loaded for him. The
exposure session proceeded, with two articles about people in his age
group who had died of heart disease. Once Robert's anxiety in reading them had substantially decreased, he was given pictures of heart
surgery and asked to look at them until his anxiety again returned to
a low level.

Robert was also encouraged to drive on a major highway while
traffic was heavy. At first we accompanied him as he drove. However, since the presence of his therapists was a kind of safety signal
that things would be all right, we later encouraged Robert to drive
alone while we waited for him at a parking lot.

Discussions with the client after the exposure sessions concentrated on how successfully exposure had elicited Robert's symptoms,
whether Robert had been able to focus his attention on the anxiety-
provoking situations and thoughts, and whether his anxiety had
decreased. In addition, we introduced a thought experiment on the
topic "living with uncertainty about health." Robert tried to get clear
what it would take for him to feel safe about his physical health.
After some thought, he concluded that definitive guarantees about
his health did not exist and that he had to accept uncertainty about
whether he was in perfect health.

The intensive phase of the exposure therapy lasted twenty-eight
therapeutic sessions. Situations that he had avoided before treatment
or that he had entered with tension and anxiety no longer provoked
strong anxiety reactions. He showed a healthier and more relaxed
attitude toward bodily sensations, and consequently he was able to
remain in places from which he could not easily leave at a moment's
notice. After the intensive phase came five sessions in which Robert
discussed his conflicts about having a child. His wife participated in
these sessions and was happy to discuss this issue in a more con-
structive and empathetic way. In the end, Robert was still a bit

uncertain whether he could be a good father. His wife had gained more insight into the reasons for his hesitation and could understand this point of view much better. The couple then made some plans for having a child in the future.

Two sessions concentrated on interactional problems at work. Role playing was used to extend Robert's communication and problem-solving skills. In the appointments following the intensive phase of exposure therapy, Robert reported further improvements with his "heart problems." We praised him for his success and encouraged him to continue with self-initiated exposure. In addition, we prepared Robert on how to cope with relapse situations.

Therapeutic gains were maintained at the one-year follow-up, but, as expected, it had not always been easy for Robert to cope with relapse situations. During a period of intense stress at work, he had begun monitoring his physical reactions again and had a recurrence of his panicky feelings. When he first heard that a colleague was seriously ill, the thought that the colleague could have had a heart attack flashed through his mind and triggered a panic attack. But the most important thing that Robert had learned during therapy was that he had to *seek out anxiety-provoking situations and remain in them for as long as it took for his anxiety to disappear.* Thus, he repeatedly exposed himself to frightening stimuli until he no longer reacted to them. This continued self-initiated exposure was probably essential for the long-term efficiency of the therapy.

EVALUATION OF EXPOSURE THERAPY

To evaluate the effectiveness of our treatment approach, we follow up clients at six weeks, one year, and five years after completion of the exposure therapy. Evaluation includes assessment of anxiety disorders as well as other psychological disorders such as those relating to depression, sexuality, and eating. We determine whether therapy has led to long-term improvement and whether other disorders have developed in the meantime. In addition, we assess adjustment to social and work life. Clients are asked to describe and rate how they have changed and write in their own words what the principal lessons of therapy have been. In order to achieve a representative sample at the time of the follow-ups, a great amount of effort is given to make sure that all clients participate. Clients who do not send back their questionnaires are repeatedly contacted by phone or mail to encourage them to respond.

As a result of these efforts, we succeeded in getting all clients in our initial sample to participate in the six-week and one-year follow-ups. We found that six weeks after therapy, the majority of anxiety patients (76 percent of a total of 282, who in most cases had been treated for panic disorder and agoraphobia) rated their psychological state as being much improved in comparison to pretreatment. Of the 176 clients who have reached the one-year time point, 74 percent continue to feel improved. Thus, our exposure therapy approach seems to lead to a meaningful improvement in psychological health for most of the clients who complete it.

Too few of the initial sample have reached the five-year mark to draw any conclusions about the persistence of improvement at that time. However, data collected from a previous study conducted at three German universities indicate that little relapse occurs even after five years. These results are in line with those of many other published studies that have demonstrated the success of exposure therapy in anxiety disorders. We encourage you to try it.

NOTES

P. 32, *assessment, client preparation for therapy, intensive exposure, and self-management:* Bartling, G., Fiegenbaum, W., & Krause, R. (1980). *Reizüberflutung. Theorie und Praxis.* Stuttgart: Kohlhammer.

P. 34, *semistructured interview:* Margraf, J., Schneider, S., & Ehlers, A. (1991). *Diagnostisches Interview bei Psychischen Störungen.* Berlin: Springer-Verlag;

Di Nardo, P. A., & Barlow, D. H. (1988). *Anxiety disorders interview schedule–revised (ADIS-R)*. Albany, NY: Graywind Publications.

P. 35, *Theories of cognitive consistency:* Eagly, A., & Chaiken, S. (1993). *The psychology of attitudes*. Orlando: Harcourt Brace Jovanovich.

P. 39, *direct confrontation, prolonged and repeated exposure, and response prevention:* Fiegenbaum, W., & Tuschen, B. (in press). Reizkonfrontation. In J. Margraf (Hrsg.), *Lehrbuch der Verhaltenstherapie*. Heidelberg: Springer Verlag.

P. 40, *more successful than the graded form:* Fiegenbaum, W. (1986). Long-term efficacy of exposure in-vivo for cardiac attacks. In I. Hand & H. U. Wittchen (Eds.), *Panic and phobias. Empirical evidence of theoretical models and long-term effects of behavioral treatments* (pp. 81–89). Berlin: Springer-Verlag; Grawe, K., Donati, R., & Bernauer, F. (1994). *Psychotherapie im Wandel. Von der Konfession zur Profession*. Göttingen: Hogrefe.

P. 40, *most important rule for mastering their anxieties:* Fiegenbaum, W. (1990). Langzeiteffektivität von nicht graduierter versus graduierter massierter Konfrontation bei Agoraphobikern. In W. Fiegenbaum & J. C. Brengelmann (Hrsg.), *Angststörungen. Diagnose und Therapie* (pp. 113–130). München: Gerhard Röttger Verlag.

P. 54, *most of the clients who complete it:* Fiegenbaum, W., & Tuschen, B. (1995). Therapie von Angsterkrankungen aus verhaltenstherapeutischer Sicht. In Bundesärztekammer (Hrsg.), *Fortschritt und Fortbildung in der Medizin* (pp. 99–112). Band 19. Köln: Deutscher Ärzte-Verlag.

P. 54, *little relapse occurs even after five years:* Fiegenbaum, W. (1986). Long-term efficacy of exposure in-vivo for cardiac attacks. In I. Hand & H. U. Wittchen (Eds.), *Panic and phobias. Empirical evidence of theoretical models and long-term effects of behavioral treatments* (pp. 81–89). Berlin: Springer-Verlag.

P. 54, *the success of exposure therapy in anxiety disorders:* Öst, L. G., Westling, B. E., & Hellstrom, K. (1993). Applied relaxation, exposure in vivo, and cognitive methods in the treatment of panic disorder with agoraphobia. *Behaviour Research and Therapy, 31*, 383–394; Clum, G. A., Clum, G. A., & Surls, R. (1993). A meta-analysis of treatments for panic disorder. *Journal of Consulting and Clinical Psychology, 61*, 317–326.

CHAPTER

3

TECHNIQUES OF COGNITIVE THERAPY

Stefan G. Hofmann and Patricia Marten DiBartolo

In the last two decades, investigation of the relationship between cognition and emotion has burgeoned. This line of research has had important implications for our understanding of the phenomenon of anxiety. David H. Barlow defines anxiety as "a diffuse cognitive-affective structure consisting of a negative feedback cycle characterized to varying degrees by components of high negative affect; a sense of both internal and external events proceeding in an unpredictable, uncontrollable fashion; and maladaptive shifts in attention." Hence cognitions, or thought processes, are thought to play a crucial role in the maintenance and development of the anxiety response. Although cognitive symptomatology is not always considered to be a central defining feature of each of the disorders in this class, it can be argued that cognitive processes (attributions, predictions) are essential to the development of an anxiety response. That is, a situation or object is only anxiety provoking if we believe it to be threatening in some way. For example, in individuals with panic disorder, the catastrophic misinterpretation of the rush of physical sensations experienced during

---

Note: We thank Dr. David H. Barlow for his editorial comments.

a panic attack will exacerbate their distress and perpetuate their difficulties ("I'm having a heart attack," "I'm losing my mind," "I'm going to lose control"). If a person were able to attribute panic symptoms to some more innocuous cause ("I've been stressed lately"), it would be less likely that clinical levels of anxiety would result.

Similar negative predictions are common in individuals with other anxiety disorders. In cases of social phobia, the focus is usually placed upon the consequences of public scrutiny and subsequent negative evaluation ("Nobody is going to like me," "I'm going to make a fool of myself"). Individuals with agoraphobia without a history of panic disorder feel distress if they will be unable to escape or get help in case they develop certain symptoms (dizziness, diarrhea) in a variety of situations (such as shopping or in crowds).

Although some of the cognitions typically associated with each diagnosis may be disorder-specific, there are a number of commonalities of cognition across the anxiety disorders. First, the maladaptive cognitions associated with the anxiety disorders tend to be future-oriented perceptions of danger or threat (what is about to happen, what will happen). This sense of danger may involve either physical threat (having a heart attack) or a psychological one (anxiety focused on embarrassment). In addition, these cognitions tend to focus upon a sense of the situation or symptoms of anxiety being uncontrollable. Another hallmark of anxious cognitions is that they tend to be automatic or habitual, such that a person puts no effort into conjuring up such thoughts. Instead, they occur instantaneously and sometimes in response to subtle cues.

Oftentimes, a feeling of anxiety is accompanied by hypervigilance or scanning of the environment to determine any potential sources of threat. Given that the anxious response typical of persons with anxiety disorders tends to be unrealistic (that is, there are no external dangers), individuals then tend to search inward to explain the reason for their distress ("I am going to be ill," "I am not performing well"). This often results in an inaccurate assessment of the cause of their anxiety as well as their ability to cope with the situation they are facing.

These maladaptive cognitions are the focus of this chapter. We review ways in which to apply cognitive-behavioral techniques that directly target the negative thoughts typically experienced by people with anxiety disorders, providing descriptions of the process of identifying and challenging these maladaptive thoughts. In addition, we discuss some potential difficulties that may arise when using this approach, as well as suggest ways of addressing such problems.

PRINCIPLES OF COGNITIVE-BEHAVIOR THERAPY

The central notion in cognitive-behavior therapy is that our behavioral and emotional responses are strongly moderated and influenced by our cognitions and how we perceive things. That is, we are only anxious, angry, or sad if we think that we have reason to be anxious, angry, or sad. It is not the situation per se but rather our perceptions, expectations, and interpretations of events that are responsible for our emotions. Epictetus summarized this observation in the statement: "Men are moved not by things but the views which they take of them."

The word *cognitive* in cognitive-behavior therapy implies that treatment mainly concentrates on thought processes. However, cognitive-behavior therapy does not mean that therapy is limited to cognitive modification. It simply means that the therapist gets to the client's emotions through cognitions. The client's emotional and behavioral responses are of equal importance. Effective cognitive-behavior therapy has to target all aspects of an emotional disorder, including emotional experience, behavior, and cognitions. For example, Aaron T. Beck distinguishes among the intellectual, the experiential, and the behavioral approaches, all of which are important aspects of cognitive-behavior therapy.

The central element of the behavioral approach is to encourage the development of specific forms of behavior that lead to more general changes in how patients view themselves and the world. For this reason, people often use the term *cognitive-behavioral intervention* in referring to this type of treatment as opposed to only "cognitive therapy," in order to emphasize the importance of the behavioral component.

THE THREE-COMPONENT MODEL OF ANXIETY

Fear is an unpleasant but natural emotional response to danger or threat. In contrast to fear, anxiety does not count as a basic emotion. A variety of complex behavioral and cognitive operations, mixed with a primary fear response, contribute to what we call "anxiety." For this reason, we provide a model of anxiety that furnishes a framework within which clients can discuss and describe their difficulties with anxiety. It consists of cognitive, behavioral, and physiological components. The cognitive component is the self-talk in which a person engages when feeling anxious (as with thoughts about danger). The behavioral component is how a person acts or what is done when feeling anxious (fidgeting, biting nails, escaping the situation). Lastly, the physiological component involves the physical sensations that are typical of anxiety (such as sweating, palpitations, dry mouth).

The anxiety model given to the patient is described as interactive. That is, each of the three components impacts the others. For individuals with anxiety disorders, the three components tend to affect one another negatively, often exacerbating the distress and inability to function. In this cycle, a potentially threatening situation such as having to speak publicly, may be accompanied by the presence of a number of physiological sensations (heart racing, flushed face). Consequently, a negative cognition predicting failure or danger ("I'm not going to remember what to say") will only serve to heighten physiological levels of arousal. As physical sensations increase, it is less likely that one will be able to focus upon the task at hand. Thus, instead of providing coping self-statements to alleviate anxiety ("If I forget my place, I can always look at my note cards"), the intensity of the maladaptive cognitions grows ("If I stumble, everyone is going to think that I'm stupid and unprepared"). The end result will likely be extreme levels of anxiety as well as poor performance or avoidance of the anxiety-provoking situation ("I'll just call in sick the day of my presentation"). Furthermore, similar situations in the future will elicit similar levels of anxiety and disruption.

Clients are also told that the three components of anxiety can exert a positive influence upon one another. Using the same example as above, once the physical symptoms of anxiety are first noticed, more rational responses (for instance, "Everyone gets nervous before these presentations") will prevent an exacerbation of these physical symptoms. With continued encouraging self-talk ("I can make a few mistakes and the talk can still go well"), anxiety will remain at a reasonable level. As a result, it is likely that functioning will not be disrupted and the outcome will be successful. Given the sense of mastery that results from this experience, adaptive responses will be predicted in the future.

As noted above, each of these three components is necessary for an adequate definition of anxiety. But when using cognitive-behavioral techniques, the focus is placed upon the cognitive realm first and foremost. We ask that clients begin to challenge their negative predictions by facing those situations which they find to be anxiety provoking.

We know there are no guarantees that every situation our patients face will be successful. In fact, providing only positive self-talk ("I'm sure that my talk will be great") may only serve to increase pressure as well as provide unrealistic standards for performance. This type of talk can be just as inaccurate as the negative cognitions that are more typical of anxious individuals. The goal of cognitive-behavior therapy is to foster patients' abilities to provide for themselves more realistic and accurate appraisals of their abilities and of the actual threat presented by the situations they face.

THE THERAPEUTIC PROCESS

Dividing the Process into Steps

In this section, we illustrate the techniques of cognitive-behavior therapy by dividing the process into six basic steps, a general framework to guide clinicians through the process of cognitive-behavioral treatment.

Step 1: Establishing a Good Therapeutic Relationship.
In cognitive-behavior therapy, positive therapist-client interactions flow from a collaborative relationship. Therapists should accept the client's problems and concerns. In general, therapists' behavior should be honest and warm. In addition, we should help clients realize that they themselves are experts in their own problems and are potentially capable of solving them. Clients are not considered to be helpless and passive but rather experts at dealing with their own problems. Therefore, we need to encourage clients to formulate and test certain hypotheses in order to get a better understanding of the real world and their own problems.

The initial role of cognitive-behavior therapists is very active as they educate patients about the underlying principles of this treatment approach. In addition, therapists often find that clients may need a great deal of guidance in the beginning stages of therapy to help them identify their automatic thoughts successfully. As treatment progresses, patients are expected to become increasingly active in their own treatment.

Step 2: Problem Focus.
At the beginning of treatment, it is important that the therapist and client reach a consensus regarding the goals of therapy, including identifying the type of interventions that will be used to reach these goals and delineating concrete observable outcomes that will indicate that each goal has been achieved.

Usually, clients seek help for a variety of problems. Therefore, it is extremely important that clients undergo a thorough clinical assessment in order to determine the precise nature of their difficulties. Chapter One describes a method of clinical assessment similar to ours. In addition, we use a case formulation approach. Within this strategy, the variety of overt psychological difficulties that patients present are viewed as resulting from one or two core irrational beliefs about themselves (as in "I must never appear weak," "I am incompetent"). The goal of this assessment is to identify these underlying core beliefs in order to intervene effectively during treatment. Regardless of the assessment method used, clinicians must establish with their patients the focus and goals of treatment.

The case of David, a client with social phobia, illustrates the general principle of problem reduction.

DAVID

David, a twenty-year-old student of history, sought professional help for his academic problems. At the first contact, he seemed depressed and introverted. During a subsequent structured diagnostic interview, it became apparent that David's principal difficulty involved being extremely nervous and panicky in certain social situations, such as meeting people in authority, initiating a conversation, being introduced, and going out on a date. In those situations, David stated, he typically experienced sweating, heart palpitations, tingling sensations, hot flushes, and feelings of dizziness and unreality. The typical cognitions that he experienced during social situations revolved around his concern that he would make a mistake or be ridiculed by others. As a consequence, David avoided most social situations. He reported that his lack of social contact made him feel worthless and depressed. David never had any panic attacks other than in social situations. He reported that he was anxious about negative evaluation by other people rather than his bodily symptoms.

This example illustrates the importance of a thorough evaluation in order to identify the main problem and to understand the relationship between several apparently independent problems. Whereas David presented with a host of difficulties (depression, academic problems, impaired self-worth), a more thorough assessment revealed that his primary difficulty was his social anxiety.

Once the major problem is identified, the therapist needs to break it up into component problems to be attacked in a given case. For example, David soon identified a number of social difficulties he wanted to target during treatment, including improving his social skills, becoming more assertive, and participating in a greater number of activities such as parties and dating. After this, concrete and appropriate therapeutic interventions would have to be determined.

The first step toward intervention varies from person to person. For a client with severe agoraphobia who is housebound most of the time, the first therapeutic approach may include exposure exercises. Within a cognitive approach, however, the ultimate goal of these exercises is cognitive modification. Thus the purpose would be to challenge and restructure the patient's anxious cognitions toward, for example, "I can leave my house without having a heart attack," or "I can handle going to the grocery store and nothing bad is going to happen."

Patients need to be clear about the formulation of their case as well as the rationale for treatment. Therapists should always elicit client feedback regarding their formulation in order to set the stage for a collaborative relationship. If some point is disputed, cognitive-behavior therapists suggest their formulation as a hypothesis that can be tested within the context of treatment. Also, the rationale for treatment needs to be clearly stated.

Step 3: Identifying Irrational Thoughts. Once clients define their problems and goals for treatment, they need to become aware of what they are thinking. David M. Clark classifies cognitions into negative automatic thoughts and dysfunctional or irrational beliefs. Negative automatic thoughts are thoughts or images that occur in specific situations when an individual feels anxious. For example, David (the client with social concerns) may think "Other people think I am boring," or "I will embarrass myself," or "Other people will think that I am stupid" when in an anxiety-provoking situation.

Many clients have initial difficulty identifying their automatic thoughts, because they can occur very rapidly and without the client's being consciously aware of them. Monitoring forms have been found to be very helpful at identifying maladaptive cognitions and irrational thoughts. At the Center for Stress and Anxiety Disorders in Albany, New York, for example, we use monitoring forms in order to assess various indices of functioning outside of session.

More-global mood questionnaires can be complemented by monitoring that provides information on more-molecular measures of patient symptomatology. For example, specific symptoms of interest can be monitored using tailored forms. In cases of panic disorder, we ask clients to monitor the occurrence of panic attacks.

Given the importance of understanding cognitive processes within the context of cognitive-behavior therapy, monitoring of thoughts, beliefs, and attitudes associated with anxiety is crucial. The "Monitoring and Challenging Automatic Thoughts" instrument presented in Exhibit 3.1 is a good example of a form that allows both clinicians and patients to identify and challenge their automatic cognitions as well as substitute irrational thoughts with rational ones. This form is particularly useful because it can be applied to each of the anxiety disorders. Furthermore, it illustrates the process of identifying, challenging, and replacing irrational thoughts.

In the first three columns of this form, clients learn how to identify automatic thoughts, their triggers, and their effects. The thought "I will have a panic attack" would not be considered an appropriate example of an automatic thought. Instead, clients are instructed to "dig a little deeper" and to ask themselves questions such as "What would happen if I had a panic attack?" "What would be the worst case scenario?" "What do these panic attack symptoms mean to me?" This identifies their underlying

Exhibit 3.1
Monitoring and Challenging Automatic Thoughts

Describe Trigger Event, Thought, or Sensation	Anxiety (0–8)	Automatic Thought	Belief in Thought (0–100 percent)	Alternative Thought	Question to Ask Self: "What is the evidence?"	Re-Rate Belief in Thought (0–100 percent)	Anxiety (0–8)	Questions to Ask Self: "What is the worst consequence?" "So what?"

automatic thoughts. This information is essential to clinicians as they help their patients begin to identify and challenge their automatic thoughts. This process is illustrated by transcripts from therapy sessions in later sections of this chapter.

Dysfunctional (or irrational, maladaptive) beliefs, on the other hand, are assumptions that individuals have about the world, the future, and themselves. These more global and overarching beliefs provide a schema that determines how a person may interpret a specific situation. For example, some of David's beliefs were "Everybody expects me to be entertaining, intelligent, and funny," "Unless I am liked by everyone I am worthless," and "I have to be perfect at any point in time." Such dysfunctional beliefs cause David to be not only very anxious about social situations, but also avoidant, depressed, and "touchy." He avoids interpersonal contact due to his anxiety about criticism, disapproval, and rejection and will likely feel inferior to others and be inhibited in new interpersonal situations because of feelings of inadequacy. Just as with automatic thoughts, therapists can identify irrational beliefs through the process of "guided questioning."

Step 4: Challenging Irrational Thoughts. By treating clients' irrational thoughts as hypotheses, they are put into the role of observers or scientists rather than victims of their anxiety. In order to challenge these thoughts, therapist and client discuss the evidence for and against a particular assumption in a debate, or what Beck calls "Socratic dialogue." This can be done by using information from patients' past experiences (for example, "What is the probability based on your past experience?"), by delivering more adequate information ("What are the high-risk factors of cardiovascular diseases?"), by reevaluating the outcome of a situation ("What is the worst thing that could happen?"), and by giving clients the opportunity to test their hypothesis by exposing them to feared and/or avoided activities or situations. Many automatic thoughts reported by clients with anxiety disorders are misconceptions due to the cognitive error of probability overestimation. We use the term "probability overestimation" if the person believes that an unlikely event is likely to happen.

As previously noted, the goal of these cognitive-behavioral techniques is neither to provide unwarranted reassurance nor to underestimate the likelihood that something negative can happen. Such efforts will surely fail. Instead, therapists emphasize that automatic thoughts typically err in the direction of overstating the danger or the aversiveness of a particular situation or event. Again, the goal of cognitive-behavior therapy is to help clients think more realistically and practically about the situations they face.

In addition to probability overestimation, another typical cognitive error is called "catastrophic thinking." Catastrophic thinking means blowing things out of proportion, or making "a big deal" out of something. In other words, a person with this cognitive error perceives an outcome as catastrophic even if it is not. The following conversation between the therapist and Bob, a forty-two-year-old client with the diagnosis of agoraphobia without history of panic disorder, helps illustrate the questioning techniques necessary to identify cognitive errors due to catastrophic thinking.

> *Therapist:* Why is it that you still avoid going shopping?
> *Bob:* I don't know. I guess I am still very scared of crowds.
> *Therapist:* What are you afraid might happen?
> *Bob:* I'm afraid that I may get anxious.
> *Therapist:* I understand, but can you tell me what you imagine happening if you were to get anxious when you are shopping?
> *Bob:* Sometimes in malls I feel very dizzy and disoriented.
> *Therapist:* Dizziness and being disoriented are simply sensations. Why is it that you are afraid of these sensations?
> *Bob:* I'm not afraid of anything. I don't know. I just don't like having those feelings.

Therapist: OK. Let's talk about some other feelings that you may get in your body. How did you feel last week when you had the flu?

Bob: Well, I had a temperature and my muscles were achy. I also felt flushed a lot and was really tired all the time.

Therapist: OK, let me ask you: did you get anxious when you experienced the symptoms that you had when you were sick with the flu?

Bob: No, those feelings were uncomfortable, no one likes to be sick, but I just tried to deal with them by taking care of myself and going to bed early every night.

Therapist: Then tell me, why do you think that there are certain physical sensations that make you anxious while others do not at all? Let's talk about what you might be telling yourself about these symptoms. When you are feeling dizzy, what do you imagine would be the worst thing that could happen?

Bob: (hesitating) Well, I guess I could faint. And I did twice in the past.

Therapist: OK. So you avoid crowds because you are afraid of fainting. In a minute, we can discuss the probability that you might faint. For right now, let's just assume that it would be fairly likely that you would faint. Now, what would happen if you fainted?

Bob: I never really thought of that. It would be absolutely terrible.

Therapist: OK, let's see what would be so terrible. Please picture the worst-case scenario. So, you are in the mall. Your heart is pounding, you feel very dizzy, your legs get weak, and you faint. Then what?

Bob: Wow, I guess people would gather around me. Somebody would probably call the ambulance. And they would come and would probably find nothing wrong with me.

Therapist: And then what?

Bob: I would be really embarrassed.

Therapist: And then what?

Bob: Well, that would be terrible. I couldn't handle that.

Therapist: Again, we have not talked about the actual likelihood of being embarrassed because you fainted. For right now, let's just picture the worst-case scenario. So you would be very embarrassed. Have you had any embarrassing situations in the past?

Bob: Oh, plenty.

Therapist: Have you had situations when you thought something like: I will never be able to look into these people's eyes again?

Bob: Some situations were really bad. Yes, I've been through situations like that before.

Therapist: And have you been able to cope with these situations and your feeling of embarrassment?

Bob: Well, I guess I have.

Therapist: OK. Now back to the fainting situation. Fainting in a big crowd of people is certainly an unpleasant experience. But, based on what we talked about, why exactly is it such a catastrophic situation?

Bob: It would be embarrassing but I guess it is not really a catastrophe. I think that I could handle it if I had to.

Notice how much effort was required of the therapist to elicit Bob's catastrophic thought. Oftentimes, this is the most difficult part of a restructuring exercise; however, it is essential. Without valid identification of the negative consequence, efforts at challenging will be superficial and likely to fail. Furthermore, in order to counter catastrophic thoughts, therapist and client need to identify the chain of anxiety-provoking thoughts and images until they reach the worst consequence. For example, Bob's chain of thinking was: (1) "If I feel dizzy in a mall, I will faint in public," (2) "If I faint in public, I will embarrass myself," and (3) "It would be a catastrophe if I embarrassed myself, because I would not be able to cope with this situation." Once the worst-case scenario is identified, therapist and client need to evaluate the actual severity of the consequence. The two main messages the therapist needs to convey are

1. Specific actual consequences are unlikely.
2. Anxiety and its effects are time-limited and manageable.

Some elements that lead to the worst-case scenario for Bob are examples of probability overestimations (such as "If I feel dizzy in a mall, I will faint in public"). Also, a particular automatic thought can be a result of both catastrophic thinking and probability overestimation. For each anxious thought, two questions need to be asked:

1. What is the probability that the anxiety-provoking event might happen?
2. Would the actual consequence be manageable?

It is best to apply the principle of probability overestimation if most people consider a particular event as catastrophic (as in "I will have a heart attack"). However, both principles (catastrophizing and probability overestimation) often need to be addressed to deal with patients' anxiety properly. This requires some creativity because clinicians must attempt to restructure automatic thoughts as well as convey these skills to patients in a logical and consistent manner. In a later section we discuss in further detail how to restructure catastrophic thinking that involves actual catastrophic predictions (death, serious disease, loss of a loved one).

As you are beginning with clients or they are first applying the cognitive-behavioral techniques on their own, the "Monitoring and Challenging Automatic Thoughts" form (Exhibit 3.1) is extremely helpful for challenging clients' maladaptive cognitions. After clients rate their anxiety and identify the trigger and their automatic thought, the monitoring form asks clients to rate the belief in this automatic thought on a scale of 0–100 percent (fourth column) and to provide other alternative thoughts a person could possibly have (fifth column). By finding evidence in favor of or against the alternative thought (sixth column), clients can challenge their old beliefs. In the seventh and eighth columns, clients are asked to re-rate their anxiety as well as their belief in the automatic thought on a 0–100 percent scale. The ninth and last column addresses cognitive errors due to catastrophic thinking. Clients are instructed to ask themselves questions such as "What is the worst consequence? So what?" in order to restructure such thoughts.

When patients first begin to apply their cognitive-behavioral techniques, you need to emphasize that effective use of this approach is a skill requiring effort and practice, especially at first. Patients should be told they are not expected to restructure their automatic thoughts during challenging situations. Instead, they may need to strengthen their skills by generating rational responses following an anxiety-provoking situation. To encourage regular application of these skills, clients can be instructed to examine their thoughts whenever they experience an increase in their level of anxiety. In this way, patients may be more likely to identify those automatic thoughts that are most problematic for them as well as set the stage for application of their cognitive-behavioral techniques.

Step 5: Testing the Validity.   Once irrational thoughts are identified and challenged, clients need to put their old beliefs to the test. By confronting themselves with anxiety-provoking stimuli (situations, sensations, images, activities, etc.), clients have the opportunity to conduct field experiments to examine the validity of their assumptions. For example, David, who is afraid of social interaction because of his fear of embarrassment, may be asked to give an impromptu speech about his hobbies in front of the clinic staff. Sarah, who has panic disorder and is afraid of heart palpitations and therefore avoids physical exercises, may be asked to run in place for one minute during a therapy session. Bob, who is afraid of dizziness because he may faint and embarrass himself, may be asked to hyperventilate for one minute to make himself feel dizzy.

Careful consideration needs to be given to developing exercises that are relevant to the patient's focus of anxiety. At times, a combination of exercises may be appropriate. For example, with David both in-vivo exposure to social situations as well as exposure to problematic physical sensations (such as breathlessness) that he experiences when trying to interact with others may combine to produce a practice that would be challenging to him and allow him the opportunity to test his automatic thoughts.

The therapy session is a controlled and safe environment in which to conduct these experiments. Following this initial practice, clients can be instructed to practice at home. Finally, it is important for patients to engage in these exercises in more challenging situations (perhaps when alone, or in an anxiety-provoking situation). Other exposure exercises for bodily sensations are mentioned in Chapter Eight.

After each exercise, clients are asked to give a rating of their anxiety, the intensity of their bodily sensations, and the similarity of these sensations to their naturally occurring panic attacks on a scale from 0 (not at all) to 8 (very much). Typically, some of the exercises produce high levels of anxiety. Those exercises give clients the opportunity to work on their "hot cognitions." In other words, after the anxiety-provoking exercise, clients are asked to identify their automatic thoughts, challenge these thoughts, and test their validity. For example, Bob may have felt very anxious after hyperventilating for one minute. One of his anxiety-provoking automatic thoughts may have been "Feeling dizzy is a sign that I will faint." By repeated and prolonged exposure to the feeling of dizziness, Bob is able to test his belief. After four or five repetitions of hyperventilation, Bob's anxiety decreased. Thus, this practice is extremely useful in teaching Bob that he can habituate to his sensations, and that he has overestimated the probability that his feelings of dizziness will lead to fainting.

As mentioned, after conducting these kinds of experiments in sessions, clients have to continue with field experiments as part of their homework assignments outside the therapist's office in a less-safe environment. But prior to this, clients have to create a list of feared or avoided activities or situations. One of the potential difficulties of such practices is that patients can return to session declaring that they failed or that the techniques did not work. It is always important to emphasize to your clients that there is no such thing as a "failed" practice. In fact, therapists should be aware that patients may sometimes catastrophize practices that do not go as well as they desire. Focus in session may need to be placed on helping clients restructure their negative interpretation of the outcome of the practice.

You want to develop reasonable goals for practices in part to prevent patients from viewing their performance through a negative filter following the exposure. Afterwards, you need to show clients that they can perform well and meet their goals even when they are anxious. If they escape or avoid the practice, you can work with your patients to problem-solve this difficulty together. Even if clients do not meet their goals, they can learn from their mistakes in order to make mistakes less likely in the future.

Step 6: Substituting Irrational Thoughts with Rational Thoughts and Eliciting Feedback. One of the most difficult steps in cognitive-behavior therapy is substituting irrational thoughts with rational ones. The fifth column of the form in Exhibit 3.1 asks clients to name possible alternative thoughts. To come up with alternative thoughts, clients need to ask themselves "What are alternative ways of interpreting this particular event?" or "How would other people interpret this event?" With repeated practice, clients learn to change their perspective, from being a passive victim of their own anxiety to an active observer. Moreover, monitoring forms reflect improvements, relapses, or setbacks. In this respect, monitoring forms indicate whether changes were correct and treatment is going to be successful. As noted before, monitoring forms are of crucial importance in cognitive-behavioral treatment of anxiety disorders for all of these reasons. Treatment success is very often highly correlated with compliance in filling out monitoring forms such as "Monitoring and Challenging Automatic Thoughts."

Like any bad habits, automatic thoughts can be very resistant to change. This is normal and to be expected. If clients quickly dismiss their automatic thoughts after only a few sessions and characterize them as ridiculous, stupid, or crazy, the therapist has good reason to worry. In this case, it is likely that clients do not take their automatic thoughts seriously, maybe because they are embarrassed to endorse them with the therapist or are unwilling to accept them for some other reason. Further, perhaps they have not fully explored the underlying automatic thought. Patients need to understand that there are many different ways an event can be interpreted. In order to interpret an event, we need to formulate hypotheses that ultimately determine our emotional response to the event.

You can ask patients to help you make a list of these automatic thoughts as well as the rational responses that they can apply. In the following dialogue, David and his therapist prepare for his conversation in the upcoming week.

> *Therapist:* Now that you have created reasonable goals for your practice, we need to discuss the thoughts that you may be likely to have when you start this conversation. In other words, we need to problem-solve by anticipating what automatic thoughts may get in the way of doing the practice or reaching your goals. Can you tell me what you think some of these thoughts may be?
>
> *David:* Like I said earlier, my main concern is that he will reject me—not want to talk with me or be my friend.
>
> *Therapist:* OK, I want you to try to challenge that thought.
>
> *David:* Let's see. I know that the first thing I am supposed to do is question the evidence for my thought. Well, I have met other people who had wanted to get to know me better. In fact, most of the times that I have had this thought it doesn't turn out to be true.
>
> *Therapist:* Let's be more specific. How many times have you

been interested in becoming friends with someone and they have rejected you?

David: That's really never happened. The only times that I have been rejected by other people has been when we've had an argument or misunderstanding about something, and even then we can usually work things out.

Therapist: Great. So you're saying that having looked at the evidence from your past experiences, it is not very likely that you will be rejected when you approach this person at work. Even though it is very unlikely, imagine the worst-case scenario. Imagine that this guy tells you that he wants nothing to do with you when you talk to him. What would happen then?

David: I'd be so embarrassed. That would be awful.

Therapist: What would be so terrible about it?

David: I'm sure that it would get around the office and then everyone would think that I'm an idiot.

Therapist: What then?

David: Well, they might not want to have anything to do with me. They would all ignore me and not want to be friendly with me anymore.

Therapist: OK, now I want you to challenge this thought.

David: I guess it's kind of silly of me to think that everyone I know in the office would be mean to me just because one person didn't like me. It's not very likely that they would let one person's opinion change their feelings about me. And even if it did happen, I could try to cope with it by talking to some of my coworkers individually. If they were unreasonable enough to let one person dictate how they should feel about me, then maybe I wouldn't want to be close to them anyway.

Therapist: Great job. Now what I want you to do as you are preparing for your practice is to review this restructuring. We'll talk about the practice next week after you've done it.

This review of automatic thoughts and possible rational responses is crucial to increasing the probability that the assigned practice will be therapeutic. Adequate preparation before a practice makes it more likely that patients will be able to identify the inaccuracies of their negative predictions, appraise their performance accurately, and enjoy their efforts and successes.

COMMON DIFFICULTIES IN COGNITIVE-BEHAVIOR THERAPY

Now that the general principles of cognitive-behavior therapy for individuals with anxiety disorders have been reviewed, it seems important to discuss some of the potential pitfalls of using this approach. Although such difficulties do occur, they can be easily managed if you are prepared to deal with them in an effective and therapeutic manner.

Catastrophic Anxiety

One challenge to the cognitive-behavior therapist is working with individuals who report being bothered by thoughts that are truly catastrophic (such as dying, developing Alzheimer's, being paralyzed). Obviously, decatastrophizing these thoughts can at times feel like an insurmountable task. The first step to dealing with anxiety is to identify and restructure the probability overestimation error that characterizes such thoughts ("How likely is this catastrophe?"). Some clients, however, describe continued anxiety resulting from even this reduced estimation. In such a case, the focus is on attempting to decatastrophize these thoughts. Focus here might be on the patient's ability to cope or even the need to cope ("If you are dead, what do you need to worry about? Although it would be tragic to be physically impaired, could you find any part of life worth living?").

Consistently reminding patients throughout this process that what we are actually talking about has little likelihood of occurring can be important. When dealing with a catastrophic prediction, the focus should be on putting things in perspective. Again, you must ask patients to remember how unlikely this outcome is and also how surprised they may be at how well they could deal with it.

Realistic Anxieties

An additional difficulty that cognitive-behavior therapists often need to face when working with individuals with anxiety disorders is the fact that patients' feared outcomes may involve realistic concerns. A variety of family, financial, employment, and medical difficulties can often be associated with clients' feared consequences. Here you need to remember to reassure patients that you recognize the stress they are currently experiencing, but you feel nonetheless that it is important to focus upon ways in which they can better deal with these real problems. In fact, this skill seems all the more urgent because of the realistic stress that they are experiencing because of their life circumstances.

A common example of realistic fears may be related to a client's deficit in certain skills. For example, with socially anxious individuals there is a proportion of such people who lack the appropriate social skills to interact successfully with others. Thus, when you ask them to challenge their estimation of the likelihood that something negative will happen in a given social situation, they may inform you that they have had a number of unpleasant experiences. When such difficulties arise, it is important to address the particular skill deficit that is interfering with your patients' ability to use the cognitive-behavioral techniques. With regard to the example of a socially awkward individual with social anxiety, time should be spent on providing social skills training in tandem with the appropriate cognitive-behavioral techniques.

Lack of Insight

A third potential difficulty of doing cognitive work is finding yourself attempting these techniques with patients who report little or no insight into their own cognitive processes or automatic thoughts. Despite repeated probing, they are unable to report to you any thoughts they have when they are anxious. Instead, they may reply that their anxiety occurs from out of the blue or independently of any stressor.

Here it might be particularly important to teach patients the skill of causal analysis. That is, they need to thoroughly examine both external and internal reasons for the anxiety that they are experiencing. You must emphasize that anxiety never occurs without a cause, and it is extremely important that the cause of anxiety be identified. Otherwise, patients begin to believe that anxiety is uncontrollable and unpredictable. Such attitudes only further contribute to their hypervigilance and the sense of vulnerability that is often reported by individuals with anxiety disorders.

In order to help clients identify their automatic thoughts in a given situation, you may find that exploring their responses to alternative situations helps you identify their feared outcome.

EFFECTIVENESS OF COGNITIVE-BEHAVIORAL TREATMENT

For a number of mental disorders, including anxiety disorders, schizophrenia, depression, and alcohol abuse, cognitive-behavioral treatment is clearly effective. Cognitive-behavioral techniques have been found particularly effective for the treatment of anxiety disorders, including panic disorder with and without agoraphobia and social phobia. As just one example, Barlow and his co-authors demonstrated that cognitive-behavioral techniques are more effective in treating panic disorder with mild agoraphobia than is applied relaxation, a credible psychological alternative. The results of this particular study showed that approximately 80 percent of patients undergoing this kind of treatment were panic-free after twelve weekly sessions. In comparison, only 40 percent improved after receiving applied relaxation, and 30–35 percent of patients from the wait list evidenced similar levels of improvement.

Cognitive-behavioral interventions have been found to be not only more effective than credible placebo or no treatment but at least as good as existing pharmacological approaches immediately after treatment. For example, cognitive-behavioral treatment for panic treatment was superior to alprazolam as well as either a wait list or drug placebo. Cognitive-behavioral treatment for panic disorder with agoraphobia combines very well with tricyclic antidepressants. Some of the high potency benzodiazepines, such as alprazolam (Xanax), may interfere with the effects of psychologically based exposure treatments over the long run. For example, Isaak M. Marks et al. showed that initial improvement was approximately equal in a cognitive-behavioral treatment that included exposure whether a drug was a part of the treatment or not. However, at follow-up periods, those treated with medication showed substantial relapse.

Similar findings have been reported for the treatment of social phobia. Results show that both cognitive-behavioral group treatment and drug treatment with a monoamine oxidase inhibitor (MAOI) are of approximately equal effectiveness, and both are significantly more effective than either a drug placebo or a credible educational support treatment. Preliminary results from follow-up show continuing comparability. However, individuals who improve on medication begin to relapse when it is discontinued, while those who improve with cognitive-behavior therapy maintain their gains.

In this chapter, we have given a brief introduction of the principles of cognitive-behavior therapy and illustrated some of its basic techniques. We also demonstrate that cognitive-behavior therapy is a short, efficient, and highly cost-effective method for treating anxiety disorders. We see cognitive-behavior therapy as one among many possible alternatives clients can use as a strategy to help them manage their anxiety. Cognitive-behavioral techniques are easy to combine with exposure treatment, relaxation exercises, pharmacotherapy, and psychodynamic psychotherapies. Controversies among different theories should not keep us from using effective treatment methods. After all, our primary goal as therapists is to help our patients.

NOTES

P. 57, *David H. Barlow defines anxiety:* Barlow, D. H. (1988). *Anxiety and its disorders.* New York: Guilford Press.

P. 59, *Aaron T. Beck distinguishes:* Beck, A. T. (1979). *Cognitive therapy and the emotional disorders.* New York: Meridian; Beck, A. T. (1985). *Anxiety disorders and phobias: A cognitive perspective.* New York: Basic Books.

P. 64, *David M. Clark classifies cognitions:* Clark, D. M. (1989). Anxiety states: Panic and generalized anxiety. In K. Hawton, P. M. Salkovskis, J. Kirk, & D. M. Clark (Eds.), *Cognitive behaviour therapy for psychiatric problems: A practical guide.* Oxford: Oxford University Press.

P. 73, *exercises that are relevant to the patient's focus of anxiety:* Barlow, D. H., & Craske, M. G. (1994). *Mastery of your anxiety and panic II.* Albany, NY: Graywind Publications.

P. 79, *Cognitive-behavioral techniques have been found particularly effective:* Craske, M. G., Brown, T. A., & Barlow, D. H. (1991). Behavioral treatment of panic disorder: A two-year follow-up. *Behavior Therapy, 22,* 289–304; Mattick, R. P., & Peters, L. (1988). Treatment of severe social phobia: Effects of guided exposure with and without cognitive restructuring. *Journal of Consulting and Clinical Psychology, 56,* 251–260.

P. 79, *Barlow and his co-authors demonstrated:* Barlow, D. H., Craske, M. G., Cerny, J. A., & Klosko, J. S. (1989). Behavioral treatment of panic disorder. *Behavior Therapy, 20,* 261–282.

P. 80, *combines very well with tricyclic antidepressants:* Mavissakalian, M. R. (1993). Combined behavioral and pharmacological treatment of anxiety disorders. In J. M. Oldham, M. B. Riba, & A. Tasman (Eds.), *Review of Psychiatry, Vol.*

12 (pp. 565–584). Washington, DC: American Psychiatric Press; Clark, D. M., Salkovskis, P. M., Hackman, A., Middleton, H., Anastasiades, P., & Gelder, M. (1994). A comparison of cognitive therapy, applied relaxation, and imipramine in the treatment of panic disorder. *British Journal of Psychiatry, 164,* 759–769.

P. 80, *Isaak M. Marks et al. (1993):* Marks, I. M., Swinson, R. P., Basoglu, M., Kuch, K., Noshirvani, H., O'Sullivan, G., Lelliott, P. T., Kirby, M., McNamee, G., Sengun, S., & Wickwire, K. (1993). Alprazolam and exposure alone and combined in panic disorder with agoraphobia: A controlled study in London and Toronto. *British Journal of Psychiatry, 162,* 776–787.

4

PROGRESSIVE RELAXATION

Paul Lehrer and Richard Carr

Progressive relaxation is a technique for teaching people very subtle awareness about muscle tension in everyday life and how to eliminate it at will. It was developed in the 1930s by Edmund Jacobson, a distinguished physician and psychologist. Variations on the technique were later invented by more recent behavior therapists.

Progressive relaxation involves training for recognition of very small degrees of muscle tension, and for voluntary cessation of that tension. It proceeds with training in one or a few muscle groups in each session, until the trainee has learned to relax the whole body progressively. Trainees also are specifically taught to tense muscles that are needed differentially (and differentially relax those that are unneeded) for any given activity (walking, sitting, driving, writing, discussing emotional topics, etc.). It encourages more efficient use of the body and reduces excessive muscle tension, which has been identified as a factor contributing to fatigue, headaches, chronic pain, stress, breathing irregularities, and acute and chronic anxiety.

WHAT PROGRESSIVE RELAXATION DOES

Brief training in progressive relaxation appears to have greater effects on problems with a pronounced muscular involvement, such as muscle contraction headaches and other forms of muscle pain, than do less muscle-focused methods such as autogenic training. But more intensive training in progressive relaxation also has been widely used for treating problems with a predominantly autonomic or cognitive base. Jacobson and his colleagues have proposed neural pathways by which cognition and autonomic arousal may be affected by progressive relaxation.

The most comprehensive explanation of the mechanisms by which progressive relaxation affects the autonomic nervous system was offered by physiologist Ernst Gelhorn. He noted that fibers from the skeletal muscles (the muscles that can be contracted voluntarily) are a large proportion of the nerve input into a part of the brain called the reticular system, which stimulates the sympathetic nervous system (controlling heart action, blood pressure, and sweating) to produce the pattern of physiological responses that are part of anxiety. Nerve fibers also go from the reticular system to the cortex, increasing alertness and a feeling of nervousness. Thus, if progressive relaxation can reduce input to the reticular system, sympathetic nervous activity, alertness, and associated cognitive activity will be dampened. Following Jacobson's early clinical observations, psychologist F. J. McGuigan showed experimentally that the process of thinking invariably involves muscular activity, and that all thought disappears during very deep muscle relaxation.

Progressive relaxation has thus been widely used for treating somatic conditions affected by the autonomic nervous system, including hypertension, irritable bowel syndrome, and asthma, as well as more purely psychological problems such as generalized anxiety and phobias. It is the behavioral treatment of choice for psychosomatic problems involving neuromuscular tension. It also is used for treating worry, insomnia, and obsessive ruminations.

Relation to Biofeedback

This chapter describes a method, quite similar to Jacobson's original one, that emphasizes training in the recognition and control of individual muscle groups with a goal of complete relaxation of all skeletal muscles. As such it is similar to the more technology-intensive method of biofeedback using the electromyogram (EMG). In fact, with the collaboration of engineers from Bell Laboratories, Jacobson was the inventor of the surface EMG recorder ("surface" in the sense that recording is from the skin over the muscles rather than from the muscle itself) that is used today in all EMG biofeedback units. He called it the "integrating neurovoltmeter."

Jacobson used zero microvolts of surface EMG as the gold standard for relaxation. He did not, however, approve of the use of EMG biofeedback itself during relaxation training. Although late in his career he tried applying biofeedback clinically, he rejected the method because he felt that it would make the learner dependent on the presence of a machine. In those days the integrating neurovoltmeter took up the better part of a large room, and a home EMG trainer—let alone a fully portable unit—was unthinkable. The modern portable surface EMG biofeedback unit might have softened his objection. More recent research suggests that EMG biofeedback may hasten relaxation learning among some individuals, particularly compared with some of the briefer progressive relaxation methods described below.

In our own clinical experience, an appreciable minority of clients find it difficult to isolate feelings of tension in habitually tense muscles, but they are helped by using biofeedback machines. The machines are particularly helpful for teaching awareness of muscle tension during sleep, as may be important in treating nocturnal bruxism. There is also evidence that some individuals react better to external signals than to internal ones. Such individuals tend to score high on tests of "external control" (that is, they tend to think that things happen to them because of outside forces rather than because of their own actions) and tend to score lower on tests of ability to become completely absorbed in an experience or to become hypnotized.

Original Versus Revised Methods

Jacobson also rejected the use of "relaxation suggestions." He did not want learners to *think* they were relaxed when, in fact, they were not. From his perspective, the salutary effects of relaxation stemmed from the muscle relaxation itself, not from any mental effects associated with *believing* oneself to be relaxed.

Since Jacobson's early descriptions, progressive relaxation has undergone a variety of changes, many of which are intended to shorten the procedure or to augment the learning of a muscle skill with hypnotic or autogeniclike suggestions. A review of the literature shows that these short cuts may alter the nature of the technique and its clinical effects. Although they may produce more immediate perceptions of being relaxed and may have quicker effects on *verbal reports* of tension, they might be expected to have smaller effects in producing actual muscle relaxation. For example, some so-called progressive relaxation methods make considerable use of hypnotic and autogenic suggestions. They also frequently give training in *all* muscle groups with the very first session, and in all sessions thereafter, while Jacobson's method trains only a few groups in each session.

In our clinical experience, most trainees do require several days or even weeks of training on a relatively small number of muscle groups in order to learn to recognize and control muscle tension down to the zero or near-zero level. Although the "revised" methods may produce greater feelings of relaxation during the initial sessions, they do not provide as thorough training in recognition and control of muscle tension itself. Indeed, the progressive aspect of progressive relaxation involves gradual expansion of training from one muscle group to another, and from control of more severe tension to control of minute levels of muscle tone. Most people who were originally trained in one of the revised methods, including highly experienced clinicians, report experiencing qualitatively greater amounts of sensitivity and control over muscles after subsequent training in Jacobson's method. However, very few empirical comparisons have been made between new and old methods, and none have been published because of their methodological weaknesses. At this time, one must rely on the clinical reports of practitioners who have used both.

Some have objected to Jacobson's method as being impractical in the usual clinical setting: too lengthy, requiring too much time commitment, and not emphasizing a "relaxation experience." Indeed, Jacobson's classic book on the topic, *Progressive Relaxation* (the revised edition was published in 1938 by the University of Chicago Press), does make it appear that most of his patients received training in only one muscle group a week and that the training lasted for many months. However, elsewhere Jacobson has described very brief methods of training, even as little as one session. Although Jacobson wrote of preferring the slower and more intensive method, he also showed how his method could be applied in training that was quite brief. In his training of one of the authors, he spent one session each in training all the muscles of a particular region of the body: arms, legs, trunk, neck, eye region of the face, speech region of the face, mouth, and larynx. He often saw people biweekly or monthly for such training.

Jacobson also avoided the use of tape-recorded training. He felt that taped instructions might distract trainees' attention from the often subtle internal cues they must attend to during learning of the technique, and that they might become dependent on the tape rather than on internal cues from the muscles for detecting tension or relaxation. Clients who are dependent on tapes for relaxing might never learn how to apply their newly learned skills and might instead succumb to "suggested" rather than genuine muscular relaxation. Also, training that proceeds *only* through the use of tape-recorded instructions does not allow for trainee variations in performance and learning, and it cannot provide the feedback and correction necessary for learning a new muscular skill. There is considerable evidence that individuals trained only by taped instructions do not learn a generalizable relaxation skill. They are unable to produce measurable relaxation effects on any physiological function, when measured in a session in which taped instruction is absent.

Revised relaxation methods also often convey the impression that an individual relaxes by tensing a muscle and then letting it go. This was never Jacobson's intention. Tense-release instructions are provided at the outset of treatment as a didactic device—to give the trainee the "feel" of tension, and to recognize what must *not* be done when trying to relax. However, tension is the opposite of relaxation. For this reason, Jacobson warned against even using the expression "relaxation exercise" when referring to progressive relaxation instruction. In fact, there is some evidence, both from Jacobson's laboratory and from our own, that several seconds of severe tension can produce *greater* levels of subsequent muscle tension, even though the trainee sometimes *feels* more relaxed.

FACTORS IN TRAINING

It may come as a surprise to readers that Jacobson's method does not necessarily require an exceptionally long period of training. Although Jacobson described many cases of prolonged training in progressive relaxation (twenty sessions or more), he also realized that this often was impractical; as mentioned above, he described cases in which training was provided in as little as one session.

The most important features of his method are that muscles are trained individually and that the trainee genuinely learns to perceive subtle levels of muscle sensations and the muscle control necessary to eliminate them. In this chapter we provide the reader with a detailed description of progressive relaxation training over the course of approximately eight sessions. First, let's consider some general factors.

Environment

Clients learning progressive relaxation should try to practice for a full hour a day. Although most trainees fall short of this ideal goal in home practice, some form of regular home practice is necessary for learning the technique. The busy lives of some stressed individuals appear to preclude adequate time for practice. We have occasionally suggested that such people wake up earlier in the morning to practice, especially because the quality of rest during progressive relaxation practice sometimes exceeds that obtained from sleep in those morning hours. There are no particular prescriptions as to the ideal time of day for home practice. However, practicing the method just before bedtime sometimes prevents genuine practice from occurring because people often go to sleep when they practice the method while tired. Although this may help relieve the irritability and stress symptoms associated with fatigue and insomnia, the trainee does not learn new muscle relaxation skills during sleep.

When practicing at home, the client should turn off telephone ringers and tell other family members that he or she does not wish to be disturbed. Apportioning part of the day to such practice is a hallmark of all relaxation methods, and it may in itself account for some of their salutary effects. When the clients acquire adequate relaxation skills, they are instructed in the use of "minipractices" prior to the stressful events (such as business meetings or social encounters) and in the use of differential relaxation while engaged in stressful activities.

For relaxation practice, the client must be dressed in loose-fitting, comfortable clothing. Clothing worn tightly around the abdomen (trousers, dresses, or belts) can adversely affect both breathing and muscular tension. Contact lenses, glasses, jewelry, and shoes should be removed. The client should lie in a supine position on a bed or reclining chair that provides proper back support as well as complete support for the head and neck. If the client is practicing at home on a bed, the head should be supported by a pillow. Lights should be dimmed so the trainee is not gazing into a bright light bulb. Usually, it is advised not to train or practice on a full or an empty stomach or right after strenuous exercise. Sensations associated with digestion or hunger can distract individuals from paying attention to muscle sensations, and muscle fatigue can decrease sensitivity for perceiving very low levels of muscle tension.

Sequence of Training

Training usually begins with the arms, because they are rarely a focus of tension problems and because there is plentiful voluntary control of arm muscles. Training is not usually begun in a problem area, where tension may initially be more difficult to perceive and control. Ensuring success early in training is good pedagogical practice; hence we begin in an area where success is readily obtained. This is usually followed by training in relaxation of the leg muscles, and then the muscles of the trunk, neck, and face.

Elevated tension is often located in areas of the body close to symptom areas. Tension may include "bracing" against pain from some bodily source. Compensatory tension also may occur at rather distant sites when the individual engages in postural shifts to avoid experiencing pain or discomfort and then strains muscles at the compensatory site. As mentioned above, even minimal mental effort can produce muscle tension. Thinking about a part of the body usually leads to tension there, along with tension in the muscles of the eyes. McGuigan found that visual thought especially involves eye muscle tension and verbal thought, especially tension of the muscles of the mouth and larynx. He believed conscious thought to be impossible in a state of complete muscle relaxation.

Comparing the Effectiveness of Various Techniques

Although some clients can be helped dramatically by the use of progressive relaxation alone, we generally combine it with other methods. Alone it appears to be a particularly effective treatment for problems in which skeletal muscle tension is a prominent symptom, for example, muscle contraction headaches. Relatively brief training in progressive relaxation (five or six sessions) has more muscular effects but fewer autonomic effects (that is, on heart rate, blood pressure, sweating) than autogenic training, and greater effect on the body than mantra meditation methods such as transcendental meditation. Progressive relaxation also produces fewer instances of "relaxation-induced anxiety" than the other two methods.

Some of the revised methods of progressive relaxation produce weaker effects on skeletal muscle relaxation (as measured by surface EMG) than does EMG biofeedback to a particular site. The classical Jacobson method, however, has not yet been compared empirically with EMG biofeedback. Also, it should be noted that many methods of relaxation may produce very generalized relaxation effects (muscular, autonomic, and cognitive) when the methods have been practiced intensively over years. Only a few individuals, however, so devote themselves to such discipline; most do not learn methods so thoroughly. Hence the differences between methods as observed after relatively brief periods of training are clinically important.

Combining Progressive Relaxation with Other Techniques.   Progressive relaxation can be combined with other methods quite easily. In treating phobias, it is often combined with systematic desensitization and exposure therapy. For problems of anger management (including marital and relationship difficulties), progressive relaxation can be combined with training in assertiveness and negotiation skills. For treating emotional difficulties of various kinds, it can easily be combined with cognitive therapy. When combining it with these methods, we often spend twenty to thirty minutes of each session (or sometimes every second session) in teaching progressive relaxation and its application in daily life, while the rest of the time is spent in practicing the other treatment methods.

Combining progressive relaxation with other *relaxation* methods is more problematic because of possible conflict in instructions; however, the experienced practitioner may be able to do this quite effectively while remaining true to the rationales for the various methods. For example, autogenic training makes use of suggestion while progressive relaxation avoids it. Autogenic training and meditation both make use of subvocal verbalization while progressive relaxation avoids it because it creates tension in the vocal muscles. Sometimes, however, autogenic instructions may be helpful in speeding learning of autonomic control, and meditation may be helpful in early sessions to control anxiety-provoking thoughts. During advanced practice of all methods, however, a state of passivity is emphasized, and all effective methods can be seen as a means to achieving that end. Thus when applying progressive relaxation in daily life, the individual no longer tenses and relaxes muscles but simply "lets go." Similarly, advanced meditators or users of autogenic training no longer subvocalize formulas or mantras. They exercise more direct control over mind and body to produce a state of relaxation, homeostasis, mindfulness, and integration.

Practice Requirements

Jacobson advised his patients to practice progressive relaxation for one hour a day and then to practice differential relaxation throughout every day during daily activities. In fact, research has shown that such dedication may not be necessary to produce therapeutic results for a variety of stress-related medical and psychological problems. After one learns the basics of the method, it appears to be sufficient to practice even just occasionally (once or twice a week), or just to use it when experiencing symptoms of stress or anticipating a stressful situation.

Learning to relax muscles is like learning any other simple muscle skill like swimming or riding a bicycle. Some practice is necessary to maintain peak performance, but once learned the skill remains within one's behavioral repertoire and can easily be called upon when needed. However, if an individual actively dislikes the method and seems unlikely to use it at all, it is best to try something else. Research has found that symptom levels return to pretreatment levels when clients completely forgo practice and use of the relaxation methods they have learned.

TEACHING THE METHOD

The following is based on a manual that we have used for teaching progressive relaxation in eight sessions.

Presenting the Rationale to the Client

As with any therapeutic intervention, therapist-client collaboration is essential. Time should be devoted to discussing the client's expectations for relaxation therapy. Then the following rationale is provided to the client:

> During the eight treatment sessions, we will instruct you in progressive relaxation. This method has been developed to help you learn to reduce anxious reactions to stressful situations. It involves learning to relax all the major muscles in your body. We will begin with learning how to relax your arms, then your legs, then your trunk (stomach, chest, back, and shoulders), then your eyes, and finally your mouth. We leave the eyes and mouth for last because learning to control muscle tension in those areas may be more difficult. Nevertheless they are important. Anytime someone is worried about or preoccupied with some upsetting event, there is an increase in muscle tension around the eye region, which sometimes produces tension headaches in the forehead region. Here are some important issues for you to consider as we begin:
>
> 1. *Relationship between anxiety and muscle tension.* Your feelings of tension and anxiety are related to muscle tension. Whenever you are tense, or even if you are just thinking about something, there is some muscle tension.

2. *Control by relaxation.* When you are feeling too anxious or aroused or tense, it is good for you to be able to control those feelings. One way that we know you can control them is by learning to relax your muscles. The problem is that most people are not aware of their muscle tension when they are anxious; even if they are aware of it, they are not able to control it. I am going to teach you to recognize your muscle tension before it causes symptoms, and teach you a way to control it.

3. *How relaxation is learned.* In this procedure, I am going to ask you to tense and relax muscles throughout your body to learn what muscle tension feels like, and how to control it.

4. *Purpose.* The purpose of this is not to give you exercise. These are not relaxation "exercises." Rather the purpose is to teach you to recognize what you are already doing so that you can stop doing it—that is relaxation. Doing things always involves tension. In this training, I will teach you how to stop doing things. That is what relaxation is all about.

5. *Goal.* Let me draw an analogy to how you run your car. When you "switch off" your muscles, you will stop doing things and relax, just as you turn off the ignition in your car and the car stops. Most of us keep our engines running all the time. The purpose of this training is to teach you how to shut them off when you want to do so. Even thoughts stop when you switch off your muscles completely. Relaxation is not doing anything. It is switching off. Do you have any questions? It is hard to understand until we do it.

The following are essential points that should be repeated throughout training:

We call relaxing switching off or "going negative" to indicate that no effort is required to relax. An effort to relax is a failure to relax. By learning to switch off when you are tense, you will not only feel more relaxed but you will also save energy that can be used more efficiently for other things. Wasting energy in muscle tension and nervous habits can cause you to be tired, much as leaving your lights on unnecessarily can run down your battery. Relaxation is a skill; practice is very, very important.

I'll be asking you to practice this technique for one hour every day. If you do so, eventually you will notice tension in your muscles automatically throughout the day, and you will be able to relax at will *while you go about your daily activities.* This is a gradual process. It may take several days or several weeks before you really start to notice the benefits from practicing this technique.

Do you have any questions? Your feelings of anxiety are related to muscle tension. When you are nervous or tense or even when you think about an anxious situation, there is muscle tension. The problem is that most people don't notice this tension so they can't control it. I'll be teaching you to recognize tension and to relax it away when you wish to do so. By individually tensing and relaxing various muscles throughout your body, you will learn to notice and control your tension. Tensing muscles doesn't *produce* relaxation. It just teaches you what it feels like when you aren't relaxing, and how to control these feelings.

Troubleshooting Problem Muscles

At any point during training, a client may experience difficulty in recognizing tension, may find it difficult to discriminate tension from other interoceptive stimuli (like the stretching of counterposing muscles), or may just not "get it." Here are four strategies to assist the client in recognizing and acquiring control of muscle tension.

1. Therapists use their own hands to offer resistance to the movement the trainee has been instructed to make. This increases muscle sensations and makes them easier to perceive.
2. Trainees touch the place where they should be feeling a signal that gives them control, and the therapist then has them make

the movement, asking if any sensation of tension can be felt there.

3. The therapist can lightly touch the spot where trainees should be feeling a control signal and then has them make the movement, asking if any sensation of tension can be felt there.

4. The therapist can tell clients that this area may be an individual "trouble spot," and if so, with practice the perception of sensations from it should become easier: the more generally relaxed the trainee is, the easier it will be to feel the tension.

We should note that Jacobson himself usually did not use steps 2–4 because he felt that telling the trainee where to experience tension might produce *suggested* sensations of relaxation, which might not correspond to actual tension sites. However, this very conservative approach can sometimes present a frustrating obstacle for the trainee. Surface EMG biofeedback can be used on occasion to verify whether the trainee's perceptions of tension are in fact valid.

The following section describes the content of individual sessions.

SESSION 1: PROGRESSIVE RELAXATION OF THE ARMS

For each of these steps, start first with the dominant arm and then repeat for the nondominant arm. Try not to tell the trainee where the sensations of tension should be felt, unless frustration appears to be setting in. Let the trainee discover this through repeated tensing. If the sensations cannot be perceived after several attempts and some counterforce, move to another muscle group. Eventually, however, the therapist may point out the correct spot. For each muscle group, have the trainee tense repeatedly until the sensation of tension is achieved. Use the "Method of Diminishing Tensions" (described below). Try very gradual reductions in tension in order to train for increased sensitivity.

The trainee should perceive the tension while moving so little that the observer can hardly see it.

1. Keeping the arm relaxed on the arm of a chair, the trainee is instructed to bend the hand back at the wrist so that the fingers point up toward the ceiling at a 45 degree angle. Observe tension in the back of the upper part of the forearm. Point out the differing sensations of tension in the forearm extensor muscle (on the back of the forearm, approximately two-thirds of the distance to the elbow). This sensation should be contrasted with the more easily perceived sensation of strain in the wrist joint and the passive stretching of the opposing muscle (on the underside of the arm). Actual muscle tension is usually perceived as a slight squeezing sensation, whereas joint strain may actually be painful, and passive sensations may appear as qualitatively different stretching sensations. When the sensations are correctly perceived, instruct the trainee to switch off.

After the forearm muscle has been switched off for about twenty to thirty seconds, ask the trainee to repeat the flexing but this time to use only about half the tension of the first try. If the trainee cannot recognize the tensions in the forearm at 50 percent tension, instruct him or her to bend the hand back just to the point where the tension can be recognized. Proceed with the Method of Diminishing Tensions.

2. Method of Diminishing Tensions. If the trainee can recognize tension at 50 percent, ask him or her to reduce it again by half. Ask if the trainee can notice the tension now. Ask to have it reduced by half again, and then again, and then again until the hand rests on the arm of the chair. Ask the trainee to switch off completely between contractions. This is the Method of Diminishing Tensions.

Finally, after allowing the arm to remain relaxed for thirty seconds or more, ask the trainee to "just begin, very slowly and very slightly, to bend the hand back at the wrist, but this time do it so slightly that I hardly see you move it. . . . There, do you notice the tension? Can you create the tension without bending the hand back at all? Good! Now switch off completely." Then step out of the room for two minutes, telling the trainee to remain switched off. Leaving the room allows the trainee to practice relaxation as will be expected at home. When reentering the room, the therapist should note whether the trainee has remained relaxed without moving. If so, the trainee should be complimented. If tension or movement has occurred, the therapist should mention this, and remind the trainee that relaxation consists of doing *nothing*.

3. The trainee should proceed with the following: keeping the arm relaxed on the arm of the chair, roll it onto its side so that the thumb is toward the ceiling. Bend the hand toward the body. Observe tension in the inside (ventral) surface of the forearm, the forearm flexor. Sensations of stretching may occur in the forearm extensor, and strain in the wrist joint may also be perceived. Compare the sensations of tension to those of joint strain and of passive stretching. Use the Method of Diminishing Tensions. After the trainee perceives the sensations and switches off, the therapist should step out for two minutes as before. Instruct the trainee to remain relaxed during this period, to observe any possible remaining sensations of residual tension, but not to "do" anything to relax. Remind the trainee that relaxation is the opposite of "doing" and that *trying* to relax may prevent real relaxation from occurring.

4. Keeping the lower arm flat on the arm of the chair and the hand relaxed, the trainee should bend the arm back at the elbow as if trying to touch the shoulder with the back of the hand. Observe tension in the biceps. Only bend the arm about halfway up towards vertical. Turn the palm up for stronger sensations. Use the Method of Diminishing Tensions. Then the therapist steps out for two minutes as before.

5. Keeping the lower arm flat on the arm of the chair, the trainee should bend the hand down at the wrist (use a book under the wrist if the tension is difficult to feel and more bending is needed). Observe tension in the back of the upper arm (triceps). Use the Method of Diminishing Tensions. Then the therapist steps out for two minutes.

6. If the trainee is not "getting" a muscle, refer to Troubleshooting Problem Muscles above.

7. Ask if the trainee feels residual tension after switching off. Explain that this will diminish with time.

Home Practice

Review the general instructions with the trainee. Over the next few days, the trainee should spend one hour a day practicing what has been learned. Also, have the trainee check the arm muscles several times during the day and release tension, particularly when experiencing emotional or physical tension.

SESSION 2: PROGRESSIVE RELAXATION OF THE LEGS

At the beginning of this and each subsequent session, review the progressive relaxation rationale. Talk about experiences during practice sessions and application of techniques between practice sessions. Compliment the trainee for paying attention to the instructions and using them.

Relaxation of the leg muscles is best done in a reclining position on a bed, couch, or reclining chair. For each of these steps, start first with one leg and then repeat for the other leg. Begin by having the trainee switch off muscle tension in their arms, and then step out for two minutes. Trainees should then proceed as follows:

1. Bend the foot at the ankle, pointing toes towards the head. Observe tension along the front of the lower leg (shin). Use the Method of Diminishing Tensions. Then the therapist steps out for two minutes.

2. Bend the foot down at the ankle, pointing the toe away from the body. Observe tension in the calf. Use the Method of Diminishing Tensions. Then the therapist steps out for two minutes.

3. Extend the lower leg, keeping foot and lower leg relaxed so that tension is on the top of the lap. Use the Method of Diminishing Tensions. Then the therapist steps out for two minutes.

4. Press the heel into the top of the footrest of the chair or the end of the couch or bed. (With beds without footboards and certain couches, this step must be omitted.) Try to bend the leg back as if trying to kick oneself in the rear end. Observe tension along the back of the thigh. Use the Method of Diminishing Tensions. Then the therapist steps out for two minutes.

5. Lying supine with one leg dangling off the side of the couch (bed, chair), raise the knee of the dangling leg. Observe tension in muscles deep in the abdomen, toward the back and near the hip. Use the Method of Diminishing Tensions. Then the therapist steps out for two minutes.

6. Place a pillow under the back of the knee. Press the back of the knee and upper leg down onto the pillow. Observe tension in the buttock. Use the Method of Diminishing Tensions. Then the therapist steps out for two minutes.

7. The therapist must apply counterforce as needed. Steps may be repeated multiple times. Use the Method of Diminishing Tensions, with a minimum of hints about where the tension should be felt.

8. Remind the trainee to keep the arms relaxed while learning to relax the leg.

In general, use the Method of Diminishing Tensions and remind the trainee that switching off is the most important part of training.

Home Practice

Review the general instructions with the trainee. Over the next few days, the trainee should spend one hour a day practicing what has been learned. The trainee begins practice by switching off tension in the arms for two minutes, and then proceeding to tension-release cycles with the legs. Also have the trainee check both arm and leg muscles several times during the day and release tension, particularly when experiencing emotional or physical stress.

SESSION 3: PROGRESSIVE RELAXATION OF THE TRUNK

This can be done in a chair or supine on a couch or bed. Again, talk about the experiences during the week's practices and how the technique was used at other times. Compliment the trainee for appropriate practice and use of progressive relaxation. Review instructions for areas the trainee deems troublesome.

Instruct the trainee to switch off and then step out for two minutes. The trainee should then proceed as follows:

1. Squeeze abdomen in. Observe tension all over abdomen.

2. Keeping the shoulders and buttocks on the chair, raise the stomach slightly and arch the back. Observe tension on both sides of the lower spine. Use the Method of Diminishing Tensions. Then the therapist steps out for two minutes.

3. Bend the shoulders back against the chair as if trying to touch the tips of the shoulders to the chair. Observe tension in the back between the shoulder blades. Use the Method of Diminishing Tensions. Then the therapist steps out for two minutes.

4. Bring the left arm over and across the chest, pointing to the opposite wall. Let the arm just fall over the chest and relax when a tension signal is noticed. Observe tension in the front of the chest, near the left arm (pectoral muscles).

5. Repeat with the other side. Use the Method of Diminishing Tensions. Then the therapist steps out for two minutes.

6. Raise the shoulders as if in a shrug. Observe the tension along the top of the shoulders and in the back of the neck. Use the Method of Diminishing Tensions. Then the therapist steps out for two minutes.

7. Concentrate on breathing for a while. Feel the sensation of tension in the chest when inhaling. When exhaling, switch off. Let go more deeply with each breath out. If the tension is not noticeable, take a slightly deeper breath. Observe a vague tenseness all over the chest and/or abdomen when breathing in. Use the Method of Diminishing Tensions. Then the therapist steps out for two minutes.

8. Remind the trainee to maintain relaxation in all previously trained muscles and to be aware of excess muscle tension throughout the day.

Home Practice

Home practice is the same as in previous sessions, with the addition of the new instructions. The trainee should remember to quickly check for release of muscle tension several times a day in the muscle groups we have covered while he or she is engaged in regular activities. The techniques should especially be used when experiencing tension symptoms.

SESSION 4: PROGRESSIVE RELAXATION OF THE NECK

This training is sometimes combined with the training in session 3. First talk about experiences during practice and use of progressive relaxation at other times during the week. Compliment the trainee for appropriate practice and use of the technique. Review instructions about areas the trainee deems troublesome.

Instruct the trainee to switch off muscle tension, and then step out for two minutes as in previous sessions. The trainee should then proceed as follows:

1. Bend the head back so that the chin points to the ceiling. Observe the tension in the back of the neck and perhaps below in the back.

2. Raising the head slightly, bend the chin down to the chest. Feel the tension in the sides of the neck towards the front.

3. Holding the head so the nose points to the ceiling, bend the head to the left as if trying to touch the left ear to the shoulder. Observe the tension on the left side of the neck. There might be some sensation of muscle stretch on the right side of the neck, which is not a sign of tension but of muscle strain. If the trainee has difficulty feeling the tension, have him or her push against the therapist's hand with the head.

4. Repeat on the other side. Use the Method of Diminishing Tensions. Then step out for two minutes.

5. The therapist then palpates the muscles on the arms and moves arms, legs, and head to test for relaxation. The trainee should try to remain completely relaxed during this procedure.

Home Practice

Home practice is the same as in the previous session, with the addition of the new instructions. The trainee should remember to check quickly for release of muscle tension several times a day in the muscle groups we have covered when engaging in regular activities. The techniques should be used especially when experiencing tension symptoms.

SESSION 5: PROGRESSIVE RELAXATION OF THE EYE MUSCLES

Talk about experiences with the technique during practices and applications of progressive relaxation throughout the week. Review areas that the trainee has had trouble with. Review the rationale of progressive relaxation. Then step out while the trainee switches off muscle tension in the areas covered thus far. The trainee is then instructed to proceed as follows:

1. Wrinkle the forehead by raising the eyebrows. Feel the tension diffusely over the entire forehead.

2. Frown or bring eyebrows together. Observe tension between the eyes.

3. Close eyes tightly. Observe tension all over and around the eyelids. Use the Method of Diminishing Tensions. Then the therapist steps out for two minutes.

4. With eyelids closed, look up and notice tension. Switch off for thirty seconds. Look down and notice tension. Switch off for thirty seconds. Look to right and notice tension. Switch off for thirty seconds. Look to left and notice tension. Switch off for thirty seconds. Look straight ahead and notice tension. Switch off for thirty seconds. Observe the tension in the muscles inside the eyeballs each time.

5. With eyes closed and without deliberating moving the eyeballs, imagine being at a tennis game, sitting right by the net. Visualize the ball as it goes from the right to the left, to the right, to the left, etc. Observe the tension inside the eyeballs when this is done. Then stop imagining and switch off everything. Use the Method of Diminishing Tensions. Then the therapist steps out for two minutes.

Home Practice

Home practice is the same as in the previous session, with the addition of the new instructions. The trainee should remember to check quickly for release of muscle tension several times a day in the muscle groups we have covered when engaging in regular activities. Pay attention to eye tension when experiencing intrusive visual imagery or when bothered by worries.

SESSION 6: PROGRESSIVE RELAXATION OF THE SPEECH REGION

Begin as in session 5. The trainee is then instructed to proceed as follows:

1. Clench the teeth. Observe the tension at the back of the lower jaw and in the temples. Use the Method of Diminishing Tensions. Then the therapist steps out for two minutes.

2. Open the mouth and jaws. Observe the tension on the sides of the lower jaw and under the jaw line of the neck. Use the Method of Diminishing Tensions. Then the therapist steps out for two minutes.

3. As if smiling, show the teeth. Observe tension in the cheeks. Use the Method of Diminishing Tensions. Then the therapist steps out for two minutes.

4. Push the tongue against the front teeth. Observe tension in the tongue. Use the Method of Diminishing Tensions. Then the therapist steps out for two minutes.

5. Press tip of tongue down to the bottom of the mouth and pull it backwards toward the throat. Observe tension in the tongue and in the floor of the mouth. Use the Method of Diminishing Tensions. Then the therapist steps out for two minutes.

6. Press lips together in a pout. Feel the tension in and around the lips. Use the Method of Diminishing Tensions. Then the therapist steps out for two minutes.

7. Count out loud from one to ten, noticing tension in the area of the vocal cords as well as in the tongue, lips, chest, etc. Muscle tension should be differentiated from the vibrations of the cords. Then say the alphabet. Begin in a normal speaking voice, and gradually speak more softly, reaching a whisper by the letter *L*, and only *thinking* the alphabet by the letter *Q*. It is helpful for the therapist to speak along with the trainee at first.

Observe tension in the cheeks, lips, tongue, jaw muscles, throat, chest, and perhaps abdomen. If trainees have difficulty perceiving this tension, they should count in a high-pitched voice to increase the tension. Then the therapist steps out for two minutes.

Home Practice

Same as in the previous sessions. Have the trainee continue to check for release of tension in all muscle groups several times a day in addition to regular practice.

SESSION 7: DIFFERENTIAL RELAXATION

The therapist should first review problem areas and try to troubleshoot, review the relaxation procedure, give additional instructions, and use the Method of Diminishing Tensions as needed, and then step out for two minutes. Upon returning, proceed with the following.

1. *Initial relaxation and troubleshooting.* Have the trainee sit upright in a chair and ask first about any difficulties in any of the muscle groups. Then ask the trainee to switch off, and leave the room for a few minutes. When you return, inquire again about residual tension and use the Method of Diminishing Tensions to gain control of any muscles that may not be completely relaxed.

2. *Review of muscles.* Mention each muscle in the body slowly, in the order in which you instructed the trainee. Tell the trainee to review each muscle in turn and check it to be sure that it is completely switched off.

3. *Differential relaxation.* Give the trainee a book to read, with instructions to continue relaxing even while reading. Give feedback, instructions, and encouragement. Talk with the

trainee about areas that may arouse some feelings of stress or emotion. Say you would like to teach him or her how to talk about things that arouse some stressful feelings while staying relaxed. Note generalized tension, particularly in the arms, legs, and facial muscles, and remind the trainee to try to keep relaxed while talking. Make sure that you give immediate feedback when you notice tension.

Home Practice

Have the trainee continue to check for release of tension in all muscle groups several times a day. Use differential relaxation during times of tension.

SESSION 8: USING PROGRESSIVE RELAXATION IN DAILY LIFE AND TO COPE WITH STRESS

Ask the trainee to relax as deeply as possible. Give additional instruction as needed where the trainee experiences difficulty. Palpate muscles in arms, and move the trainee's arms, legs, and head to test for relaxation. Speak with the trainee about applications of differential relaxation in daily life and the use of scheduled relaxation periods during times of stress.

Sexual Issues in Physical Contact with Clients

Unlike usual psychotherapeutic practice, progressive relaxation training sometimes entails physical contact between therapist and client, particularly when the therapist offers resistance against the client's movement in order to increase the vividness of the control sensation. The possible sexualization of treatment is promoted by the fact that the client's eyes are closed and muscle relaxation may increase feelings of vulnerability to advances by the only other person in the room: the therapist. The history and personality of the client may enhance these feelings. Similarly, the situation may prompt sexual countertransference thoughts from the therapist.

Prohibition of sexualized contact between therapist and clients is so basic to ethical practice that it hardly needs to be reiterated here. It is advisable to touch the client only on the extremities or the head, and to ask permission even for this kind of contact each time it is made. Jacobson's procedure of leaving the room when the client is switching off the muscle between instructions also reduces transference and countertransference.

Individual Examples

A good way to get the flavor of how progressive relaxation is actually used in clinical practice is to read case reports. Here are the stories of three clients the authors treated.

CASE ONE

C. was a twenty-year-old college student living at home with both biological parents. Her older sister was married and living on her own. C. had had no previous psychiatric treatment, although she came to us with a long history of social anxiety and avoidance, unassertiveness, and spontaneous panic attacks. She denied any history of major depression but reported a chronically dysphoric mood and general dissatisfaction with her current life situation. At the time of referral, C. had been involved in a relationship for about three years. She presented for treatment of her social anxiety for two reasons. First, she wanted to pursue graduate studies and was finding that her social inhibitions and social avoidance were presenting a serious obstacle to fulfilling her educational goals. She found it almost impossible to ask questions in class, initiate conversations with fellow students, or approach the professor after class or schedule appointments with him. Second, her social anxiety gave her boyfriend's friends the impression that she was "snobbish," "aloof," or constantly angry. She was embarrassed by these perceptions, which were disclosed to her by her boyfriend, and was fearful of her relationship ending because of this.

Following a clinical interview, Richard (the second author) asked C. to keep a daily diary of anxiety-provoking situations, people, events, or places. The interview revealed that C. was bothered most by situations or circumstances in which she could clearly be evaluated in some way. Thus she was not bothered by interactions with anonymous people in stores, at check-out counters, or with salespeople. She was, however, very anxious about meeting her boyfriend's friends because she believed that their opinions of her impacted on her relationship with him. Her behavior in class, she believed, was always subject to evaluations by other students and by the professor, who might think that her questions and comments were "stupid" or poorly articulated. She procrastinated over homework assignments, especially term papers, because she said her "ideas" might be judged inadequate or stupid.

While C. was self-monitoring her symptoms, we began the process of training in progressive relaxation to be used as a coping technique during systematic exposure to situations from her list of anxiety-provoking social cues. Because of C.'s school and work schedule, she was unable to schedule weekly sessions. We both knew at the outset that treatment was going to be irregular; therefore, it was decided at the outset to initiate progressive relaxation training for both the arms and face (eyes and speech region) in session 2, and for the trunk and neck in session 3. It was because of the unpredictability of her schedule that Richard decided to forego training in her legs. This allowed for training to move quickly into those areas that are more involved in general anxiety than the legs. If C. had experienced training difficulties, Richard would have slowed down and followed the regular schedule so as not to frustrate her with failure at the onset.

Sessions 2 and 3 were separated by two weeks. Session 4 occurred one month after session 3. At that time, C. reported that she no longer was having panic attacks and her general anxiety was significantly reduced. She reported that relaxation of her abdomen and adopting diaphragmatic breathing were especially helpful. She also had a significantly reduced concern about others observing her "shakiness," since she believed that she had "really learned how to control the muscle tension that was causing the trembling." Because of the marked response to just two training sessions and because she found the relaxation of the torso and shoulders so helpful, Richard did not continue the progressive relaxation treatment to cover the remaining muscle sites. Her inability to schedule more frequent sessions was also a consideration.

Richard helped C. construct a hierarchy of between-session homework activities for her to follow. This hierarchy progressed from the easiest to the most difficult, including such things as (1) asking one question in each class, (2) initiating a conversation with a classmate, (3) commenting to the professor about class material or the homework assignment, and (4) discussing her career interests with one of her boyfriend's friends. Richard also addressed her physical presentation and social skills. He introduced differential relaxation as a way to help C. smile and make appropriate eye contact while relaxing her shoulders, neck, and arms and displaying "interested" nonverbal cues (such as head nodding). Some of these conversations were role-played in the session. Periodically, the role play would be halted and C. would be asked to scan her body for muscle tension, after which the role play would resume. Finally, she was given a list of situations to attempt while simultaneously engaging in differential relaxation.

During the next three months, C. was seen only three times, but during that time she experienced great relief in her ability to interact comfortably in social situations. Even her boyfriend (who was unaware of her seeking treatment) had commented positively about her behavior around his friends. Interestingly, she also reported a change in her treatment goals: they became more modest and realistic. She had been shy and socially anxious almost all her life, and she initially sought treatment for the goal of becoming more like her boyfriend, who happened to be very socially skilled and outgoing. She had not verbalized this goal at the start of treatment but stated that "in the back of my mind I was just thinking that I need to be more like him." She disclosed these thoughts toward the end of treatment, when she announced that she felt much more comfortable around people even if she didn't "try to be really outgoing with everyone." Rather than responding to the pressure of carrying on conversations or of having to be as outgoing as her boyfriend, she felt satisfied that she could control many of her anxiety symptoms with progressive relaxation and could simply feel better and more confident around people. Instead of having to develop a whole new personality and to transform herself from shy to extroverted, C. had learned the necessary progressive relaxation skills that enabled this still-reserved individual to be herself (as she put it), but with confidence and a sense of self-control.

CASE TWO

E. was a sixty-seven-year-old married man with a long history of asthma and emphysema. He came to see Richard following a severe asthma attack that led to a lengthy hospitalization and a difficult rehabilitation. E. had been physically very active in his retirement, but from November until July of the year following his asthma attack he avoided almost all unnecessary physical activities. His medical doctor referred him for treatment of depression, but a clinical evaluation revealed severe anxiety and phobic avoidance. E.'s medical doctor had informed both him and Richard that there was nothing to prevent him from resuming his previous activities. Nevertheless, E. was afraid to climb stairs, go outside when the temperature was above 75 degrees, or ride his stationary bicycle. Each morning, E. experienced significant bouts of anxiety as he prepared to climb out of bed, believing that his early morning congestion was a sure sign of another asthma attack.

A number of behavioral strategies were used in E.'s treatment. Richard asked him to use a peak flow meter regularly, to improve his ability to discriminate anxiety symptoms from asthma symptoms, and a detailed plan for gradual exposure was implemented. This included increasing his daily activities by small increments and confronting a variety of situations that triggered anxiety and avoidance. Central to this process was training in progressive relaxation. At the same time he was instructed to begin daily exposure to the least anxiety-provoking situation, he began training in progressive relaxation. Because of his breathing-related symptoms, E. benefited greatly from training in diaphragmatic breathing. He learned to relax his shoulders and upper body while inhaling slowly and deeply using his diaphragm. As he exhaled, he relaxed his abdominal muscles while exhaling as far as possible. He also received progressive relaxation for his arms, legs, neck, and eye and speech regions. This training was accomplished in about five sessions.

E. practiced progressive relaxation regularly in the morning by arising twenty minutes earlier than usual. This was a time when he was typically very anxious. He also used differential relaxation of his shoulders and diaphragmatic breathing when experiencing breathing difficulties or symptoms that were not associated with decreased peak flow. After two months of weekly treatment, he was significantly less anxious in the morning and had begun using his exercise bicycle. He climbed stairs with no fear and showed significant improvements in his mood. During planned exposure exercises, he used differential relaxation skills. When exercising, he might pause, relax those muscles that were not involved in the activity, and attempt to regulate his breathing. He said he found this of significant help. When he experienced anxiety, he used differential relaxation and diaphragmatic breathing "to control myself." He also reported using less medication than previously, since much of his medication usage had been triggered by anxiety.

CASE THREE

T. was a forty-five-year-old divorced woman, living at home with her two teenage sons and working as a secretary. She was referred for relaxation therapy by her physician because of a long-standing problem with severe headaches. The patient reported that her headaches had started in adolescence and that they could be elicited by periods of stress and/or fatigue. Her stress had been growing during the previous six years of a bad marriage, but decreased somewhat after she obtained a divorce decree eight months prior to her initial session. Despite the decrease in stress, her headaches were continuing unabated. Her description of them suggested that they were of a mixed migraine and muscle contraction type. They were severe, like having her "head and neck in a vise" and with a bilateral "squeezing" pain and feeling of pressure inside her head "as if everything will pour out of my ears." The headaches usually occurred at night and were accompanied by nausea, vomiting, diarrhea, and photophobia. They usually occurred monthly in synchrony with her menstrual periods. One day prior to each headache she often experienced an aura (consisting of "seeing lights"), poor appetite, and feelings of general malaise. When she did not have headaches her hands were chronically cold, but during headaches they were warm.

The report from her physician stated that apart from the headaches the patient had a normal medical history and test findings, including negative CAT scan and EEG results. Although various medications for migraine had been tried, they provided only moderate relief and produced unacceptable side effects.

Her initial progressive relaxation session occurred in the non-headache state. Paul (the first author) made physiological measurements after a half-hour psychological interview, which showed elevated trapezius muscle tensions (24 and 15 microvolts, peak-to-peak, from the right and left respectively) and moderately cool fingers (88 degrees F. from the pad of the right middle finger). Her MMPI had an elevated score on defensiveness (the K scale), but the pattern of scores was otherwise normal and not suggestive of psychopathology. Because of the prominent degree of muscle tension in her psychophysiological test and the reported relationship between headache symptoms and stress, Paul initiated a course of progressive muscle relaxation.

The second session was devoted to instruction in relaxation of the muscles in the arm. T. was directed to practice for one hour a day, to become aware of muscle tension in the arms throughout each day, and to try to relax these muscles continuously except when they were need to perform a motor act.

Approximately one week later, she returned in the headache state and was given instruction in relaxation of the muscles of the eye region. She reported that she had fallen asleep several times during the relaxation practice during the previous week. No changes in headache symptoms were reported while relaxing in this session.

At the following session, one month later, she said she had experienced only one headache since the previous session. Although this represented a major improvement over the preceding weeks, T. reported that temporary improvements for so long a period had occurred frequently in the past. She noted mild discomfort in her shoulders at the beginning of the session, but no headache. Paul gave her relaxation training in muscles of the trunk. He observed no changes in surface EMG levels, but by the end of the session the feelings of discomfort in her shoulders had disappeared.

One month later, T. returned for relaxation treatment and said that she had had no symptoms since the previous session. She said she had practiced her relaxation instructions frequently (but not daily) at home, and that she had "headed off" one headache by deliberately relaxing. Headache-free periods of this duration had been unprecedented during the preceding few years. Relaxation instructions for the eye, speech, and shoulder regions were reviewed in this session, and Paul took surface EMG measures. Although at the beginning of the session the EMG was as high as before, levels dropped to moderate by the end (about 5–8 microvolts peak-to-peak, bilaterally).

T. opted to end treatment with this session. When Paul contacted her by telephone three months later, she reported no recurrence of headaches.

These three cases are a sampling of how progressive relaxation is applied in clinical practice. As you see, the method is not limited to treating somatic symptoms or psychosomatic illnesses. In the first case, Richard successfully treated classical psychological symptoms of depression and social anxiety. The other two cases did suffer from bodily symptoms, but not ones that were simply muscular. The second patient had become anxious about respiratory symptoms with a definite organic basis that had limited his activities more than they should have. Although progressive relaxation could not completely remove his disability, it made the condition more tolerable and he was able to function better. It managed to completely eliminate the headaches of our last case, at least for the duration of our follow-up, although there was probably a significant vascular component in addition to the muscular one.

These cases also illustrate that progressive relaxation can be combined with other methods to advantage. For case one, Richard prescribed systematic exposure in addition to progressive relaxation right from the outset. Learning to breathe from the diaphragm to reduce hyperventilation was an important additional lesson in this case and in case two. In case one, Richard encouraged greater self-acceptance and more realistic goals just as an insight-oriented therapist might. In cases two and three, we donned the white coats of the physiologist using brass instruments (in case two, a respiratory peak flow meter, and in case three, surface EMG). In our opinion, such eclectic flexibility is an essential part of successful clinical practice.

In summary, although it would be a mistake to believe that progressive relaxation alone can solve every psychological or stress problem, this technique usually has a contribution to make. At the very least it serves as a helpful therapeutic adjunct, and in some cases, progressive relaxation turns out to be the key intervention that turns the tide toward improvement and recovery.

NOTES

P. 83, *developed in the 1930s by Edmund Jacobson:* Jacobson, E. (1938). *Progressive relaxation* (rev. ed.). Chicago: University of Chicago Press; Jacobson E. (1963). *Tension control for businessmen.* New York: McGraw-Hill; Jacobson,

E. (1964). *Anxiety and tension control: A physiologic approach.* Philadelphia: Lippincott.

P. 84, *psychologist F. J. McGuigan showed:* McGuigan, F. J. (1991). *Calm down: A guide for stress and tension control* (rev. ed.). Dubuque, IA: Kendall/Hunt; McGuigan, F. J. (1993). Progressive relaxation: Origins, principles, and clinical applications. In P. M. Lehrer & R. L. Woolfolk (Eds.), *Principles and practice of stress management* (2nd ed.) (pp. 17–87). New York: Guilford Press.

P. 86, *Since Jacobson's early descriptions:* Bernstein, D. A., & Borkovec, T. D. (1973). *Progressive relaxation training: A manual for the helping professions.* Champaign, IL: Research Press; Bernstein, D. A., & Carlson, C. R. (1993). Progressive relaxation: Abbreviated methods. In P. M. Lehrer & R. L. Woolfolk (Eds.), *Principles and practice of stress management* (2nd ed.) (pp. 53–87). New York: Guilford Press.

P. 86, *these short cuts may alter:* Lehrer, P. M. (1982). How to relax and how not to relax: A reevaluation of the work of Edmund Jacobson. *Behavior Research and Therapy, 20,* 417–428; Lehrer, P. M., Carr, R., Sargunaraj, D., & Woolfolk, R. L. (1994). Stress management techniques: Are they all equivalent, or do they have specific effects? *Biofeedback and Self-Regulation, 19,* 353–401; Lehrer, P. M., Woolfolk, R. L., & Goldman, N. (1986). Progressive relaxation then and now: Does change always mean progress? (pp. 183–213). In R. Davidson, G. Schwartz, & D. Shapiro (Eds.), *Consciousness and self-regulation* (Vol. 4). New York: Plenum; Lehrer, P. M. (1996). Varieties of relaxation methods and their unique effects. *International Journal of Stress Management, 3,* 1–15.

P. 87, *Jacobson's classic book:* Jacobson, E. (1938). *Progressive relaxation* (rev. ed.). Chicago: University of Chicago Press.

5

AUTOGENIC TRAINING

Wolfgang Linden and Joseph W. Lenz

By letting go, it all gets done;
the world is won by those who let it go.

TAO TE CHING

For us as authors, this chapter provides a good opportunity to describe something that we know really well and that we have applied for many years to a variety of different patient problems. But we are also challenged to newly conceptualize some of these experiences as they apply to a more narrowly defined area of application, that is, the anxiety disorders. Surprisingly, there is not much literature that directly links autogenic training to the anxiety disorders.

Before we can make a case for how autogenic training (AT) may fit into good clinical management of anxious patients, we need to explain what AT is, how it is presumed to have its effect, and how it is taught. The obvious intent is to be informative about the nature of AT so that its rationale can be tied to our understanding of how people become anxious and what maintains this anxiety.

The opening quotation from the *Tao Te Ching* encourages people to let go rather than to try frantically to control their lives and environment. This attitude toward accomplishment appears paradoxical in a time and place where "taking charge," "forging the future," "seizing opportunities," and "empower-ment" are the catchwords supposed to describe successful peo-ple. In this light, autogenic training (AT) would have appealed to writers of the *Tao Te Ching*, but it seems quite out of place for Westerners approaching the year 2000. Yet the authors of this chapter see no contradiction; we believe that AT and its self-reg-ulatory rationale may serve as a potentially useful tool for the treatment and prevention of anxiety in our fast-paced culture.

What is autogenic training (AT)? AT was pioneered by Johann Schultz in the early 1930s. Today, it is often classified as a stress management technique, or as a psychophysiologically based form of autonomic self-regulation. The more "mechanical" aspects of AT are easy to explain: the client learns a set of six for-mulas or phrases that are subvocally repeated. Each formula sug-gests a specific autonomic sensation.

Since its inception, much of the research and clinical writing on AT has been published in German. As a result, the North American audience has had limited access to the literature. In 1990, Wolfgang Linden published a comprehensive resource book in English that contained a summary of the background research on AT and a detailed how-to manual for practitioners. This clinician-oriented book has contributed to a growing inter-est among practitioners in AT as a clinical tool. We think the serious AT practitioner should use such a manual to broaden knowledge before extensive clinical use of AT.

Each of the six AT formulas suggests a different sensation and targets a different autonomic function. The six AT formulas and their target areas are as follows:

1 = "My arm is very heavy" (muscular relaxation)

2 = "My arm is very warm" (vascular dilation)

3 = "My heart beat is very regular" (stabilization of heart function)

4 = "It breathes me" (regulation of breathing)

5 = "Warmth is radiating over my stomach" (regulation of visceral organs)

6 = "There is a cool breeze across my forehead" (regulation of blood flow in the head)

Supporting research has shown that measurable physiological changes accompany the practice of these imagery exercises and that these noticeable changes are also instrumental in symptomatic improvement. Extensive and often fascinating discussions have been published on how these sensations may be evoked and how autonomic functions may be influenced by the elegantly simple formulas. These topics are mostly beyond the scope of this chapter, but the reader interested in underlying conceptual issues may want to see reviews by Wolfgang Luthe, Kenneth Lichstein, or Wolfgang Linden.

HOW AT WORKS

A clear understanding of AT may be best achieved by first providing a rationale in the same way we offer it to our clients, and then phrasing it in more scientific language.

The general idea is to begin in a structured manner to individualize techniques after the basics are learned. Our clients are told that learning AT is like using a shoehorn. When shoes are new, the user needs help slipping into them; once they've been worn for a while, the shoes become comfortable and one no longer requires the shoehorn to slip into them.

Clients are instructed that the objectives of AT are threefold. First, one needs to learn the technique in a structured format. Clear instructions are required so that clients know what to do in a step-by-step fashion. Once the method is familiar, clients also discover that they have somehow made the method their own; small changes to the method are made, habits develop, and the method is used in novel ways. Lastly, clients begin to discover that using AT habitually, but in a way that works best for them, influences how they look at stress in general. Whereas before learning AT they usually felt overwhelmed by the strains of life, continued practice and the inherent, developing conviction that it is OK to take twenty minutes out of a busy day for relaxation are accompanied by a growing sense of control over stress. Clients feel comforted in knowing that they have a new tool for coping with stress. The confidence in that new tool may be one of the more powerful components of the treatment.

Stated in more scientific terms, AT is supposed to enable autonomic self-regulation by removing environmental distraction, by training the imagery that accompanies autonomic self-regulation, and by providing a facilitative, structured set of exercises that are easy to learn and remember. The underlying model is homeostasis, as proposed by Walter Cannon in the 1920s. He taught that self-regulatory powers are naturally built into living physiological systems, so that when influences that disrupt self-regulation are removed the organism finds its way back to a healthier, more balanced state. Homeostasis is essentially a self-established balance; in the case of AT, the balance is thought to be between sympathetic nervous system and parasympathetic nervous system arousal. Through the practice of AT, excessive sympathetic arousal (as is typical in anxiety states) is expected to return to lower, more functional levels. In some cases the opposite can occur as well, and lack of arousal can also be regulated "upwards" to a more functional, adaptive level. As you can see, the concept of autonomic homeostasis is thoroughly compatible with the *Tao Te Ching's* letting-it-go motto.

AT COMPARED TO OTHER TECHNIQUES

AT has at times been considered a self-hypnotic procedure. What is hypnotic about the procedure? Each AT formula suggests a specific somatic function. The images and sensations accompanying this function are commonly reported by patients in deep relaxation or in hypnotic trances. Therefore, the formulas suggest sensations that an AT trainee may naturally experience anyway, thus creating positive expectations and subsequent validations of distinct, predicted somatic experiences. The actual experience of the sensation then reinforces the effort and lends further credibility to the formulas. In this manner, the "magic" of hypnosis is woven into the self-directed learning process of AT. As with self-hypnosis, the AT instructor functions as a teacher of the technique, helping to maximize compliance and monitoring the progress. But the instructor does not verbalize the suggestions, except very briefly during the teaching of each new formula. To preserve the vital sense of self-control and self-regulation, we strongly suggest that AT trainees *not* be given audiotaped instructions to listen to at home.

A clear understanding of AT requires distinctions between it and a variety of frequently practiced, and interrelated, biobehavioral treatments. In particular, biofeedback, meditation, and autogenic biofeedback need to be distinguished. (Note that another popular method, muscle relaxation, is covered in Chapter Four). By its very definition, biofeedback involves technical equipment to sample, process, and display physiological signals not normally subject to the direct awareness and voluntary control of human beings. Meditation is more similar to AT than biofeedback in that the letting-go philosophy holds for both. Techniques of AT and meditation are, however, quite different in that meditation typically uses some fixed, simple stimulus for a target of mental focus. Unlike AT, meditation does not attempt specifically to sensitize the practitioner to physical symptoms or sensations. Meditation is characterized by a long history of Eastern religious practices and cannot be easily separated from its philosophical and religious origins. AT carries no such associations.

TEACHING THE BASICS OF AT

AT can be taught to individuals or to groups. Individual training is expensive but allows easy adjustment to individual differences in the pace of learning and personal preferences. Group training is clearly more cost-effective; in the age of managed care, this may be an important consideration. Groups also have the potential advantage of encouraging clients to function as mutual supports for each other, and this in turn will have a positive impact on motivation. Our personal preference is to teach AT in groups of six to ten participants, provided a group can be assembled that has more or less homogeneous needs and learning paces.

The whole learning process is positively affected by realistic expectations. At the outset of AT, trainees should be alerted to the probability that learning will be uneven, with much apparent change in one week and sometimes little observable benefit for two or three weeks in a row. We always tell clients that the great majority of practitioners feel little if anything during their first practices and that this is true even for the keen learner who is fully compliant with the instructions to practice twice per day. It is often the case that one or two people in a group experience strong sensations almost immediately. Although they are usually very excited about their experience, be aware that one person's excessive delight can easily create a sense of failure in others. We try to divert attention from this kind of "instant success" in favor of emphasis on learning the formulas and establishing regular practice habits.

The Physical Setting and Posture

The ideal physical setting is one of comfort, with minimal likelihood of disruption, a room temperature of 20–24 degrees C., a couch or exercise mattress (plus pillows) to stretch out on, and adjustable lighting conditions (a slightly darkened room is best). Training success is facilitated by an environment that permits trainees to concentrate on their inner sensations with a minimum of distraction. Accordingly, speech interferes with the basic principle of *auto*genics. If the trainer talks during the exercise or plays a record or cassette, the trainee cannot really learn to exercise autogenically (that is, independently).

For training in session, a very comfortable sitting—or, even better, lying—position is necessary. The entire body position must be comfortable, since body position itself may lead to muscle tension, which interferes with progress in the exercises. It is advantageous to exercise in a supine position, with the neck especially well supported. The arms should be placed flat beside the body with slightly bent elbows, and the interior of the hands should be placed on the ground. The tips of the feet should fall slightly toward the outside. If lying is not possible (perhaps if a trainee wants to practice in the clinician's office), a chair with a high back and armrests is best, so that the head and arms are supported. If seated, the elbows should be bent at nearly a right angle. The feet should rest flat on the ground and close to each other, and the knees should fall slightly toward the outside.

In one of these positions, the trainee can now begin with the first exercise. The eyes should be closed to facilitate passive concentration, and the trainee should now try to imagine the sensation in the formula as well as possible, without making any movement or trying to speak or do anything else. The ideas, images, and memories that necessarily develop in each individual should not be fought off, because this attempt in itself will lead to tension. Ideas and images other than the formula-based sensations should simply be ignored. We tell clients that watching their thoughts go by may be like standing by the road watching the traffic. "A lot of buses may go by, but you don't have to get on every one. If you happen to find yourself riding on an idea, just stop at the next corner and get off."

First Exercise: The Heaviness Experience (Muscular Relaxation)

The first AT exercise involves the musculature because muscle activity is familiar to people and is most easily influenced by conscious efforts. In addition, experience with hypnosis and relaxation suggestions has shown that notable muscular relaxation can be achieved rapidly. Muscular relaxation is experienced as a heaviness of the extremities. Intentional concentration on outside stimulation is associated with muscular tension (looking, speaking, and reaching out are based on muscular movement). Attentional anticipation likely results in tension because muscles are tensed in anticipation of movement. Even profound thinking may be associated with muscular activity, and many individuals crease the forehead while thinking. Each intention—or even vivid imagination—of a motion results in increased tone of the musculature in the extremities.

It is not advisable to use the entire body as an object of training at once because the necessary focus would be difficult to achieve. The training should begin with the dominant arm. If this arm has been trained for a reasonable period of time, the experience of heaviness during muscle relaxation generalizes to the other arm, the legs, and other body systems because all extremities and organs are enervated by the same nervous system. In keeping with this rationale, the first exercise is practiced on the arm until it has generalized to the other three extremities. It is important to achieve maximal concentration on one arm and to permit a generalized "overflow of relaxation" into the other extremities before moving on to other formulas.

Because the six formulas are structured in a similar manner, mastering one makes learning the others easier. The steps for the heaviness formula are as follows:

1. "My right (left) arm is very heavy." (This is repeated six times.)
2. "I am very quiet." (This is said only once.)
3. Repeat steps 1 and 2 above alternatively until six cycles have been completed.
4. Complete the "taking back" steps explained below.

In most normal individuals, a noticeable experience of heaviness soon develops, particularly in the area of the elbow and lower arm.

After six repetitions of the heaviness formula, the instructions are "taken back." *Taking back* refers to a systematic set of activities designed to bring the trainee gradually from a state of relaxed, low muscle tone back to an alert state. This needs to be performed in a consistent manner to facilitate the reflex nature of the process. It is executed in the following steps:

1. The arm is bent and stretched a few times with an energetic pull.

2. The individual briefly breathes in and out profoundly.

3. The eyes are opened.

Trainees can easily expedite this portion of the practice by using a very simple verbal cue to suggest and initiate each of the three steps. A brief self-suggestion version of taking back follows:

1. "One. Bend my arm."

2. "Two. Breathe deeply."

3. "Three. Open my eyes."

Once the taking-back response is strongly established, simply counting "One. Two. Three" can replace the series of suggestions.

It is important that the trainee pay attention to the timing of the exercise and avoid pushing too hard for results. Training should be repeated in two practice sessions per day. We encourage trainees to go through the heaviness formula twice for about one minute each in a training session; this is preceded by about three or four minutes of general relaxing and one- to two-minute intervals of quietness in between the formula-based exercises. Many trainees are particularly focused on doing the exercise very well or on getting it just right. If the individual steps are extended with this focus on results, semiconscious tensions may arise and trainees will realize that, instead of increasing, the experience of heaviness decreases more and more with excessively long practices.

This tendency to extend practice and push towards results is very common and is incompatible with good results from AT. To reduce perfectionism and keep clients from getting in the way of AT, we tell clients the following during the first session: "There is only one reason to do extra practice: because you really *enjoy* it. If the exercise feels great and you want to stay with it to experience more of it, OK. If you are tempted to do it again just to get it right, then resist that thinking, do your scheduled repetitions, and no more."

Within the first week of training, the feeling of heaviness in the trained arm becomes more pronounced and occurs more rapidly. Also, the same feeling is experienced in the other extremities, usually at the same time as in the other arm. When the experience of heaviness in both arms is quite pronounced, the formula can now be changed to "My arms are heavy." When this change in the formula is made, the taking-back procedure is modified slightly. The steps follow:

1. "Make a couple of fists."
2. "Bend the arms a few times."
3. "Breathe in deeply."
4. "Open the eyes and sit up."

Once these steps are learned, the trainee takes back both arms by counting from one to four, associating each number with a specific instruction. Most trainees experience heaviness in the legs as well as in the arms, but the legs do not require a particular taking-back procedure, since legs appear to be more directly responsive to the autonomic state and respond to the taking back of the arms. Normally, within a week the exercise has proceeded so far that with only a brief moment of inner concentration, arms and legs can be perceived as quite heavy. It is then time to approach the second exercise.

Second Exercise: Experience of Warmth (Vascular Dilation)

Muscular exercises are something that the naïve individual finds natural because muscular activity is a voluntary act. It is more novel to be told that blood vessels may constrict or dilate through conscious effort, and some trainees have trouble believing this will happen for them. We try to point out simply that all emotional activity tends to be associated with a change in blood flow. Although they don't usually do it on purpose, people flush or turn pale as part of their reaction to purely internal events such as an embarrassing or frightening thought. The second AT exercise, which aims at the warmth experience, affects the entire peripheral cardiovascular system. It affects blood flow through arteries, capillaries, and veins in the skin, organs, and musculature. The distribution of blood in the vessels is regulated through constriction and dilation, which take place as a response to nerve impulses.

Once the first exercise with the heaviness experience has been well trained and can be induced rapidly and reliably, training sessions can then be extended by adding the second formula. With the second formula added, the trainee thinks as follows:

1. "My arms (legs) are very heavy." (This is repeated a total of six times.)
2. "I am very quiet." (This is said once at this point.)
3. "My right (left) arm is very warm." (This is repeated six times.)
4. "I am very quiet." (This is said one more time.)

With the warmth suggestion, most individuals rapidly notice an inner, streaming, flowing sensation of warmth. It typically occurs first in the area of the elbow and the lower arm. Quite frequently, trainees who master the heaviness sensation also spontaneously report warmth sensations before they are instructed to imagine them. Specific instructions for taking back the experience of warmth are not necessary. The blood vessels are elastic and governed by a compensatory self-regulation which triggers a return to their usual state automatically with the return of increased muscle tone when the heaviness is taken back.

The first and second training exercises are executed in the same manner for a period of at least one week each, until warmth is experienced easily and rapidly in the trained arm first and then in all four extremities. The experience of heaviness and warmth then also generalizes to the entire body. The blood vessel dilation and associated relaxation have a particularly tranquilizing and sleep-inducing effect. Training exercises directed at blood vessel dilation are not necessarily innocuous, since the changed distribution of blood influences the entire organism. For this reason, warmth exercise should be instituted only in healthy individuals for whom no vascular risks are known to exist.

Each time a new exercise step is added in AT (for example, when the experience of warmth is added to the feeling of heaviness), the trainee should always concentrate initially on the exercise he or she already knows how to do, and then the new exercise should be added only for brief periods (typically about one minute). New exercises are added only briefly to keep the overall exercise length short and to prevent trainees from attempting to achieve "perfect success" (or taking it too seriously). The choice of one-minute segments is somewhat arbitrary, but it is suggested because it is an even unit of time, and because when all training steps are added together they amount to a reasonable practice length of ten to fifteen minutes. Once heaviness and warmth are achieved rapidly and reliably, the third exercise can be added.

Third Exercise: Regulation of the Heart

The awareness of heart activity varies considerably among people. Some are easily aware of their heart or pulse nearly all the time. Many other individuals are aware of it in times of strain, excitement, and fever. Trainees who do not perceive their heart activity at any particular point in their bodies can use their pulse for orientation. With further training they, too, can experience the activity of the heart itself. If this help is not sufficient, a trainee may try to become aware of heart activity by other means. This can be done by lying flat on the back so that the right elbow is fully supported and lies at the same height as the chest. The right hand is placed in the heart area with the left arm positioned as for an AT session. Now the trainee can go into the usual state of heaviness, warmth, and quietness and can concentrate on the sensations in the chest area just where the hand touches the skin. The pressure caused by the weight of the hand on the chest is usually sufficient to allow the trainee to sense heart action. After a few exercises, the trainee is now likely to recognize heart activity, and with continuing repetition of the entire exercise the experience becomes more obvious.

The heart formula is, "My heart is beating quietly and strongly." This formula is repeated six times, followed by one repetition of "I am very quiet." There are a few individuals who are very easily aroused; they may respond with increased arousal to a suggestion that their heart is beating "strongly." In cases like this, the formula should be modified slightly to "My heart is beating quietly and regularly." We have not found anyone unable to use this last formula, but it should be noted that some people (notably those who have been called "cardiac phobics," and some sufferers of panic disorder) are highly sensitive to their cardiac sensations and may experience increased anxiety when learning this formula. In our experience, this anxiety subsides quickly with a little practice or, alternatively, with continued exposure to the sensations. (See the section on interoceptive exposure in the treatment of panic disorder later in this chapter for more ideas on how to conceptualize and manage difficulties like this.)

When the heart sensation has been learned (or "discovered"), the hand no longer needs to be placed in the area of the heart, and the exercise can be continued in the usual position. It should be strongly emphasized that the intent of the exercise is not to slow down the heartbeat, since this would prevent self-regulation, but to create regular and strong beats. We tell trainees that their heart *may* slow down, but that is not the intent. The intent is simply to feel the steady, self-regulated pace of the heart with no interfering thoughts or expectations.

Fourth Exercise: Regulation of Breathing

Breathing is partially intentional and partially an autonomous activity. In AT the muscular, vascular, and heart relaxation becomes immediately integrated with the rhythm of breathing, much as heaviness and warmth automatically generalize from the trained arm to all the other extremities. The trainee must simply allow this regulation to happen on its own. As with the heart formula, the AT trainee avoids any intentional influence on or modification of breathing, because intentional change in breathing would be associated through a reflex-type mechanism with tension and voluntary activity. The wording of the fourth formula underscores this concept.

As before, the trainee is to enter all the previously learned exercise levels before adding the new, fourth formula. The fourth formula is: "It breathes me." (This is repeated six times.) As before, a single iteration of "I am very quiet" is added.

As noted earlier, we always emphasize the passive nature of this formula. This is particularly important since it is very seductive for many trainees to attempt voluntary changes of breathing, as they may in a systematic breathing exercise such as yoga. This intentional modification needs to be prevented in AT, since breathing is supposed to function autonomously and in a self-regulatory system without any active adjustment. In order to discourage intentional change, we point out that "It breathes me" means "There is nothing you have to do. Just observe quietly and the breath happens on its own." This statement is intended to make it clear to the trainee that relaxation and the regulation of breathing come by themselves—that the trainee is carried by, and is to give in to, his or her natural breathing rhythm. It typically takes another week to make good progress with this exercise.

Fifth Exercise: Regulation of Visceral Organs ("Sun Rays")

For self-regulation of visceral organs, the trainee focuses on the area of the solar plexus, which is the most important nerve center for the inner organs. The image associated with this nerve center is that of a sun from which warm rays extend into other body areas. The solar plexus is found approximately where you think the center of your stomach is.

After practicing the four previous formulas, the trainee now concentrates on the solar plexus area and adds the fifth formula: "Sun rays are streaming quiet and warm." As before, the formula is repeated six times, followed by one repetition of "I am very quiet." This exercise also takes approximately one week for normal individuals to learn. The image that the breath is streaming out of the body when the subject breathes out can also help with this particular exercise.

Sixth Exercise: Regulation of the Head

The well-known relaxing effect of a cool cloth on the forehead forms the basis for the sixth exercise. In order to learn the sixth exercise, the subject engages in the first five exercises in the same careful and progressive manner as described above, and then (initially only for a few seconds for this formula) proceeds with the formula "My forehead is cool" (repeated six times). Just as warmth is associated with vasodilation, the experience of freshness on the forehead leads to a localized vasoconstriction and thereby to a reduced supply of blood, which in turn accounts for the cooling effect. It is probable that a very simple phenomenon serves to reinforce this somewhat unusual sensation. Since most walls are not entirely airtight, there is always a slight movement of air in any room. With the heightened awareness cued by the suggestion in formula six, coolness on the forehead may be sensed and described as a cool breeze.

Because all the blood vessels of the entire organism are interconnected, localized vasoconstriction may generalize to other blood vessels. This effect can be demonstrated by placing a finger in a basin filled with cold water. In response, the entire hand (and at times even the opposite hand as well) is likely to feel cool and look pale. During AT, the suggestion of coolness on the forehead results in changing the distribution of blood within the body. The "cool forehead" exercise can be learned in about the same time as the other exercises, although Mensen, a German physician, has reported that up to a third of trainees never acquire a strong response to this formula. Our experience has been similar.

Summary of Exercises

We have described AT in its most basic but complete form. The entire sequence of six exercises can now be summarized. For this summary, we have abbreviated the sentence "I am very quiet," and you may find that many trainees prefer this and think simply "quiet" when they practice. Here is the full sequence:

1. "My arms and legs are heavy" six times; "quiet" once.

2. "My arms and legs are very warm" six times; "quiet" once.

3. "My heart is beating quietly and strongly" six times, "quiet" once.

4. "It breathes me" six times; "quiet" once.

5. "Sun rays are streaming quiet and warm" six times; "quiet" once.

6. "My forehead is cool" six times; "quiet" once.

7. Taking back: Make fists, bend arms, breathe deeply, open eyes.

After about eight weeks of training, most individuals have acquired the complete set of sensations, and emphasis can be placed on ease in achieving the described sensations reliably and rapidly. Daily training for another four to six months leads to more distinct and stronger sensations, and generalization of training to different environments can be targeted. It is important to go through the taking-back procedure after each session (except when the trainee has fallen asleep during AT). Thus the trainee acquires a readily available mechanism for switching from active tension to deep relaxation and from relaxation to activation.

Troubleshooting and Maximizing Effectiveness

Any therapist attempting to apply a standardized treatment such as AT soon finds out that clinical reality and full standardization are often incompatible: trainees lose motivation, have unpredictable and confusing training experiences, have medical or psychological problems that interfere with learning and practicing AT, or have other obligations that may prevent regular practice. Good general clinical skills are required to complement the training manual and still bring training to a fruitful end. A case example may best illustrate how general clinical skills may be usefully applied to help a client deal with an unexpected obstacle in the training program.

CASE ONE

A thirty-seven-year-old nurse took part in one of Wolfgang's AT workshops involving one hour of teaching per week, with twice-daily home practices, over an eight-week period. She wanted to learn AT herself in order to use it as a practitioner while working with chronic patients. She quickly learned and enjoyed the heaviness, warmth, and breathing exercise but had a great deal of difficulty with the heart exercise. Initially, I encouraged her to place her hand on her rib cage over the heart in order to feel the heart beats more directly. Given her nursing background, explanation of anatomy or physiology was unnecessary.

Even with the hand placement over the heart, however, she remained detached and aloof to this exercise. Finally, she admitted that any direct sensation about heart activity made her anxious because she somehow associated awareness of heart activity with the possibility of disturbing the heart rhythm. At this point, I continued to have her learn and master all AT exercises but left out the heart exercise. Toward the end, I did encourage her one more time to try to locate pulse sensations but intentionally asked her to seek the sensation elsewhere in her body because direct attention to the heart area continued to be anxiety arousing. Finally, she did learn to locate a pulsing sensation in her earlobe and become comfortable with directing attention at it. She no longer experienced any fears of disturbing the heart's rhythm.

While this case example describes a unique situation, some other problems are well known to experienced teachers of AT and are endemic either to specific exercises of AT or to the practice of relaxation at large. Although a full discussion is beyond the scope of this chapter, typical problems are briefly addressed below. For a more thorough treatment of these and other issues, see Linden's manual.

Trying Too Hard

Most trainees find themselves trying to *make* relaxation happen rather than *let* it happen. This ubiquitous obstacle to success in AT can hardly be overemphasized. Because it is such a common difficulty and so central to the concept of AT, we address it at length during the first training session. See in the previous section the discussion of formula number one for specifics concerning how we deal with the issue at the outset. We mention it again at this point to emphasize its importance and to remind AT trainers to remain continuously vigilant to the issue through the course of training.

Relaxation-Induced Anxiety and Panic

It has been observed with keen interest that occasionally a client experiences sudden levels of high anxiety or panic attacks while practicing relaxation strategies. Physiological recordings during relaxation biofeedback sessions sometimes indicate radical increases in arousal that can occur almost instantaneously. When severe, these are referred to as relaxation-induced panic attacks. Although true panic attacks while relaxing are relatively infrequent, it is not at all unusual for clients to report that sometimes when they are relaxing they experience disturbing thoughts or new and peculiar body sensations that give rise to anxious feelings. This paradoxical response has been referred to as relaxation-induced anxiety. Most of the research on relaxation-induced panic and anxiety has been based on techniques such as progressive muscle relaxation and biofeedback; we know of no published research on relaxation-induced panic in AT.

There is, however, an extensive listing of a wide variety of unexpected sensations that have been reported during AT. They are given the overall descriptor of "autogenic discharges." The AT trainer should be familiar with a variety of autogenic discharges: muscle spasms, twitches, restlessness, myoclonic jerks, and also recurring cognitions that relate back to unpleasant somatic experiences somewhere in the client's past. In most cases, autogenic discharges are minor occurrences that result more in puzzlement than concern. A case example may illustrate how these personally relevant experiences may occur and how they can be handled during training.

CASE TWO

A sixty-seven-year-old retired woman was using AT to reduce general anxiety. She had practiced for five weeks with some difficulties. The warming formula had been expanded to include her feet because each time she had used the "warm hands" formula, she had become distracted by her cold feet—a chronic problem that she badly wanted solved. After a good deal of practice, she was excited to be able to induce warming sensations in both hands and both feet.

At this point she reported with some amusement that when she warmed her feet she felt and heard a popping or clicking noise in her face just to the side of and behind her nose. It was obviously in her sinuses. She had suffered from periodic vertigo and wondered whether the popping and clicking in her sinuses might have some impact on her inner ear since, as she put it, "everything's connected up there anyway." Then she laughed to explain, "But I don't have any idea what this has to do with warm feet!" A brief explanation of the concept of autogenic discharges, and a declaration that these were both frequent and harmless, was sufficient for her to accept these odd sensations and not worry about them.

For more information and for ways of using anxiety and panic to clinical advantage, see our note on interoceptive exposure in the treatment of panic disorder later in this chapter.

Monitoring Progress and Maximizing Compliance

Compliance and monitoring progress are intricately linked and are therefore discussed jointly in this section. Clearly, a trainee who does not see any progress despite twice-daily practice and weeks of training can quickly lose the motivation to continue. In some ways, this section could also be entitled "Maximizing Motivation," because motivation is the cornerstone of progress and compliance. In fact, we do not much like the term *compliance* because of its connotation of passively submitting to another's agenda, but we use it occasionally for want of a better term. As with our earlier emphasis on self-regulation, it would be far better for trainees to think of practicing to accomplish something for themselves than to simply "comply" with our instructions.

Because progress is not immediately obvious, a trainee with high initial motivation is more likely to succeed, and it is extremely important that the therapist radiate confidence and a firmly anchored belief in the effectiveness of AT from the very beginning of training. It is recommended that the therapist give an optimistic but reasonable picture of the success to be expected: "I have trained x number of people or groups, and there is hardly anybody who has not benefited considerably.

Even after *y* years I still practice it myself. Within two weeks or so, you can expect the first training effects, which only become stronger and easier to trigger as you keep on practicing."

On the basis of empirical findings on compliance and our experience with AT, we recommend a number of concrete steps for monitoring progress and enhancing compliance.

Keeping a Training Diary

Trainees should keep a diary in which they record their daily practices and particular success or failure experiences. We recommended that trainees rate the intensity of their perceived sensations in order to maximize the principle of the self-fulfilling prophecy. When trainees rate each practice after being told that the sensation will get stronger and stronger, they are likely to expect improvement, which becomes even more obvious when they see the progressive ratings they have made. The diary is of course very useful for review of the past week's training experiences, which should be undertaken at the beginning of a therapy session.

Scheduling Regular Home Practice

We ask trainees to think about and commit themselves to such practice times in the first training sessions. We would rather deal with their scheduling difficulties before they start practicing than find out a week later that they did not practice at all because they could not find the time. We have better results when we plan and negotiate reasonable scheduling with trainees at the very beginning than when we just allow them to "fit AT in" on their own.

AT trainees may find the rule of twice-daily practice for two months (or more) overly compulsive. When AT is combined with all the other facets of their lives that compete for their time, they may be tempted to cut down on practicing. Our recommendation is to be understanding if one or two practices a week are skipped; however, trainees should be urged to stick to their agreed-on schedule. Frequent practicing is more likely to occur if trainees clearly understand the reason for learning AT in the first place and the necessity of repetition while learning.

Examining Reasons for Dropout

Although AT is popular, patients drop out for a variety of reasons. They move away, there is too much competition for their time, the training effects are too slow in coming, and so on through a variety of other reasons. Even the most experienced therapist has to face dropout and noncompletion rates of 20–25 percent in AT, but this does not appear to be appreciably different than for other relaxation-related behavioral techniques. If the dropout rates are noticeably higher than this, therapists should question their own ability to motivate patients. Lack of trainer enthusiasm, poor communication skills, or poor session planning is sometimes the culprit. We have also seen—although rarely—that for no identifiable reason some groups simply never develop cohesion.

A useful method for maximizing compliance is to highlight success. Nothing succeeds like success, as the old saying goes. The therapist can use this principle by making it a habit to underscore any and all success stories. Trainees may report a variety of effects of their AT practice, including use of AT in acute stress situations (anticipating an exam, or facing a confrontation with a superior), improvement in ability to fall asleep or relax after a hard day of work, or reduction in occasional tension headaches. Also, the trainer should frequently praise the learners not only for apparently positive outcomes but also for coming regularly to the training sessions and keeping up with the home practice.

USING AT TO TREAT ANXIETY DISORDERS

Given the empirical support for the linkage between imagery and physiology, it appears that AT has multiple strengths that recommend it for inclusion in a treatment package for anxiety disorders. It not only serves as one of many techniques that can lead to a generic relaxation response, as Herbert Benson described, but it may actually have differential treatment effects for a variety of disorders. But how about the evidence for the effectiveness of AT?

Evidence That AT Can Help Reduce Anxiety Levels

In 1994, Wolfgang Linden published a comprehensive review of the clinical benefit of AT for a variety of disorders. The technique was a combined narrative and meta-analytic review that focused only on controlled clinical trials published both in German and English. This review concurred with earlier reviews of AT outcome conducted by Kenneth Lichstein and Howard Pikoff, who both found that AT was a useful treatment for a wide variety of psychological and psychosomatic dysfunctions. The meta-analysis led to the conclusion that AT was most effective with reducing the discomfort of childbirth, and that it led to improvements in infertility, angina, eczema, and headache. AT was also useful for rehabilitation from myocardial infarction. The main point here is that one cannot help be struck by the wide variety of disorders that AT has been shown to help alleviate and by the number of different organ systems involved. The only sensible conclusion is that AT reduces the body's general vulnerability to stress.

While there is good evidence that AT can be a useful clinical tool for a diversity of stress-related disorders, stress and anxiety—although related—are far from identical. For this chapter, the critical issues have to do specifically with anxiety disorders. Although we might wish for a great deal more research on this topic, there is a limited but consistent body of evidence that AT is useful for treating anxiety. AT has been subjected to controlled tests for panic and for more circumscribed anxiety reactions, including test anxiety. In addition, it has been researched both in group form and individually, and it has been compared with other biobehavioral treatments such as biofeedback and muscular relaxation. There have also been studies of AT outcomes in nonclinical populations in which anxiety-related constructs were the target of measurement. The results of this somewhat fragmented body of research show consistently that AT leads to anxiety reduction, but there is no demonstration of a distinct advantage for AT over other relaxation methods.

Treating Specific Anxiety Disorders

Having discussed how AT works, how to train clients in AT, and what the outcome research has to say about the effectiveness of AT, we now discuss how to use AT to treat specific anxiety disorders.

One point bears strong emphasis: *when it comes to anxiety disorders, we do not see AT as a unitary or stand-alone treatment technique.* The problems faced by sufferers of anxiety disorders are far too complex to be addressed with one single technique. Instead, we propose using AT as a central component of a treatment package. Since many of the facets of learning AT are related to other anxiety management strategies, we often use AT as a springboard for addressing issues such as interpretation of bodily sensations, threat appraisal, and general stress reduction, management of worrisome cognitions, etc.

Even though each anxiety disorder may have its own etiology, it is of use to consider what the various disorders have in common. In each anxiety disorder, there is some level of increased arousal, some degree of cognitive disturbance related to this arousal, and some behavioral component. We see AT to be useful primarily in reducing arousal, and this is borne out by research. To a lesser extent we find that AT is also useful in correcting certain cognitive patterns—especially cognitions of being unable to change undesirable patterns of fear and avoidance. To the best of our knowledge, this latter application has not been researched, but clinically we have had good results modifying maladaptive patterns of thinking by combining cognitive techniques with AT. Although the rationale for cognitive therapy rests on a different foundation than that of AT, in practical application, we have found the two approaches to be very compatible.

Generalized Anxiety Disorder. Generalized anxiety disorder is characterized by chronic levels of distressingly high sympathetic arousal and by a pervasive tendency to worry about a wide range of things, large and small. The GAD sufferer often sees life as an endless chain of anxiety-provoking events, and he or she frequently complains of inability to find relief or to change the continually negative response to external events. Therapy in a cognitive vein often confronts worry directly, and AT could be expected to add little to this aspect of treatment. AT can, however, be quite useful in reducing chronic arousal. In addition, the mastery of AT can promote feelings of being more in control and of having some impact on breaking the overwhelming chain of worrisome events.

We focus on two problems when discussing anxiety with clients. First, there is the level of anxiety at any given time, and with GAD the level is distressingly high. Second, we introduce a concept that is new to many of our GAD clients: the idea that anxiety levels normally fluctuate. This is a vital understanding, and we often underscore it by making an impromptu sketch showing anxiety levels fluctuating over time. We may trace anxious fluctuations something like this:

> Anxiety may be high as you are getting out of bed and thinking about all the problems you may have to face. Then, as you get busy in the bathroom and kitchen, anxiety may decline for a while. An unexpected phone call, and the anxiety is up again and goes higher still as you have to race the clock to get out of the house. On the way to work it may be more routine, and you relax a bit, only to get hit all at once by a burst of anxiety as the day's work stares you in the face, or when your schedule is suddenly shifted. This up-and-down course is typical, and it shows that there are two separate skills to learn. The

more obvious is to learn not to respond too strongly to things that upset you. The other is just as important: you have to learn to recover once the upsetting event is past.

This type of explanation sets the stage for introducing AT. With the GAD client, we emphasize that we are trying to reduce anxious arousal and that we are teaching a method of recovering from acute anxiety. In our view, this outlook sets realistic and therapeutically sound expectations: we are telling the client that it is *not* our goal to make anxiety go away, but rather that we are teaching him or her how to recover from anxiety *when it happens. When*, not *if*.

In our experience, as GAD clients reduce habitual high levels of anxiety, they begin to discriminate between things that make them anxious and things that are more calming. This fluctuation opens the door for cognitive work, and at times for exposure. Clients tend to progress from reports of constant anxiety to reports of good and bad days, to a more varied texture with responses to particular events and worries. In other words, progress is shown when the pattern of chronicity is broken, and we help induce changes in anxiety levels by using AT in session—especially when anxiety-provoking issues have surfaced.

A case example of a client with strong perfectionistic tendencies demonstrates the considerable struggle some clients may have with the "relative improvement" rather than perfect healing approach of psychological therapies in general, and in this particular case AT.

CASE THREE

A fifty-year-old technician in treatment for stress management and generalized anxiety disorder responded to AT in a manner typical of GAD clients. During training he asked many detailed questions and showed great concern with getting it just right. During the first week, he spontaneously extended practice sessions from nine minutes to twenty to thirty minutes, and he tried to practice at least three times per day rather than the assigned twice. All this effort contributed to disappointment with results.

With this client, training emphasized letting go and the idea of doing frequent but imperfect practice sessions. He began to use the suggestion "I am very calm" when driving in traffic and at work and reported good results with this application.

AT served as only a small part of the treatment program for this client. It helped reduce overall arousal in at least two ways. First, it allowed him to return to a relaxed state more frequently than before. Secondly, it gave him tools to reduce responsiveness to a variety of situations and worries.

Even more important than arousal reduction, for this client AT provided a handy set of in-session stimuli that facilitated work on his generally anxious approach to life. This approach combines assessment and treatment techniques and involves seeing AT as a microcosm in which the client's general response patterns can be evoked, examined, and changed. For this client, the tendency to establish perfectionistic standards and then try distressingly hard to reach them became apparent as soon as AT was taught. Discussion of his responses revealed such thoughts as "This is my last chance" and "I *have* to get it right this time." Other cognitions with a more existential flavor became apparent later. The cognitive work that followed AT was both lengthy and vitally important to reducing the client's distress.

For this client, the outcome of treatment was necessarily disappointing but clinically good: relief was significant but far less than complete. It is interesting that although the client continued to get caught in occasional cycles of worry, he continued to practice AT long after treatment ended. He characterized it—with some satisfaction—as imperfect practice of an imperfect solution to his problems.

Many of those with GAD find anxiety or arousal in any form particularly aversive. A few have told us openly that they would like to become relaxed once and for all and simply stay that way. It may sound silly when stated blatantly like this, but our guess is that a great many clients feel this way and never verbalize the sentiment. The therapist has the considerable challenge of deflecting this unrealistic goal or desire—whether or not it is stated openly. We try to empathize by reflecting that remaining uncomfortably—perhaps intolerably—anxious for a long, long time probably makes the beginning of any kind of arousal seem frightening. We also use the taking-back procedure to emphasize the need for fluctuation in levels of arousal. We introduce the idea of taking back by saying that a certain level of arousal is necessary, that we don't go through the day like a limp dishrag; instead we need a certain edge in order to be able to perform well.

Phobias. In recent years, there has been a great deal of theorizing and research concerning the etiology of phobias. Early psychoanalytic models were quickly replaced with conditioning models such as those proposed by Joseph Wolpe and Stanley J. (Jack) Rachman. These theories have proved especially useful in the development of effective behavioral interventions. Specifically, there is overwhelming evidence that exposure to the feared stimulus is a potent therapeutic method. Some explain the mechanism of exposure treatment by claiming that exposure to the feared stimulus without the habitual avoidance or escape behavior begins an extinction process. Others emphasize the role of cognitions in the development and treatment of phobias.

Regardless of *how* exposure works, it clearly does work, and we would never replace it with AT in the treatment of specific phobias. Instead, we use it along with exposure. Exposure treatments can be offered either imaginally or in the natural environment (in vivo). They can be presented as flooding methods (beginning with exposure to the most fear-arousing stimulus) or by gradually escalating toward the most anxiety-arousing stimuli (that is, graduated exposure as in systematic desensitization). Although in vivo exposure is usually preferred, it is often quite impractical; flooding generally works faster than graduated exposure, but it can overwhelm the client and backfire by reinforcing the fear and avoidance. Exposure is by definition very arousing however it is conducted. Even the anticipation of exposure makes most phobics highly anxious, and this anticipatory anxiety is of course is at the heart of the patient's avoidance behaviors that have effectively contributed to the maintenance of the disorder. Sometimes drugs are used to reduce initial anxiety levels preceding exposure. But as clinicians we prefer not to use drugs for fear that our patients will attribute their therapeutic gains (such as decreases in arousal) to the drug and not to their own coping or mastery efforts. When direct reduction in arousal levels is indicated during exposure exercises, we use AT. We find this superior to medications because it enhances rather than reduces self-efficacy. Thus, we see that the most useful role for AT in the treatment of phobias is in the preparation for in vivo or imaginal exposure.

In addition, AT can be used outside of the therapy session. We have repeatedly heard phobic clients explain that the worst thing about running into what they most fear—whether it be a spider, a crowded bus or elevator, a dog, a balloon, or a Coke truck—is the inability to calm down afterwards. Sudden exposure to a phobic stimulus can and does ruin the phobic's day. A portion of the avoidance often has to do directly with anticipation of this difficulty in recovery after exposure, and we have encouraged clients to use AT to solve this problem. Once phobic clients have mastered AT for use during exposure exercises, they can use the techniques to decrease arousal and regain composure after sudden, unplanned exposure to the feared stimulus.

As you may well imagine, once a phobic can think about a feared stimulus and encounter it naturally without undue upset, anticipatory anxiety usually declines quickly. This is especially true if cognitions of mastery and coping are encouraged. As noted earlier, AT appears to potentiate feelings and cognitions of self-efficacy and can thereby add a nonphysiologic component to recovery. We always emphasize that the real benefit of AT (and of other relaxation techniques as well) is preventive, and we try always to emphasize long-term practice.

Panic Disorder. Panic disorder appears to respond best to a fairly complex treatment package (see Chapter Eight). The package includes education about anxiety and physiological reactions, relaxation training, cognitive restructuring, and two kinds of exposure: in vivo and interoceptive. The relaxation and structured breathing components of the therapy have much the same rationale as we proposed above for using AT to treat phobias: general autonomic arousal is reduced and the sense of mastery of physical sensations is enhanced. The client is taught that panic is most likely when stress levels are high, and that reducing general tension helps make panic attacks less likely.

Interoceptive exposure involves inducing bodily sensations that are associated with panic attacks. It is a double-barreled approach in that cognitive restructuring and behavioral desensitization occur at the same time. Developing comfort with interoceptive exposure may be more difficult for some clients than for others. A case example follows where the client did have initial difficulties with this approach.

CASE FOUR

A twenty-eight-year-old male laborer suffered from panic disorder with an unusual presentation. His attacks were preceded and cued by a flushed feeling that began in the back of his neck and then ran quickly up his scalp. Soon his face would feel flushed and hot all over, and, like many panickers, he would begin to experience fairly severe cardiac and respiratory sensations. Since he attributed the sensations to being overheated and restricted by clothing and jewelry, he felt an overwhelming urge to strip. Usually his cap, watch, and ring were the first to go, followed by shoes and socks. During especially severe attacks, he reported stripping to his underwear, and he laughed to admit that at home he would take that off also.

For this client, the flushed feeling at the back of his neck signaled two highly aversive events: (1) he was about to experience the acute distress of a panic attack, and (2) he was at risk of embarrassing himself by stripping down or by beating a sudden retreat to find a place where he could strip. Of the two events, he had come to dread the stripping more than the panic.

After a careful behavioral assessment and some thorough education about anxiety and about the cognitive theory of the etiology of panic, this patient was taught AT. He learned the heaviness formula without a problem, but like many beginning practitioners he felt a bit hurried and nervous while practicing. During the second AT session, the warmth formula was introduced. The client stiffened visibly, reporting simply, "I really don't like that. I don't think this is a good idea."

Interoceptive exposure was explained once again, and although the idea itself made sense to him, the notion of inducing flushed feelings was met with stiff resistance. He practiced heaviness for one more week, and during the next session he reported that his hands had felt a little warm when he was using the heaviness formula. Using a "foot-in-the-door" approach, the therapist was finally able to convince him to try the warmth formula.

By the third repetition of the warmth formula, the client tore off his watch. A minute or two later he caught himself trying to get his ring off without the therapist noticing, and he broke into laughter. The laughter was a turning point. Building on this lightening tone, the therapist convinced him to attempt interoceptive exposure with the statement "The back of my neck is becoming warm and tingly." The formula induced the warm rush he associated with a panic, without any severe cardiac or respiratory sensations.

A variety of exposure and response prevention procedures were used during the next few sessions, and the client became quite amused by how easily his fears could be induced. He began testing his limits by practicing AT in the truck he drove for a living, and in the restroom at work.

With this client, AT practice never proceeded beyond the third formula (heartbeat). It is uncertain whether he significantly reduced his arousal with AT, but over just a few weeks the frequency of his panics reduced from three to five per week to one or two per month. His concern with them dropped even more dramatically: his severe worry and self-criticism turned to amusement and detachment. It is quite certain that the increased sense of self-control he gained with AT played a vital part in his recovery.

Although to the best of our knowledge there is no research on this issue, we see AT as a particularly useful component in the treatment of panic disorder because of its emphasis on physical sensations. We have had several patients whose panic-inducing sensation was a flushed, tingling feeling in the back of the neck, scalp, or upper arms. When they learned to induce warm, tingling feelings purposely, their catastrophic reactions to the sensations quickly abated. As mentioned earlier in this chapter in the section on relaxation-induced panic and anxiety, the practice of AT has been reported to lead to a wide variety of sometimes bizarre sensations. Since the treatment of panic disorder involves purposely evoking sensations for interoceptive exposure, we simply use the sensations that occur during AT in session—the autogenic discharges—as exposure. These experiences make excellent springboards for the examination of cognitive and emotional reactions to odd physical sensations.

The objective of this chapter has been to show how AT can be usefully applied in the treatment of anxiety disorders. Despite a scant research literature, there are many clinically applicable ways for using AT; these applications should vary with the type of anxiety disorder being treated. Although we may often begin treatment with AT, invariably we combine AT with other techniques before we finish with therapy. Depending on the disorder and the client, it appears that AT can play multiple roles:

• As a relaxation procedure, AT may be broadly inter-changeable with other relaxation-inducing techniques when the goal is to bring about a generalized relaxation response and a corresponding sense of control. For example, research shows that muscular relaxation is equally as potent as AT. However, some individual clients, if given a choice, may find the rationale and method of AT more appealing. Whenever this happens in therapy, we find that the enhanced credibility of a method and the resulting enthusiasm may accelerate successful treatment in and of itself.

• As a tool for interoceptive exposure and desensitization to physical symptoms, AT fits well in a conceptual framework that emphasizes the importance of the panicker's experience and labeling of physical sensations. Although there are no data show-ing that AT is more likely than other techniques to induce panic attacks or anxiety, the literature on autogenic discharges suggests that AT may be especially useful for interoceptive exposure. To the best of our knowledge, this is the first published description of this particular use of AT.

• Finally, we have emphasized the nonphysiological bene-fits of AT, such as increased sense of mastery of anxiety sensa-tions, the use of AT rationale to teach about normal fluctuations in anxiety levels, and increased confidence in recovering from anxiety-provoking situations.

NOTES

P. 118, *AT was pioneered by Johann Schultz in the early 1930s:* Schultz, J. H. (1932). *Das autogene Training (konzentrative Selbstentspannung) [Autogenic training: Concentrative self-relaxation].* Leipzig: Thieme.

P. 118, *Today, it is often classified as a stress management technique:* Lehrer, P. M., & Woolfolk, R. L. (1993). (Eds.), *Principles and practice of stress management* (2nd ed.). New York: Guilford Press.

P. 118, *a psychophysiologically based form of autonomic self-regulation:* Pikoff, H. (1984). A critical review of autogenic training in America. *Clinical Psychology Review, 4,* 619–639.

P. 118, *In 1990, Wolfgang Linden published a comprehensive resource book:* Linden, W. (1990). *Autogenic training: A clinical guide.* New York: Guilford Press.

P. 119, *reviews by Wolfgang Luthe, Kenneth Lichstein, or Wolfgang Linden:* Luthe, W. (1970). *Autogenic therapy. Vol. IV: Research and theory.* New York: Grune & Stratton; Lichstein, K. L. (1988). *Clinical relaxation strategies.* New York: Wiley; Linden, W. (1994). Autogenic training: A narrative and quantitative review of clinical outcome. *Biofeedback and Self-Regulation, 19,* 227–264.

P. 120, *proposed by Walter Cannon in the 1920s:* Cannon, W. B. (1929). *Bodily changes in pain, fear, and rage* (2nd ed.). New York: Appleton-Century-Crofts.

P. 131, *although Mensen, a German physician:* Mensen, H. (1975). *ABC des Autogenen Trainings.* München: Goldmann-Verlag.

P. 134, *Linden's manual:* Linden, W. (1990). *Autogenic training: A clinical guide.* New York: Guilford Press.

P. 139, *as Herbert Benson described:* Benson, H. (1975). *The relaxation response.* New York: Morrow.

P. 139, *In 1994, Wolfgang Linden published a comprehensive review:* Linden, W. (1994). Autogenic training: A narrative and quantitative review of clinical outcome. *Biofeedback and Self-Regulation, 19,* 227–264.

P. 139, *Kenneth Lichstein and Howard Pikoff:* Lichstein, K. L. (1988). *Clinical relaxation strategies.* New York: Wiley; Pikoff, H. (1984). A critical review of autogenic training in America. *Clinical Psychology Review, 4,* 619–639.

P. 144, *Joseph Wolpe and Stanley J. (Jack) Rachman:* Wolpe, J. (1973). *The practice of behavior therapy.* New York: Pergamon Press; Rachman, S., & Levitt, K. (1985). Panics and their consequences. *Behavior Research and Therapy, 23,* 585–600.

6

PSYCHODYNAMIC THERAPIES

Richard Almond

Psychodynamic, or psychoanalytic, psychotherapy has been developing since Freud first experimented with asking patients to "talk out" their problems. Psychoanalysis has two valuable aspects:

1. It offers a model for understanding personality function and specific symptoms such as anxiety.
2. It offers treatments that can help the long-standing symptom patterns and life problems that often accompany anxiety disorders.

The psychoanalyst or psychoanalytically oriented psychotherapist uses a *dynamic* approach: a view of behavior and conscious experience as part of a more complex, interconnected system of thoughts, feelings, attitudes, and motives. Psychodynamic understanding does not conflict with biological theories of human behavior. In fact, it assumes there is a biological level to all mental activity, but also that our understanding of the links between psychological experience and the biological substrate is still limited. We can learn much about psychodynamics—the causal pathways of thoughts, feelings, and motivations—through psychological approaches, primarily by listening to patients carefully and observing their responses to the questions and comments we make. Combining this approach with psychoanalytic theory provides a rich source of working hypotheses for the clinician.

In this chapter, I

1. Describe how anxiety is thought of in psychoanalytic theory
2. Present a categorization of anxiety
3. Suggest how this understanding can be used in evaluation and treatment

A psychoanalytic approach differs from that embodied in the *DSM-IV.* The latter is a *phenomenological* view of patients' experience and behavior: what the professional can see directly, and what the patient reports. This is the diagnostic approach usually employed by therapists treating with medication, or those using behavioral or cognitive/behavioral psychotherapies discussed in other chapters. This chapter focuses on the psychodynamic understanding and treatment of anxiety. Ideally, a clinician synthesizes these different ways of understanding and treating a patient.

ANXIETY AS THE TIP OF THE ICEBERG

To a psychoanalyst, conscious experience—the symptom of anxiety or panic, for instance—is the tip of the iceberg of mental activity. Each person has an extensive unconscious psychological life. This "dynamic unconscious" has its own mode of thinking, a mode that is different from the rational thinking of waking consciousness. We see evidence for this unconscious activity in dreams, in the many irrational aspects of human behavior, and in the form of symptoms.

An awareness of the role of unconscious mental activity can help the clinician, whether using a psychotherapy approach or a more symptom-oriented approach. Psychodynamic theories, sometimes called psychoanalytic or "depth" psychologies, study the large part of mental function that is unconscious (inaccessible) and preconscious (not in consciousness, but accessible). These theories can help us understand much of human behavior that appears illogical and pointless, including anxiety as a symptom.

A central idea in this view of the mind is that people learn from their experience. The most formative aspect of this learning occurs early in life, in the central relationships of childhood. We know that children, however, do not develop the capacity for abstract thinking until adolescence. Nevertheless, they are avid theorizers, speculating about how best to obtain what is pleasurable and how to avoid unpleasant feelings and other dangers. Children's interpretations of their world make sense if we appreciate their particular point of view, and the kinds of thinking they use. Freud's famous "Little Hans" illustrates such thinking.

LITTLE HANS

Hans was the four-and-a-half-year-old son of colleagues who consulted with Freud. Hans loved each of his parents. But like most boys of his age, he harbored a wish to have his mother for himself. This led to fantasies in which something would happen to his father.

When Hans saw a horse fall down dead in the street, it confirmed the possibility that his death wishes towards his father could come true. But this event was also frightening because Hans also loved and feared the father he wished to usurp. He felt guilty and feared punishment for his wish. Out of these feelings Hans became anxious. Then, to protect himself from these thoughts, he developed a phobia of horses. This mental maneuver, however, did not fully solve his conflict of both loving and wanting to get rid of his father, since the ideas were in his head, and thus avoiding horses could not truly protect him. As the phobic avoidance increased in a further attempt to defend himself, he became frightened of going out on the street at all.

When Hans's father, with Freud's coaching, interpreted Hans's wishes and fears to him, the phobic ideas ceased. The interpretation of his wishes and fears, made conscious and verbal by father, relieved Hans's guilt and fear. The symptom was no longer needed.

Like Hans, all children develop theories or "fantasies" about the world, especially concerning their closest relationships. These theories involve conclusions about which thoughts, feelings, and actions will lead to gratification and which to danger. While growing up may correct some of these ideas, many persist unconsciously in their childhood form. These unconscious ideas, though based on ideas formed long ago, then become part of the person's reactions to current life events.

ROGER

Roger came to see me because, despite his successful professional career, he did not feel satisfied. He was the oldest of five sons. He repeatedly developed projects outside his work that involved influencing large, publicly visible organizations. Usually, these projects ended in failure after much expenditure of time and energy. Yet Roger would quickly find another project to launch.

In our therapy together, it emerged that Roger had felt massively and increasingly rejected and displaced by each of his younger brothers' arrivals. To ward off rage and depression as a child, he had identified with his mother. *He* would produce amazing projects, just as his mother had, magically, produced children from inside herself. But he had also internalized his failure to accomplish enough to overcome his early disappointment. As an adult he replayed this scenario over and over, never succeeding enough to allay his unconscious need, and at the cost of his time and involvement with his family.

The Dynamic Origins of Anxiety

Anxiety plays an important and complex role in the mental processes that develop around unconscious fantasy and defense. We next distinguish between two different forms of anxiety determined by the intensity and meaning of the original source.

In one type, *signal anxiety*, the ego has learned to recognize certain situations as dangerous (that is, as potentially overwhelming emotionally) and to produce small amounts of anxiety to alert the person to danger. In another type, *traumatic anxiety*, the ego is overwhelmed by danger and loses control. Note that what we refer to as a danger may be an external event or an internal one, such as a very powerful sexual or aggressive impulse.

Roger, for example, had murderous impulses toward his younger brothers. Competitive situations triggered a recurrence of these feelings and the danger of losing control of his rage. His ego would then produce a signal of anxiety, and he would undertake another project to defend against the danger of his feeling. If one of Roger's siblings had actually died in childhood, he might have experienced traumatic anxiety.

Signal Anxiety

Anxiety plays an extensive and normal part in mental life. In the formative years of childhood, important dangers become associated with a special form, signal anxiety. This is an anticipatory fear that is triggered when a situation has some feature that is associated with a past situation of danger. It triggers a self-protective reaction, that is, a defense mechanism.

Suppose a mother regularly became rejecting and cold in the face of a child's anger. The child would develop an ability to generate an anxiety signal when feelings of anger threatened to emerge. By adulthood, this process would be largely unconscious and automatic. Anxiety would be felt before there was any awareness of anger. The anxiety signal would stimulate a defensive reaction, for example, becoming especially kind or compliant (reaction formation), or turning the anger against the self (masochism). Thus, while anxiety may appear as a symptom itself, it also may trigger other thoughts, symptoms, and behaviors.

A case study illustrates reaction formation as a response to signal anxiety.

PAUL

Paul came from a happy family, but one where both parents avoided the expression of strong feelings. He sought therapy because he found himself anxious about his work situation, which offered advancement if he could assert himself strongly in a highly competitive situation. Paul had managed to get ahead by doing his job well and being of service to others. When the work situation changed, he was paralyzed at the prospect of acting in his own behalf. To act aggressively aroused fantasies of rejection and disapproval by his internalized parents. Signal anxiety, experienced unconsciously, led Paul to act altruistically to convince himself that he was not being competitive.

Signal anxiety can also operate in more massive ways to inhibit development in major areas of life, as in another case.

MARY

Mary was the child of a hard-working father who drank heavily once he arrived home from work and a tense, paranoid mother who slapped the children at moments of frustration. To protect herself, Mary developed a highly compliant manner. When she reached adulthood, Mary moved away from home and began to develop a career and friends. But she found herself overwhelmed with anxiety at every step she made in the direction of increased autonomy. She felt that she was "not really a person."

The difficulty was that Mary had not had the normal experiences of testing out intense loving and angry feelings with her family. To Mary, acting on such feelings might well be a dangerous provocation that would lead to violence or rejection, as had happened in her family of origin. The result was that when Mary began to act in ways appropriate to adult development—taking action to develop a career, or dating—she became anxious.

In our psychotherapy, Mary gradually came to trust me enough to become assertive and even angry. As she did this, she gradually felt safe enough to become more vigorous in her own life, with less and less anxiety.

Mary's anxiety served as a *signal* to her to keep dangerous feelings and thoughts repressed. The extent of her anxiety and its many potential triggers related to Mary's not having developed ego capacities to assess and manage her feelings realistically. She was still unconsciously trying to prevent the actualization of childhood fears of abandonment and destruction.

Signal anxiety operates constantly in human psychological life. In some individuals like Mary, however, signal anxiety is not well-contained by defensive responses. In such people anxiety can spiral out of control, even though the stimulus might be minimal. The result may be a panic attack, massive somatic symptoms, obsessive-compulsive behaviors, pervasive and unfocused anxiety, phobias, hypochondriacal preoccupations, or even aggressive or self-destructive behavior.

Traumatic Anxiety

In another type of anxiety state, traumatic anxiety, there may also be an inappropriate reaction to a minimal stimulus. In this case the anxiety results from an earlier experience of being emotionally overwhelmed. Unlike signal anxiety, which *protects* the psyche from being overwhelmed, traumatic anxiety reactions *repeat* an earlier experience of being overwhelmed.

Posttraumatic stress disorder (PTSD) is an example of such a phenomenon that may result from adult experience. Children, having less developed abilities to protect themselves psychologically, are even more vulnerable to trauma and traumatic anxiety than adults are. Mary can be contrasted with Lucy, who experienced traumatic anxiety.

LUCY

When Lucy was an adolescent, her beloved fifteen-year-older sister committed suicide. The sister had taken special interest in Lucy as a young child, engaging her in fantasy games and lavishing attention on her. When the suicide occurred, Lucy's entire family was too upset to attend to her special feelings of loss. Lucy coped for a time by being a good student, like her sister. She went on to do well in high school and college, marry, and hold a good job, although she remained emotionally quite immature. She avoided having children.

In her late thirties, Lucy began to have episodes in which, with almost no provocation, she became agitated and would think that the only solution was to kill herself. In therapy, this pattern quickly turned on the therapist: every separation aroused so much anxiety that Lucy considered suicide. Exploration revealed that disavowed feelings of loss, guilt, and rage were triggering a near-*repetition* of the sister's behavior. Because she had been unable to tolerate these feelings when her sister died, they were repressed. Only anxiety and the impulse to imitate her sister were visible symptomatically.

Lucy actually experienced far less conscious anxiety than Mary. For her, a feared event had actually occurred. The affective (feeling) memory and emotional meaning of this event, however, had been fended off for many years. When they began to break into consciousness, the reaction was to repeat the trauma with herself as the object, probably as a symbolic form of rejoining the lost sister, and guiltily turning her anger about the loss on herself. This tendency to repeat traumatic experience seems to result from the ego being overwhelmed at the time of the trauma. In effect, the event has not been fully processed—it has not become memory yet! Once it can be remembered (meaning: with the appropriate feelings), then the person can begin to build defenses, that is, move from traumatic anxiety to signal anxiety.

DEVELOPMENTAL STAGES OF ANXIETY

Another way to conceptualize anxiety involves consideration of a hierarchy of severity. Since anxiety is present from infancy onward, its impact on the adult may depend upon at what point in childhood the greatest stress, deprivation, trauma, or conflict occurred.

Freud pointed out that children experience a series of danger situations, relating to the internal meaning of their anxiety. These begin with fear of loss of the object (abandonment by the mother), then fear of loss of the object's love (emotional rejection by mother or father), then fear of bodily damage (usually from a parent-competitor), and later, fear of the superego's disapproval (guilty conscience). In actual clinical practice, one usually sees a mix of these different levels of anxiety operating in the same person.

The normally developing child must contend with each of these forms of anxiety, usually with the parents' help. Appropriate defenses develop, each with signal anxiety as a component. Thus, even in the healthiest person, life events often produce anxiety, or other symptoms secondary to anxiety. If the life events are not overwhelming, the person uses defenses in an effective adaptation to the situation. It is when these adaptive efforts fail that people come for treatment.

Freud's levels are useful in the detailed work with patients in therapy. For our purposes it is more useful to focus on the broader qualities of anxiety: fragmentation anxiety, separation anxiety, conflictual anxiety. These are closer to subjective experience, yet they reflect a sequence that moves from earlier, more primitive forms toward more mature forms of anxiety.

Fragmentation Anxiety

This form of anxiety is not on Freud's list, but it can be added as perhaps the most primitive, disturbing kind. It occurs largely in schizophrenics or other psychotic individuals. It is often the initial experience of acute psychosis, untreated with medication. The different aspects of experience—internal states, sense perceptions, thoughts, external events, the impact of other people— lose their usual sense of relation to each other. To put this more theoretically, the "synthetic function of the ego"—the capacity to put the different elements of daily experience in their place from one moment to another—is lost.

The danger is immense: confidence in internal controls is lost, there is no firm sense of body intactness or psychological boundaries from others, and there is no sureness about contact with others. The various specific symptoms of schizophrenia—catatonic immobility, paranoid delusions, hallucinations—are restitutive attempts to organize experience in primitive ways.

Separation Anxiety

Fear of loss of contact can be an issue for individuals with very different levels of personality structure. We all feel some anxiety when we leave those we love. This feeling is intensified if the separation involves a significant step towards autonomy, such as beginning school or leaving home for college. Such steps may generate unusual levels of anxiety under several circumstances. If a parent, usually the mother, is herself anxious about the child becoming more autonomous, she may give the child an emotional message that discourages normal psychological growth.

FRANK

Nine-year-old Frank was sent to a special camp for children with emotional problems, to help with separation from his close-binding mother. He immediately began to write postcards home describing beatings by his counselors and his constant unhappiness. In fact, with mild encouragement from the staff he was having a fine time.

Mother wrote him several letters each day, addressed to "My Oopsie-Poopsi Bubsie-Wubsie," commiserating with his proclaimed suffering, and telling him that "soon all this will be over, and you will be back at home away from the bad counselors."

Of course, the maternal message need not be this blatant. A parent may convey some disturbing feeling-signal to a child at moments of separation in a way that would not be noticed by an observer. If repeated regularly, the child will begin to have separation anxiety as a warning of the possibility of eliciting this disturbing parental message.

Separation can also be a problem in the opposite situation, where parents have been distant, unloving, or sadistic. In this case the patient, as a child, does not feel the support of the parent in making maturational steps, especially those that involve leaving the physical presence of the parent. (Mary is an example.) In adulthood these inner experiences may emerge strongly, not only in making major life changes but in a clinging tendency in close relationships. Borderline patients and narcissistic patients frequently have such difficulties, because their internal experiences of relatedness are so problematic.

Borderline patients are often acutely anxious in relation to their feeling of contact with others. Their tendency to use anger as a major defense leads to a fear that they are alienating others (often accurate!). Yet when they are close, because of difficulty tolerating their own feelings they project their anger onto the other person. This person then becomes a dangerous threat, and flight is necessary. This begins the cycle once more. At each step it is an anxiety signal—and with borderline patients this may reach panic proportions easily—that moves the person on to the next step.

The appearance and management of separation anxiety is quite different with a narcissistic personality.

MORT

Mort was first child of a large family. His mother was preoccupied with his many younger siblings as they arrived, and with her husband's needs. Father was a businessman who loved his children, but he left most of the child rearing to mother and servants.

Mort received his mother's attention in concentrated doses, such as when he was ill. But at other times he did not feel in control of their contact and had to suppress rage at being frequently shunted aside. The result was an intense need for a mothering woman, coexisting with marked hostility because of feeling so dependent.

Separation from a wife or girl friend for more than a day led Mort to feel shaky and needy. Single, he felt a desperation that led him to feel frightened about functioning, and paradoxically made him feel inadequate in meeting new women. When he was with a woman he wanted to feel in control of the relationship.

This pattern exemplifies the way separation anxiety appears in someone with narcissistic problems. That is, Mort felt that separation meant the loss of mother's love, and his self-esteem plunged correspondingly when he was without a woman. He needed a woman to feel all right, but his fears of not being in control led to real or feared rejections. He felt this as a combination of anxiety and depression.

For narcissistically disturbed patients like Mort, therapeutic contact and minor tranquilizers as a supplement usually suffice during periods of acute anxiety. Unlike borderline patients, these persons often find a psychotherapeutic relationship very helpful. The noncritical quality of psychotherapy helps restore their self-esteem and trust in others after narcissistic injury. Working with the patient to identify the source of destabilization of the patient's self-feeling is usually the immediate therapeutic goal.

Adult children of alcoholics also may have serious separation problems. These individuals have usually been precociously mature in their families by necessity, and have developed rigid, controlling personality styles. Change from routine can be anxiety provoking.

Separation anxiety in an adult child of an alcoholic is illustrated in the case of Mary, the woman with a cold, abusive mother (see above). Mary turned for closeness to her more loving but alcoholic father. His drinking after work often led to sleepy or passed-out states. Even when up and about, Mary's father had a short attention span, and he tended to forget important events and situations in her life, like her high school graduation.

This unpredictability was mirrored in Mary's difficulty in trusting that I would sustain my involvement between sessions, or during longer breaks. At such times she would become so anxious she felt depersonalized, and she would abort whatever steps she had begun so as to make changes in her life.

Relatively healthy patients whose conflicts involve wishes for specialness with the opposite-gender parent may also have separation anxiety.

GEORGE

George was treated as a special child by his mother, but he felt left out of the close relation between his father and older brother. He

admired them, but to get too involved made him feel inferior, especially compared to the special status his mother made him feel. Transitions like kindergarten, camp, starting high school, and going off
to college were times of fear, sadness, and longing.

After George's mother died when he was a young adult, he began
to abuse stimulating drugs and act in other self-destructive ways.
When he entered treatment and was able to control these behaviors,
he began to be aware of feeling anxious about separations from his
girlfriend or the therapist.

In this case, maternal emotional seductiveness made it hard
for the patient to make normal developmental transitions, which
involve some degree of relinquishment and mourning for the
parent, and for the past. Further, George experienced amounts
of anxiety far greater than normal about feeling inadequate in
relations with men. His emotional reliance on his mother had
interfered with his feeling confident with his father about closeness and competition.

Anxiety can also frequently arise out of guilt, again as a signal
of danger. In this case the danger is to someone else, a loved
person.

LYDIA

Lydia had been close to her father when he died during her adolescence. She had a tense relationship with her demanding, self-cen-
tered mother. Although she eagerly moved away from home to
college and professional training, Lydia found it difficult to develop
a long-standing relationship with a man. She entered therapy because
of chronic anxiety as well as frustration about her personal life.

Her anxiety calmed, and she talked about her guilt at moving
ahead in her life, leaving both parents behind in symbolic ways.
Once she could recognize that it was this "survivor guilt" that was
making her anxious, Lydia was able to leave an exploitative job, meet
and marry an appropriate man, and plan a family.

Conflictual (Neurotic) Anxiety

Both George and Lydia demonstrate separation anxiety at a neurotic level, although the trauma of loss played an additional etiological role for each. By neurotic we mean that personality development has been relatively complete: there are complex and flexible coping abilities (defenses, ego skills) and a strong, but not overly punitive, conscience (superego). The unconscious sources of anxiety here involve fears of parental retaliation or disapproval.

Both of these patients functioned well professionally and had stable social relationships. They each had difficulties with intimacy caused by unconscious conflicts about the consequences of closeness. Signal anxiety occurred every time one of these people formed a strong one-on-one relationship with an appropriate partner. Unconsciously, each feared the loss of love of the parent of the opposite sex, and the anger and attack of the parent of the same sex (the oedipal conflict). Neurotic anxiety can also appear in a person who does not have any significant traumatic history.

BUD

Bud grew up in a stable home, the oldest of three. His father, a high-powered businessman, was caring but very competitive with Bud. Mother was frustrated at having given up her career possibilities and envious of her husband and children, and she gave Bud mixed messages about his success. He did well in school, married, and had children. Many of his career moves were accompanied by intense anxiety.

Treatment revealed the ways in which success evoked anxiety at imagined competitive threats or envy in others. Bud unconsciously would limit or undo successful efforts to ward off this anxiety. He sought treatment for depression, but treatment revealed the underlying fears about success.

If there is significant impairment of functioning, as was the case for George and Lydia in their personal lives and for Bud in his work and mood state, treatment of neurotic anxiety is, optimally, long-term psychotherapy or psychoanalysis. While such treatments are demanding in time and expense, they provide the best possibility of sustained, significant change. If such treatment is not part of the person's health coverage, it is important to make them aware of the benefits of "talking therapies," and the choice of paying for this service themselves, if possible. Many therapists will adjust fees to make psychotherapy affordable for patients on tight budgets. Sometimes a reluctance to pursue personal therapy is a sign of resistance to change, or fear of stigmatization. Open discussion of these fears and attitudes is the best approach. Low-fee psychoanalytic and psychotherapy clinics are available in many areas.

If, on the other hand, an anxiety episode appears to be a temporary state in an otherwise well-functioning individual, brief contact may suffice. Minor tranquilizers may be offered not only to combat anxiety, but to give the person a sense of renewed control of internal states. Often, therapeutic contact alone is sufficient.

One major goal in treatment is to identify the life event(s) that triggered the disequilibrium, and then help the person identify the sequence of feelings and meanings that lie behind the anxiety. Obvious precipitants are bereavement, divorce, job loss. Because of their internal meanings, promotions, parental divorce, children leaving home, moving, and other life events can also be followed by anxiety.

CLAIRE

Claire was in middle age when her husband died after a long struggle with cancer. She mourned appropriately, and returned to a music career she had interrupted during the illness. However, when after several years a man she was dating suggested marriage, she became acutely anxious. Exploration in once-a-week therapy brought out two significant issues.

One was an episode of molestation from childhood that had been buried for years but was activated by the fact that the man she was dating was an "older man." She also struggled with fears about losing a hard-fought autonomy she had attained in her marriage and that she could now fully enjoy as a single person. The acute anxiety passed quickly, but Claire remained in therapy for over a year to work out her feelings about these issues. She decided for the time being not to marry again and worked hard and with satisfaction at expanding her career and friendships.

TREATMENT

The contribution of a psychodynamic understanding to evaluation of anxiety is in the search for underlying causes in the psychology and life situation of the patient. The statements, "I'm anxious!" or "I'm afraid to . . ." tell us little. If we consider only the symptomatic treatment of anxiety, we may miss its underlying cause, and the patient will experience a recurrence or continue to suffer from the underlying problem in some other way.

In most of the case vignettes in this chapter, anxiety—acute or chronic, mild or severe—indicated the presence of strong unresolved feelings and meanings that were either unconscious to the patient or not being given sufficient attention. The initial interviews with a patient may give an indication of the nature of these underlying issues. They usually provide the therapist with some sense of the level of anxiety the patient is feeling. This will provide an indication about therapeutic direction: whether to be thinking of brief therapy only, whether longer therapeutic exploration would be important, how much support versus uncovering to do, whether a trial of medication is worthwhile.

Realistically, the important psychological issues and even diagnostic questions may not be definitively determined in a few sessions. If medical coverage limitations do not allow for a more thorough, extensive diagnostic psychotherapy trial, a more symptom-oriented approach may be necessary.

Simply talking to a concerned, insightful professional often reduces the most intense anxiety in a few visits. But acute anxiety, as we have said, is usually the tip of the iceberg of more extensive problems. The option of seeking psychotherapy independently should be discussed while the patient is still motivated to look at underlying causes of the acute episode. The therapist may have to be an advocate of continued treatment with the managed care provider. If it *is* possible to continue in an extended evaluation, much more will be learned about the patient's central conflictual areas, and the patient may do important therapeutic work on the root causes.

Psychodynamic Psychotherapies

For some time it has been fashionable to debunk psychoanalysis and psychodynamic psychotherapies. These attacks usually focus on the older aspects of psychoanalytic theory, rather than on the question of the utility of psychoanalysis and psychotherapy as it is now practiced, or the value of therapies built on the theoretical structure Freud pioneered.

Studies of psychoanalytic psychotherapies indicate that they are effective in a high percentage of cases, even under less-than-ideal conditions. A psychoanalytic viewpoint stresses the complexity of the mind. It assumes that behind any particular symptom is a network of conflicts, defenses, wishes, unconscious fantasies and belief, and developmental and character patterns. This view also stresses the maximum respect for the patient's autonomy: the exploration of these underlying factors proceeds in a way that is determined largely by the patient, within conditions of treatment that the therapist recommends and maintains, once the patient agrees to treatment. Psychoanalytic therapists minimize the imposition of their own goals on the treatment. While they recognize the discomfort of symptoms and may use other modalities such as medication to reduce their intensity, they do not attempt to alter the symptoms directly. This happens when the underlying personality factors have altered so that the symptom is no longer needed.

Psychoanalysis usually involves three to five sessions of forty to fifty minutes each week. The patient lies on a couch, to reduce the tendency to engage in a more conventional social, doctor-patient sort of dialogue. Instead, the patient is asked to "free associate," to say whatever comes to mind. The analyst comments on the patient's mental process in a way that gradually helps the patient understand his or her deeper, hidden fears, processes of defense, and patterns of relating. Many of these emerge in the relationship with the analyst (transference); because of the frequency of visits the patterns become apparent to the analyst and to the patient. This enables the analyst to interpret for the patient some of the meanings of the patient's behavior. Again, the frequency of visits makes it easier for the patient to absorb interpretations and make use of them.

The process of change in psychoanalysis is complex and still under study. In a way, each psychoanalysis is a sort of personal research study of one individual. However, the understandings reached by the team of patient and analyst are used not simply for intellectual understanding, but for enabling change at a deep and enduring level of personality.

There are presently a large number of therapists who have been trained in psychoanalysis or in psychodynamic psychotherapy and are able to provide this service, or serve as consultants to therapists who want to further such skills. These therapists can be identified by calling the nearest psychoanalytic institute (usually located in large metropolitan centers) or the American Psychoanalytic Association in New York City. Psychoanalytic training is a lengthy undertaking involving personal psychoanalysis; seminars in theory, development, and technique for several years; and several hundred hours of supervision of psychoanalytic cases. Thus, treatment or supervision from a trained psychoanalyst ensures that he or she brings a large body of knowledge and clinical experience to the consulting room.

Psychoanalytically oriented psychotherapy uses the same principles as psychoanalysis, but usually visits are once or twice a week, and the patient is face-to-face with the therapist. The psychotherapist tends to be more active than the psychoanalyst, and the focus may be kept more on one or two specific areas of conflict. There are many programs for training in psychotherapy that offer a mix of theoretical and clinical courses.

With both techniques, the length of treatment is usually measured in months or years. This is understandable if we bear in mind that the goal of such treatments is the change of lifelong patterns of thought, feeling, and action. Unlike almost all other therapies, psychoanalysis and psychoanalytic psychotherapy are not simply for symptomatic relief, but for basically altering personality.

Resistance

Because the conflict issues underlying anxiety are associated with danger, they may not emerge easily. This "resistance" to self-knowledge seems self-defeating, but it makes sense if we recall the early origins of the danger. "I don't want to think about it," is an understandable response to sensing a threat, especially threats in childhood. The result is repression of the dangerous idea into the unconscious. The possibility of the reemergence of the idea, even in adulthood, awakens the original anxiety signal of danger, and this leads to resistance. By identifying and helping the patient understand resistance, psychotherapy may lead to major reductions in anxiety levels since the patient is working on the issues behind the scenes of conscious thought.

What we see in therapy is often the defensive effort by the patient to *ward off* conflicts. By working on the resistance, the underlying issues are mobilized, and the intrapsychic dangers are indirectly tested and reduced. It is this defensive activity that accounts for patients' frequent paradoxical behavior in avoiding treatment, forgetting appointments, coming late, or talking about seemingly unimportant subjects. We should not view these necessarily as lack of involvement but as indicators of the anxiety being stirred up by discussing potentially frightening issues. It may be helpful to gently point out to the patient that the avoidance may stem from anxiety about what is behind the manifest behavior.

Medication

The treatment of acute disintegration anxiety now includes antipsychotic medications as a mainstay. It may also be important to provide a sense of control by structuring the patient's environment through hospitalization, day treatment, or a halfway-house-type facility. Psychotherapy also has a place, since these patients have many psychological problems secondary to their underlying psychotic disorders.

Psychotherapeutic contact should emphasize reality issues such as the management of daily planning and clarification and counseling on relationships, limits, and feelings. The therapist is active and does not try to facilitate the emergence of unconscious ideas—they are all too near the surface, and frightening!

Treatment of anxiety in the borderline is particularly important, but also difficult because of its intensity. Both minor tranquilizers and antipsychotics may have a place. Regulating personal contact with the therapist can be a challenge, since too much can be as problematic as too little. Particularly important is maintaining a concerned, but not overreactive, involvement; this is not an easy task with patients who stir up the most intense feelings in therapists.

YVETTE

Yvette, who was functioning at a borderline level, had great difficulty whenever her therapist went on vacations. When he returned, her anxiety about having been left turned to rage rather than relief, because closeness made her afraid of her murderous feelings. After a particular vacation, she abruptly ended treatment. A few days later she resumed, but now she developed persistent anorexia that served to vent the rage safely at herself, yet indirectly at the therapist by creating a worrisome, life-threatening symptom.

Prescribing anti-anxiety drugs, whether done by the therapist or someone else, carries psychological as well as physiological effects. The best known of these is the placebo effect, the finding that a significant proportion (usually about 30 percent) of patients treated with an inactive substitute show a positive response. This response seems to derive from faith in parental figures' capacity to heal internal states—a capacity that indeed exists for small children, whose pain can often be relieved by a maternal kiss.

But there are other meanings to medication that the therapist should be aware of. There may be resentment or fear of dependency. The patient may feel control is being taken away by the prescribing physician, or even a referring therapist. This can lead paradoxically to an increase in anxiety.

Mort (the narcissistic patient discussed earlier) requested and received tranquilizers for anxiety and difficulty in sleeping. Because he feared his dependent longings, he took only small fractions of the pills at a time. When he reported this, he was able to explain directly his "fear of getting addicted."

When the therapist pointed out that he was achieving a sense of control by depriving himself of a therapeutic amount of medication, he was able to talk about the fear of dependency and begin to use the recommended dosage.

Whether or not the therapist is prescribing the medication, it is important to be aware of the possibility of these sorts of meanings. For example, it is easy for a patient to interpret a medication referral by a non–M.D. therapist as an indication that "I'm sicker than you're telling me," or that the therapist does not feel confident or wants to get rid of the patient. Asking how the patient feels about the recommendation of medication often leads to a direct answer along these lines, or to some indirect indication. This makes it possible for the therapist to clarify the recommendation and convey that it does not mean a rejection or devaluation of the patient.

TRACY

When Tracy was initially put on medication, she developed lapses in concentration, even at low doses. Since she had a sensitive job, the drug was discontinued. After some months of psychotherapy, it became clear that Tracy struggled with authority figures, usually in the form of subverting their efforts rather than open opposition. After this issue had been discussed, medication was again offered, and the previous "side effects" did not appear, even at higher doses.

Anxiety is a part of human existence, no doubt because in evolution it paid off to have a distressing affect that would warn of danger. As a result of the prolonged period of childhood dependency for humans, anxiety becomes closely associated with the status and meaning of relationships and the developing sense of self.

One way to think of anxiety from a psychodynamic perspective is as a radar in the psyche giving early warning of internal disequilibrium. When the warning is appropriate, and the psyche relatively strong, anxiety is a helpful stimulus to engage new parts of the personality to deal with the stress. But if there has been trauma, or if there is weakness in coping abilities, or if general personality function is distorted, then anxiety may get out of control.

This is where the professional enters the picture. The patient with acute panic, nebulous milder anxiety, or phobic avoidance often has no idea why he or she is anxious and therefore feels powerless to alleviate it. The capacity to evaluate the quality of the anxiety, search for causes in the life situation and history, and provide a safe place to talk about oneself are what the dynamically informed therapist can offer.

FOR FURTHER READING

Freud, S. (1955). Analysis of a phobia in a five-year-old boy. In J. Strachey (Ed.), *The standard edition of the complete psychological works of Sigmund Freud* (Vol. 10, pp. 5–149). London: Hogarth Press. (Original work published 1909)

Freud, S. (1959). Inhibitions, symptoms, and anxiety. In J. Strachey (Ed.), *The standard edition of the complete psychological works of Sigmund Freud* (Vol. 20, pp. 77–175). London: Hogarth Press. (Original work published 1926)

Lofgren, L. (1964). Excitation, anxiety, and affect: some tentative reformulations. *International Journal of Psychoanalysis, 45,* 280–285.

Roose, S. P., & Glick, R. A. (1995). *Anxiety as symptom and signal.* Hillsdale, NJ: Analytic Press.

Smith, M. L., Glass, G. V., & Miller, T. I. (1980). *The benefits of psychotherapy.* Baltimore: Johns Hopkins University Press.

Wallerstein, R. (1986). *Forty-two lives in treatment.* New York: Guilford Press.

Zerbe, K. J. (1990). Psychoanalytic theory in the psychotherapy of anxiety. *Bulletin of the Menninger Clinic, 54,* 171–183.

7

THE ROLE OF MEDICATION

Matig R. Mavissakalian and Martin T. Ryan

Medications are effective in the treatment of anxiety disorders. Whether used alone or in combination with other modes of therapy, this effectiveness is demonstrated in well-controlled research studies and in widespread clinical practice. There are special characteristics of the pharmacotherapy of anxiety disorders that make it a particularly important and exciting modality to understand, even if it is not the predominant therapeutic modality used in a given practice.

The anxiety disorders, as grouped in the fourth edition of the *DSM-IV,* include panic disorder, specific phobia, social phobia, obsessive-compulsive disorder, posttraumatic stress disorder, acute stress disorder, and generalized anxiety disorder. Viewed from one perspective, the phenomenological and clinical differences among these subtypes of anxiety disorders are significant enough to allow considering them as discrete syndromes. On the other hand, it is possible that these disorders represent different levels of complexity and severity of the same basic process. This latter view is supported by observations that there is considerable overlap in the symptoms of panic disorder, agoraphobia, generalized anxiety disorder, phobias, and obsessive-compulsive disorder. For example, panic attacks nearly always occur concurrently with the excessive anxiety, worry, and apprehensive expectation that characterizes generalized anxiety disorder. Avoidance is prominent in agoraphobia, phobias, and posttraumatic stress disorder. Obsessive-compulsive disorder often includes generalized anxiety, panic, and phobic avoidance as well as obsessional thinking and compulsions.

Research in the use of medication in anxiety disorders lends further support to the view that the subtypes of anxiety are more similar to each other than different. Findings from drug research in one subtype of anxiety disorder have been generalized to the other subtypes, with the main exception of simple phobia, where little pharmacologic research has been conducted and where behavioral treatments are believed to be sufficient. Because of this commonality of drug effect crossing the specific classification boundaries among the anxiety disorders, this chapter avoids taking a "this drug for this subtype" approach to the subject. Instead, it is more useful to view how certain general classifications of medications (for example, antidepressants, anxiolytics) can be useful in the treatment of anxiety. Unless otherwise noted, the reader can assume that the class of medication being discussed is efficacious for all of the subtypes of anxiety disorder.

At the end of this chapter, we make an effort to develop an integrated model of treating anxiety disorders with the use of combined psychological and pharmacological approaches, used together or in sequence.

THE PRIMARY ANXIOLYTICS

The class of medications grouped together under the title "benzodiazepines" are the primary anxiolytic (anti-anxiety) agents. The benzodiazepines are also referred to as minor tranquilizers and as sedative-hypnotics. These names are somewhat misleading, however. Calling a drug a minor tranquilizer might imply that it is on a continuum with the so-called major tranquilizers, the antipsychotic drugs. This is not the case. Benzodiazepines work at different brain sites, on different neurotransmitter systems, and they relieve different symptoms than do the antipsychotics. Likewise, calling the benzodiazepines sedative-hypnotic is somewhat misleading, too. Although benzodiazepines do induce sleep in higher dosages, daytime sedation and drowsiness need to be avoided in the effective management of anxiety. Also, some of the benzodiazepines are commonly used as muscle relaxants or to treat seizures.

Benzodiazepines are an efficacious treatment for all of the anxiety disorders except for obsessive-compulsive disorder. In that case, there is no body of research evidence either in favor of or against using benzodiazepines. Furthermore, the individual benzodiazepines appear to be equally effective in the anxiety disorders. The differences between individual benzodiazepines are in the onset and duration of action of each agent.

Table 7.1 lists the primary anxiolytic agents, their common dosage ranges, and their durations of action. The short-acting agents are rapidly absorbed, begin exerting their anti-anxiety effects within thirty minutes of administration, and typically reach peak levels in the blood in one to three hours. Lorazepam (Ativan) and oxazepam (Serax) are representative of the short-acting benzodiazepines. The rapid onset of effects and relatively rapid metabolism make the short-acting agents suitable for treating episodic bursts of anxiety, but poor choices for situations requiring more consistent and reliable anxiety reduction. Long-acting agents, on the contrary, have a slower, more gradual onset of action and are more slowly metabolized. Depending on the patient's age and overall health, this characteristic allows long-acting benzodiazepines to be administered once or twice a day. The ease of dosing and more even effect make long-acting agents such as clonazepam (Klonopin) and chlordiazepoxide (Librium) better choices for patients who require anxiety relief extending over weeks or months. Intermediate-duration agents, such as alprazolam (Xanax) and diazepam (Valium), have onsets and durations between the two extremes.

Many characteristics of the benzodiazepines make them sound choices for managing anxiety. In comparison to older agents,

Table 7.1
Benzodiazepine Anxiolytic Medications

Generic Name	Trade Name(s)	Common Total Daily Dosage	Duration of Action
Alprazolam	Xanax	1.0 to 6.0 mg	Intermediate
Chlordiazepoxide	Librium	15 to 100 mg	Long-acting
Clonazepam	Klonopin	0.5 to 2.0 mg	Long-acting
Clorazepate	Tranxene	5 to 30 mg	Long-acting
Diazepam	Valium, Valrelease	4 to 40 mg	Intermediate
Flurazepam	Dalmane*	15 to 30 mg	Long-acting
Halazepam	Paxipam	20 to 60 mg	Intermediate
Lorazepam	Ativan	0.5 to 4.0 mg	Short-acting
Oxazepam	Serax	10 to 60 mg	Short-acting
Prazepam	Centrax	5 to 60 mg	Long-acting
Quazepam	Doral, Dormalin	7.5 to 15 mg	Long-acting
Temazepam	Restoril*	15 to 30 mg	Short-acting
Triazolam	Halcion*	0.25 to 1.0 mg	Short-acting

*Mainly used as a hypnotic.

such as the barbiturates (which had previously been used to treat anxiety), benzodiazepines have a greater dosage margin between anxiety reduction and sedation. That is to say, it is easier for the patient and prescribing physician to determine how much of the medicine is required to effectively reduce anxiety without causing cognitive impairment or sedation. Likewise, the benzodiazepines have a relatively high therapeutic index, a measurement of the ratio of a typically lethal dose of the medicine to the average effective dose. The higher the therapeutic index, the less chance for significant risks in the case of accidental overdose.

Perhaps most importantly, *benzodiazepines work* in controlling anxiety. Response rates vary according to study and disorder, but in general 70–90 percent of patients treated show substantial improvement. Furthermore, the beneficial effects of benzodiazepines can be felt as early as the first dose. This may have important overall therapeutic implications in terms of compliance because patients feel encouraged and are more apt to have confidence in their treatments and are therefore more likely to remain compliant.

A common concern of patients, and a matter which needs to be always in the mind of the clinician, is a medication's potential for dependence and addiction. All benzodiazepines are classified by the U.S. Drug Enforcement Agency as Class IV drugs. As such, they are recognized as having less abuse potential than higher-schedule drugs such as barbiturates, and as having limited dependence liability. Although this concern is a valid one, there appears to be minimal risk of addiction when the medications are properly administered in this population. However, in therapeutic doses, physiological dependence can develop within six months, and in less time with short-acting benzodiazepines. Hence, an open-ended medication plan is ill-advised.

Table 7.2 compares the addiction potential of the classes of medications used in the treatment of anxiety disorders. Screening patients for a history of drug or alcohol abuse, close follow-up of patients for reporting side effects and symptoms, monitoring

Table 7.2
Addiction Potential of Medications
Used in Treating Anxiety Disorders

Medication Group	Risk of Physiological Addiction
Benzodiazepines	slight to moderate
Beta-blockers	none
Buspirone	none
Monoamine oxidase inhibitors (MAOIs)	none
Selective serotonin re-uptake inhibitors (SSRIs)	none
Tricyclic antidepressants	none

for unsupervised dose acceleration, careful titration of dosage to symptoms, and a plan for slow tapering of the drug at the end of treatment are all techniques that help safeguard the patient from becoming addicted. As an example, studies reveal that virtually all patients can be successfully tapered off benzodiazepines if sufficient time is given to the process; the success or failure of tapering patients off benzodiazepines is essentially a time function. And, if needed, cognitive and pharmacological treatments can help in the withdrawal process.

Patients rarely experience side effects on benzodiazepines when they are carefully and rationally prescribed. Drowsiness is the most common adverse effect; it occurs in approximately 10 percent of patients. Because of this, patients should be advised not to drive or operate any dangerous machinery during their first few doses of the medication, until they can assess whether or not they experience sedation or impairment. Dizziness, incoordination, stomach distress, and allergic skin reactions occur in about 1–2 percent of patients. As is the case when taking any medication, patients need to make the prescribing physician aware of all other medicines currently taken and any current physical illnesses, so that potential adverse reactions can be avoided.

Beta-blockers

Although beta-blocking agents have been used for a variety of anxiety disorders since the mid 1960s, their efficacy for generalized anxiety, panic, agoraphobia, social phobia, and obsessive-compulsive disorder has not been clearly demonstrated in controlled studies. There was early promise that beta-blockers would be helpful in the treatment of social phobia; however, this has not been demonstrated in controlled studies.

A useful niche for this class of drugs would be performance anxiety, including public speaking, although the clearest evidence supports their usefulness in the treatment of musicians during their performance. The effect that beta-blockers have is not that surprising since these agents have among their pharmacologic effects the alleviation of palpitations, tremor, and sweating. The common dosage ranges listed in Table 7.3 are for the treatment of hypertension and are furnished for comparison.

Buspirone

Buspirone (Buspar) is an anxiolytic drug that must be considered apart from the benzodiazepines. Its site of action in the central nervous system is different from that of the benzodiazepines; this fact is reflected in buspirone's differing from the benzodiazepines

Table 7.3
Beta-Blocking Medications

Generic Name	Trade Name	Usual Daily Dosage
Atenolol	Tenormin	25–50 mg in 1–2 doses
Metoprolol	Lopressor	50 mg twice a day
Nadolol	Corgard	40 mg twice a day
Pindolol	Visken	5 mg twice a day
Propranolol	Inderal	40–80 mg 4 times a day
	Inderal-LA	80 mg twice a day
Timolol	Blocadren	10 mg twice a day

in efficacy, onset, and addiction potential. Whereas the effects of benzodiazepines are felt in the first day of use, buspirone's full clinical response usually takes one to three weeks. Also, it has not been clearly demonstrated that buspirone is effective for anxiety disorders other than generalized anxiety disorder.

Advantages of buspirone are that there are no indications it has abuse potential, even when used in individuals at high risk for dependence and addiction, and buspirone has no sedative effect. Because of buspirone's short half-life in the blood, it needs to be dosed two to three times a day. Typical daily dosages range from 15 to 60 mg. The most common side effects of the medication are nausea, headache, and dizziness. No deaths from overdose have been reported.

THE ANTIDEPRESSANTS

Although in many patients the symptoms of anxiety are intermingled with the symptoms of depression, it is important to understand that the effectiveness of antidepressant medications in treating anxiety disorders *is independent of their antidepressant properties.* In other words, when a patient with an anxiety disorder, such as panic disorder, is treated with an antidepressant medication, relief of panic symptoms is independent of any antidepressant effect the medicine has. The antidepressants, like the benzodiazepines and behavior/cognitive therapy, are effective treatment for the majority of anxiety disorders. The choice of whether to utilize an antidepressant alone, a primary anxiolytic alone, or a combination of the two depends on several considerations.

In our anxiety disorders clinic, for example, we choose antidepressants as the main long-term pharmacologic treatment and utilize benzodiazepines for acute crises when the rapid onset of relief is needed. We address these combined uses of medications and behavior techniques at the end of this chapter.

Choosing between an antidepressant and a primary anxiolytic also requires consideration of various clinical factors. Table 7.4

makes a comparison of these two types of medications. As an example, consider a patient who complains of severe panic attacks. After a thorough history and medical workup, the clinician is faced with deciding what treatment to prescribe. From Table 7.4 we can see that antidepressant medication and anxiolytic medication are both effective treatments for panic. The difference in the speed of action between the antidepressants and the benzodiazepines is put into use in two ways. One is to provide fast relief in the symptoms of anxiety, as mentioned above, by prescribing a benzodiazepine, until the onset of the symptom relief which the antidepressants provide, which usually occurs in four to eight weeks. The other is that at the initiation of treatment with antidepressants, there are often side effects that mimic anxiety. These side effects can be relieved by administering a benzodiazepine during the first few weeks of treatment. In our anxiety disorders clinic, we primarily rely on the antidepressant medication in the long term, owing to the fact that those medications are well tolerated and are without addictive potential.

Table 7.4
Comparison of Anxiolytic and Antidepressant Medications

Condition	Antidepressants	Anxiolytics
Reduction/elimination of panic attacks	effective	effective
Reduction/elimination of nonpanic anxiety	effective	effective
Reduction/elimination of phobic avoidance	effective	effective
Speed of onset of symptom relief	weeks	hours
Relief of depressive symptoms	effective	not consistently effective
Likelihood of sedation and cognitive impairment	unlikely	common at higher doses

Antidepressant Mechanism of Action

While a complete discussion of the pharmacodynamics of medications used to treat anxiety disorders is not appropriate here, it is important to be familiar with the basic notions of the mechanisms by which these medicines work. Whereas the benzodiazepine anxiolytics exert their primary effect in the central nervous system through gamma-aminobutyric acid (GABA) neurotransmitters, antidepressant medications primarily affect the noradrenergic and serotonergic neurotransmitter systems. It is too simplistic to conceptualize one neurotransmitter as being responsible for one disorder. All three neurotransmitters mentioned—GABA, norepinephrine, and serotonin, as well as perhaps other neurotransmitters—play major roles in mediating the anxiety response.

Recently, the serotonin system has been identified as the primary key in panic disorder and in obsessive-compulsive disorder. There is strong evidence that the anti-obsessional properties of the antidepressants are largely serotonin-mediated, and this is clinically demonstrated by the experience that clomipramine (Anafranil) and the selective serotonin re-uptake inhibitors are effective in treating obsessive-compulsive disorder.

A similar trend is seen in the treatment of panic disorder, especially panic with agoraphobia, as demonstrated by clinical studies showing the effectiveness of clomipramine and selective serotonin re-uptake inhibitors such as fluvoxamine (Luvox). However, this is still somewhat controversial because, unlike the certainty that desipramine (Norpramin) is equal to placebo in obsessive-compulsive disorder, some studies have reported beneficial antipanic effects with desipramine. However, a study that has compared the selective noradrenergic drug maprotiline to the selective serotonergic drug fluvoxamine has shown that the latter was effective whereas the former was not, suggesting again that agents with serotonergic action should be considered as the treatment of choice in panic disorder.

An important conclusion is that, unlike the nearly equal efficacy of the various antidepressants in the treatment of major depression, these agents are not at all equal in their effectiveness in treating anxiety disorders. Those antidepressants which have effects on the serotonin system have generally been shown to be the ones most effective in treating anxiety disorders. This is most clearly the case in obsessive-compulsive disorder.

Practical Considerations in Choosing an Antidepressant

Beyond the larger principles outlined in the previous section, there is no one best antidepressant for treating anxiety disorders. Rational prescribing requires numerous considerations. As mentioned in the previous section, antidepressants that exert strong serotonergic effects are most effective in treating obsessive-compulsive disorder and panic disorder. Certainly, a patient's previous response to a particular medication would make that medication a promising treatment choice. Even a previous positive response in a patient's first-degree relative with the same disorder increases the likelihood of the patient responding to the drug.

The patient's tolerance of the more common side effects of a drug is also an important consideration in choosing therapy. As Table 7.5 shows, there are important differences in likely side effects among the medications used to treat anxiety disorders. It is helpful to consider side effects in two broad categories: those that are a problem in terms of initiating and maintaining acute treatment, and those that create more problems in the long term. Good examples of the latter are sexual side effects (e.g., decreased libido, anorgasmia, erectile dysfunction, and impotence) and weight gain.

Of the side effects that occur early in treatment, an interesting note is that in these anxious patients there is a large incidence of reporting side effects even when on placebo. Nevertheless, certain measures can be taken to maximize compliance and tolerance of the side effects, which usually diminish over time. Patients with anxiety disorders, perhaps more than patients with other medical conditions, are often very apprehensive about

Table 7.5
A Comparison of Medication Side Effects

Side Effect	Tricyclics	MAOIs	SSRIs	Benzodiazepines
Anticholinergic (dry mouth, constipation)	++/+++	0	0	0
Nausea	0	0	++	0
Diarrhea	0	0	++	0
Sexual dysfunction	+	++	++	0
Sedation	+/++	0	0	+/++
Weight gain	++	++	0	0
Headache	0	0	+	0
Insomnia	0	+/++	0/+	0

 0 = very infrequent
 + = infrequent
 ++ = common
 +++ = very common

pharmacotherapy. Reassurance by the physician and by other treating clinicians about the efficacy and relative safety of the antidepressants and major anxiolytics increases patient comfort and compliance.

The fact is that worrisome side effects are the exception, not the rule, in therapy with these agents when rational prescribing guidelines are followed. Patients need to be instructed that allergic reactions (such as development of a skin rash), distressing side effects, administration of additional medications for other conditions, or a change in health status should be reported to the physician prescribing the medication for the anxiety disorder. Often, a change in dosage or medication can allow relief of the troublesome side effect without an interruption in treatment.

The Tricyclic Antidepressants

The tricyclics, so called because they have molecular structures based on a three-ring nucleus, are considered the classic, traditional antidepressants. As stated earlier in this chapter, their effectiveness in anxiety disorders is independent of their antidepressant effects. Two antidepressants usually grouped with the tricyclics are actually tetracyclic. The tetracyclics are amoxapine (Asendin) and maprotiline (Ludiomil). For purposes of this discussion, we consider them as tricyclics. Table 7.6 lists the common drugs in this group and typical daily doses for comparison.

The tricyclics are the drugs most extensively studied in the treatment of anxiety disorders. Although they share many general characteristics, some important differences exist. All tricyclics have the short-term effect of reducing re-uptake of serotonin and norepinephrine. Other receptor effects occur after weeks of administration and appear to correlate with the anti-anxiety and antipanic clinical effects. Clomipramine (Anafranil) is the most potent serotonergic agent of the tricyclics and is the most effective tricyclic for the treatment of obsessive-compulsive disorder. Imipramine (Tofranil) is the most studied tricyclic in the treatment of panic disorder, although other tricyclics have also been shown to be effective. Amitriptyline (Elavil) has a long history of use in what used to be called "anxiety neurosis," but it is no longer in common use because of the development of other, more effective tricyclic medicines that have fewer side effects.

Because the tricyclic antidepressants have been in use longer than the other antidepressants, there is a much larger body of knowledge regarding their use; better-defined clinical guidelines, dosing strategies, and plasma level-response relationships have resulted from extensive long-term experience with these medications. More recently, in our anxiety disorders clinic, we have completed a placebo-controlled dose-ranging study of imipramine (Tofranil) for the treatment of panic disorder with

Table 7.6
The Tricyclic Antidepressants

Generic Name	Trade Name(s)	Typical Daily Dose
Amitriptyline	Elavil, Endep	100–200 mg
Amoxapine*	Asendin	100–200 mg
Clomipramine	Anafranil	100–200 mg
Desipramine	Norpramin, Pertofrane	100–200 mg
Doxepin	Adapin, Sinequan	100–200 mg
Imipramine	Tofranil	100–200 mg
Maprotiline*	Ludiomil	100–150 mg
Nortriptyline	Pamelor, Aventyl	50–100 mg
Protriptyline	Vivactil	15–40 mg
Trimipramine	Surmontil	100–200 mg

*Tetracyclic.

agoraphobia. This study has not only elucidated the optimal dosage and plasma level of imipramine for panic but has underscored that there exists a "therapeutic window" for the medication, which maximizes clinical response while minimizing drug side effects. Another study has suggested that similar effects can be obtained using clomipramine (Anafranil) at dosages generally half that which are used with imipramine.

There are other advantages to treatment with tricyclic antidepressants. They are almost all available in generic form, so they are among the most cost-effective medications produced. They are generally dosed once a day, which increases patient compliance with treatment. Therapeutic serum levels have been established for a number of the tricyclics, which allows for more exact monitoring and titration of the dosages. A potential disadvantage of the tricyclics is that they can be lethal in overdose, especially if taken in combination with alcohol. If a patient is felt to be at risk for intentional overdose, no more than a week's worth of the medication should be dispensed at a time. To minimize the potential for side effects, therapy with tricyclics is initiated with low doses that are gradually increased over weeks.

Monoamine Oxidase Inhibitors

Monoamine oxidase inhibitors block the action of the enzyme monoamine oxidase, which catabolizes amines at the intracellular level in various organ systems in the body including the liver, gut, and central nervous system. Monoamine oxidase inhibitors (MAOIs) are believed to exert their antidepressant and anti-anxiety effects by slowing the metabolism of serotonin and norepinephrine, which would have the effect of making those two neurotransmitters less available at the nerve endings of the brain. Table 7.7 lists the MAOIs used in the United States and their typical dosages.

MAOIs have been demonstrated to be effective in depression and most chronic anxiety disorders and are the most widely studied antidepressants for the treatment of social phobia. Because scientific evidence is relatively lacking in the treatment of social phobia with other antidepressants, the proven effectiveness of MAOIs, and in particular phenelzine (Nardil), makes them the antidepressants of choice in our clinic for social phobia, especially generalized social phobia. One study indicates that they may be effective in obsessive-compulsive disorder as well. Tranylcypromine (Parnate) is the most energizing and activating of the group, and that fact should be considered before it is prescribed since it might initially worsen the symptoms of a patient who is anxious, hypervigilant, and not sleeping well before starting treatment.

Because of the effects MAOIs have on enzymes in the gut and liver, patients on MAOIs must restrict the amount of tyramine (an exogenous amine found in some foods) they ingest. If a patient taking an MAOI ingests a sufficient quantity of tyramine-rich food, he may experience headache, stiff neck, nausea, and potentially life-threatening hypertension. Education in diet is

Table 7.7
The Monoamine Oxidase Inhibitors

Generic Name	Trade Name(s)	Typical Daily Dose
Isocarboxazid	Marplan	10–30 mg
Phenelzine	Nardil	45–90 mg
Selegiline*	Eldepryl, Deprenyl	10 mg
Tranylcypromine	Parnate	10–30 mg

*Generally used to treat Parkinsonism, although positive results in the treatment of depression have been reported.

essential in patients considering MAOI treatment. Table 7.8 is an example of the dietary restrictions patients need to follow.

Finally, the potential for drug-drug interactions is greater with MAOIs than with other antidepressants, and patients need to be cautioned accordingly.

In the last five years, there has been considerable research interest and enthusiasm of the so-called *reversible* MAOIs (moclobimide, brofaromine) because they would obviate many of the dietary restrictions currently imposed by traditional MAOI therapy. Despite the demonstration of efficacy for social phobia in early trials, the reversible MAOIs are not currently available for clinical use in the United States.

As is true with tricyclic therapy, MAOIs are started in small doses and titrated upward over a period of weeks to therapeutic doses. Like tricyclics, MAOIs begin to bring relief of clinical symptoms of anxiety and panic after four to six weeks.

The Selective Serotonin Re-Uptake Inhibitors

The selective serotonin re-uptake inhibitors, or SSRIs, are the third group of antidepressants effective in the treatment of anxiety disorders. As their name implies, these medications have a

Table 7.8
Tyramine-Rich Foods to Be Avoided
while Taking MAOIs

Very High Tyramine Content	*Moderate Tyramine Content (may have 1–2 servings/day)*
Alcohol (especially beer and Chianti wine)	Yogurt
	Tomatoes
Fava beans	Spinach
Aged cheese	Green bananas
Chicken or beef liver	Soy sauce
Smoked or pickled meats	Sour cream
Fermented sausages	Avocados
Packaged soups	Eggplant
Yeast vitamin supplements	Plums
Summer sausage	Raisins
Orange pulp	Chocolate
Caviar	
Canned figs	
Sauerkraut	

narrower and more specific biochemical effect on neurotrans-mitter systems. Studies of their effects show the most robust evidence implying the serotonergic neurotransmitter systems role in anxiety disorders. Relative to the tricyclics and MAOIs, these antidepressants are newer, and there are fewer studies of their efficacy in treating anxiety disorders.

One major disadvantage of the SSRIs is that dosing depends entirely on individual response because dose-response and plasma-concentration guidelines have not been as well established as for the MAOIs and tricyclic antidepressants. To date, a number of different SSRIs have been shown to be effective in the treatment of obsessive-compulsive disorder, with two agents, fluvoxamine (Luvox) and fluoxetine (Prozac), having received FDA specific indication for the treatment of this disorder. Table 7.9 lists the six SSRIs in use in the United States.

The SSRIs have a number of advantages over traditional anti-depressants, the main one being that they have a better-tolerated side-effect profile. However, given the peculiar sensitivity of some anxiety disorder patients to side effects, we recommend starting any SSRI at a lower dose than normally used in the treatment of depression and titrating the dose slowly. For example, fluoxetine (Prozac) could be started at a dose of 5 mg and slowly increased. The SSRIs are relatively safe in overdose and require no dietary restrictions. Three of the six medications can be dosed once a day, as can the tricyclic antidepressants.

TREATMENT STAGES

Having completed a survey of the medications effective in treating anxiety disorders, we can now illustrate a typical strategy for medication management during the course of treatment. Although the following division of treatment stages is made in the service of conceptual clarity, there are no rigid schedules in clinical treatment, and it is understood that treatment must foremost be adapted to the needs and progress of the patient. Unlike the episodic course of depression, anxiety disorders are marked by a chronic, fluctuating course; hence the continuation and maintenance phases of treatment, respectively conceptualized as preventing relapse and recurrence in depression, cannot be as easily distinguished in the anxiety disorders.

The Evaluation Stage

Prior to starting treatment, there is an evaluation phase where the diagnosis is clarified, goals of treatment are set, and contraindications to specific pharmacotherapeutic agents are ruled out. Also, it needs to be stressed that anxiety disorders are

Table 7.9
Selective Serotonin Re-Uptake Inhibitors (SSRIs)

Generic Name	Trade Name	Typical Daily Dose
Fluoxetine	Prozac	20–40 mg
Fluvoxamine	Luvox	100–300 mg
Nefazodone	Serzone	300–600 mg in divided doses
Paroxetine	Paxil	20–30 mg
Sertraline	Zoloft	50–200 mg
Venlafaxine	Effexor	75–300 mg in divided doses

chronic disorders; treatment should last a minimum of six months. Patients need to be oriented to an integrated approach to their treatment. (This subject is explained at the end of this chapter.)

The Acute Stage

The acute stage is best defined by its aim, and it may take from four weeks to three to six months. The aim is to provide the maximum therapeutic benefit in symptom control and remission. This is done quite rapidly with benzodiazepines, but it takes eight to sixteen weeks with antidepressants. A crucial concern in this phase is the tolerability of treatment and the provision of maximum therapeutic benefits. This is usually achieved with sound clinical guidelines of dose escalation, of cautioning patients not to be overly impatient with therapeutic results, and—in the case of most antidepressants—of warning patients of a period of trade-off where in earlier weeks of treatment mainly side effects are felt before therapeutic effects set in. When there is a sense of urgency or when the antidepressants produce activating and anxiety-producing side effects, we adopt a treatment approach that uses a benzodiazepine along with an antidepressant, with the proviso that the benzodiazepines will be tapered off after four to eight weeks of treatment and afterwards the antidepressant will be continued by itself.

If the level and frequency of panic has been debilitating, it is reasonable to begin treatment with a benzodiazepine, such as alprazolam (Xanax), in addition to an antidepressant, so that rapid symptom relief can occur. If a benzodiazepine is used in this way, it should be used on a *scheduled* basis, every day, and not left as a "take-when-needed" medication. By reducing anxiety and blocking panic attacks, the medication can enable the patient to reexperience those situations which he or she had come to avoid because of anxiety. During this acute stage of treatment, patients need close follow-up for monitoring any side effects and to receive encouragement and reinforcement. Benzodiazepines can also be used to relieve the physical distress of an acute attack, for example, when a patient with a new onset of panic attacks presents to an emergency room because of palpitations and chest pain.

Continuation/Maintenance Stage

The primary aim of the continuation stage of treatment is to maintain the remitted state with the fewest side effects. During this segment of treatment, the patient has consistent relief or considerable reduction of symptoms. In our example, the patient stops having panic attacks and experiences much less anticipatory anxiety. The patient stops avoiding previously dreaded situations, such as shopping or driving. The goal at this stage of treatment is to maintain the patient's improvement with the minimum amount of medication and few or no medication side effects. Usually the remitted state continues as long as there is an adequate dose of medication. Two prospective studies in the treatment of panic/agoraphobia and in the treatment of obsessive-compulsive disorder have shown that continued treatment with one half of the dosage of imipramine or clomipramine that was required during the acute stage is sufficient to continue the relief of symptoms.

The main problem in this stage is that although it may have a beginning which is well defined (at least conceptually), it has an indefinite ending because very little information exists regarding what is the optimum duration of treatment for anxiety disorders. Sometimes this stage may be lifelong, especially in the severe disorders such as panic/agoraphobia and obsessive-compulsive disorder that have a more chronic nature. In practice, however, life circumstances, the desire of the patient, or clinical judgment brings the planned continuation/maintenance phase to an end. Examples are when a female patient wishes to become pregnant, or certain illnesses contraindicate the use of these medications, or a patient is noncompliant in taking the medication. However, in an ideal clinical setting, the ending of this stage would be mutually agreed upon by patient and treatment professionals.

Termination Stage

It is not known with certainty how long a particular patient may need to continue on medication for the relief of anxiety symptoms. Many patients, after being symptom-free for four to six months, can be tapered off the antidepressant medication and not experience relapse of symptoms. Other patients experience long periods of remission off medication, perhaps years, before having a relapse of their anxiety symptoms.

If relapse occurs, the patient has a good probability of responding to the previous medication regimen. Consideration should be made for extending treatment for a longer period after symptom remission, perhaps indeterminately, although this may be done with a lowered dosage of the antidepressant. Some studies of relapse after treatment have shown higher relapse rates after medication treatment than after behavioral treatments. One criticism of such a comparison is that although medication termination can be clearly defined objectively, termination of behavioral techniques arguably cannot be as clearly shown, because patients typically continue to practice the exposure techniques they have learned despite the cessation of formal sessions of behavior therapy.

There is a fair amount of clinical experience suggesting that many, if not most, patients relapse following termination of effective anti-anxiety medications. This is true whether the medication used is a benzodiazepine or an antidepressant. With antidepressants, particularly with imipramine as used for panic disorder with agoraphobia, there is fairly persuasive evidence that duration of treatment may make a difference and that relapse within six months of discontinuation of imipramine after eighteen months of treatment is substantially less than relapse after only six months of treatment. Therefore, patients need to be informed about the risk of relapse and instructed to contact their clinician if their symptoms return before the regularly scheduled follow-up appointment to monitor symptoms and side effects.

There is much to be learned about the process of relapse. In panic-disorder patients it is likely to expect that before panic attacks themselves return the patient may experience a period of decreased sense of well-being and more generalized anxiousness. If the clinician is not impressed with the severity of symptom return, and if the patient is willing, the patient may be asked to return in a week or two weeks to reassess symptoms.

THE INTEGRATION OF MEDICATIONS WITH BEHAVIOR THERAPIES

Up to this point in this chapter, we have attempted to elucidate the unique role that medications play in treating anxiety disorders. Other chapters of this book have dealt with the effectiveness of behavioral, exposure-based techniques. Although the integration of medication and behavior therapy for anxiety disorders is widely practiced clinically, there are not many controlled studies of the combined use of medication with behavioral techniques. The preponderance of those studies supports the claim that antidepressants enhance behavior techniques in treating obsessive-compulsive disorder and panic/agoraphobia. Specifically in panic/agoraphobia, exposure-based behavioral techniques and medications mutually potentiate. In treating social phobia, though, evidence supporting a combination of treatments is scant. In the treatment of generalized anxiety disorder, a review of the few controlled studies did not show clear evidence of the superiority of combined treatment except in the most severe cases of the disorder.

Table 7.10 makes the dramatic point that the three empirically validated therapeutic modalities of exposure, antidepressants, and benzodiazepines for the treatment of agoraphobia are also effective in virtually all of the anxiety disorders, with the possible exception of antidepressants in simple phobias and benzodiazepines in obsessive-compulsive disorder. Consequently, it would be more important to understand the unique contribution that each modality makes to an integrated approach to treatment than to ask the question of which modality is best.

It is important to differentiate not only globally between pharmacological and psychological approaches but within these

Table 7.10
Comparative Treatments of Various Anxiety Disorders

Disorder	Antidepressants	Benzodiazepines	Behavioral Therapy
Panic Disorder	effective	effective	effective
Panic/Agoraphobia	effective	effective	effective
Social Phobia	effective	effective	effective
Specific Phobia	effective?	effective	effective
Obsessive-Compulsive Disorder	effective	effective?	effective
Posttraumatic Stress Disorder	effective	effective	effective
Generalized Anxiety Disorder	effective	effective	effective?

treatments as well. Here, a lesson derived from simple phobias points to a fundamental principle of treatment: the natural tendency to escape from and avoid phobic situations temporarily reduces or eliminates phobic anxiety or fear, but the disorder persists. It follows that reduction or suppression of phobic, panic, and anticipatory anxiety with psychological or pharmacological treatments, even though clinically desirable, may not always be considered optimal treatment. Indeed, psychological techniques aimed at anxiety management may run the risk of becoming the functional equivalents of escape/avoidance mechanisms, which, similar to compulsive behaviors, need to be relied on continually for the control of anxiety symptoms. These procedures may not therefore differ in principle from the need for maintenance pharmacotherapy. On the other hand, treating anxiety with exposure to the very same stimuli that elicit anxiety under conditions that prevent sensitization and foster habituation is to facilitate a learning process, even perhaps at the molecular level, that can be permanent.

Our approach is to minimize sensitization and to foster habituation to anxiety-eliciting stimuli, which takes into account both behavioral and constitutional factors contributing to the maintenance of the disorder. Exposure treatments counter maintenance of the anxiety by escape/avoidance mechanisms, and medications counter the hypersensitivity and impaired habituation that seem to characterize chronic anxiety states.

The relevant outcome studies of panic disorder with agoraphobia suggest that antidepressants achieve both of these aims, whereas benzodiazepines minimize sensitization but can interfere with the processing of the habituation of fear during systematic exposure treatments. This also suggests that benzodiazepines and antidepressants, even though of equivalent efficacy, may not be considered equivalent treatments in combination with exposure treatment. Indeed, two different paradigms of combination treatment can be conceptualized.

In the first, a medication such as an antidepressant facilitates and enhances the fundamental mechanism of habituation of anxiety that underlies exposure treatment. In this case, the treatments are mutually potentiating, and the combined treatment is more effective than either the medication or the exposure treatment individually. In this first paradigm, relapse after the discontinuation of combined treatment is less likely than it would be after discontinuation of medications used alone, without behavioral treatment.

In a second paradigm, the two treatments (pharmacologic and behavioral) act independently, with a drug such as a benzodiazepine decreasing phobia, panic, and anxiety, while the behavioral treatment encourages approach behavior. In this second paradigm, even though improvement may be more complete than with either treatment modality used alone, the likelihood of relapse upon discontinuation of treatment may be as high as it is when medication is used alone.

With benzodiazepines, therefore, it is of paramount importance to continue with exposure treatment while the medication is being tapered and discontinued in order to provide the full and lasting benefit of the processing of the habituation of fear. Alternatively, anxiety-coping strategies can be substituted to effectively diminish withdrawal and relapse problems during the tapering of benzodiazepines, although patients are then likely to have to depend on these measures for an indeterminate period of time for the relief that they formerly obtained from the benzodiazepines. Therefore, particularly with the longitudinal perspective in mind, in our clinic antidepressants are the agents of choice for use in combined treatment.

On the other hand, the rapid and potent anxiolytic effects of benzodiazepines may be particularly useful in clinical situations that require immediate effects, or during the beginning stages of the disorder when prevention of the sensitizing effects of anxiety-eliciting cues or of panic attacks themselves may be of primary importance. An additional role for benzodiazepines in combination therapy occurs when a patient cannot tolerate exposure to the feared stimulus. In these cases, the administration of a small dose of benzodiazepine prior to initiating exposure can allow treatment to proceed. The timing of the dose needs to be such that the anxiolytic effect occurs before and during the exposure exercises.

To determine the dosage needed to achieve this goal, having the patient try a small, single dose of a benzodiazepine during a time when he or she is not required to work, drive, or operate machinery, and then having the patient report any problems or side effects (such as excessive drowsiness) can allow precise titration of the dosage. In subsequent exposure trials, the dosage can be gradually decreased and stopped. Furthermore, when a patient has developed a fear of something which he or she only needs to do occasionally, such as a patient who fears air travel but who needs to fly only once or twice a year, benzodiazepines can be used judiciously on those few occasions, dosed similarly to the way described above for exposure treatments.

Medications alone are effective treatments of anxiety disorders, but they are more likely to require long-term maintenance treatments for indefinite periods of time. Although nearly equivalent in efficacy, benzodiazepines and antidepressants should not be considered equivalent when combined with behavioral treatments. Combined treatment, guided by some of the general principles outlined in this chapter, offers the best chance for relief and long-term recovery from anxiety disorders. The rationale in this chapter for integrating exposure and pharmacological treatment has been well received by patients and is invaluable in providing trainees with a comprehensive conceptual framework for the treatment of anxiety disorders.

NOTES

P. 176, *the subtypes of anxiety:* Mavissakalian, M. R. (1993). Combined behavioral and pharmacological treatment of anxiety disorders. In J. M. Oldham, M. B. Riba, & A. Tasman (Eds.), *American Psychiatric Press Review of Psychiatry* (Vol. 12, Chapter 20). Washington, DC: American Psychiatric Press.

P. 177, *benzodiazepines appear to be equally effective:* Rickels, K. (1979). Psychopharmacological approaches to treatment of anxiety. In W. E. Fann, I. Karacan, A. D. Porkorny, & R. L. Williams (Eds.), *Phenomenology and treatment of anxiety* (pp. 325–335). New York: SP Medical and Scientific Books; Sheehan, D. V., & Ashok, R. (1993). Benzodiazepine treatment of panic disorder. In R. Noyes, Jr., M. Roth, & G. D. Burrows (Eds.), *Handbook of anxiety* (Vol. 4, pp. 169–206). New York: Elsevier.

P. 179, *benzodiazepines have a greater dosage margin:* Arana, G. W., & Hyman, S. E. (Eds.). (1991). *Handbook of psychiatric drug therapy* (p. 128). Boston: Little, Brown.

P. 179, *Response rates vary according to study and disorder:* Perry, P. J., Alexander, B., & Liskow, B. I. (1991). *Psychotropic drug handbook* (p. 157). Cincinnati: Harvey Whitney.

P. 179, *minimal risk of addiction:* Uhlenhuth, E. H., DeWit, H., & Balter, M. B. (1988). Risks and benefits of long-term benzodiazepine use. *Journal of Clinical Psychopharmacology, 8,* 161.

P. 181, *There was early promise:* Dommisse, C. S., & Hayes, P. E. (1987). Current concepts in clinical therapeutics: Anxiety disorders, part 2. *Clinical Pharmacology, 6,* 196–215; Birkett, P., & Tyrer, P. (1993). Beta-blocking drugs for the treatment of generalized anxiety disorder. In R. Noyes, Jr., M. Roth, & G. D. Burrows (Eds.), *Handbook of anxiety* (Vol. 4, pp. 147–168). New York: Elsevier.

P. 181, *treatment of musicians during their performance:* Lader, M. (1988). Beta-adrenoceptor antagonists in neuropsychiatry: An update. *Journal of Clinical Psychiatry, 49,* 213–223; Welkowitz, L. A., & Liebowitz, M. (1993). Pharmacological treatment of social phobia and performance anxiety. In R. Noyes, Jr., M. Roth, & G. D. Burrows (Eds.), *Handbook of anxiety* (Vol. 4, pp. 245–247). New York: Elsevier.

P. 181, *Its site of action:* Kaplan, H. I., & Sadock, B. J. (1993). *Pocket handbook of psychiatric drug treatment* (p. 71). Baltimore: Williams & Wilkins.

P. 182, *buspirone's full clinical response:* Kaplan, H. I., & Sadock, B. J. (1993). *Pocket handbook of psychiatric drug treatment* (p. 72). Baltimore: Williams & Wilkins.

P. 184, *the serotonin system has been identified:* Roy-Byrne, P., Wingerson, D., Cowley, D., & Dager, S. (1993). Psychopharmacologic treatment of panic, generalized anxiety disorder, and social phobia. *Psychiatric Clinics of North America, 16*(4), 721; Westenberg, H., & Boer, D. (1989). Serotonin-influencing drugs in the treatment of panic disorder. *Psychopathology, 22,* 69–77.

P. 184, *effective in treating obsessive-compulsive disorder:* Chouinard, F., Goodman, W., Greist, J., Jenike, M., Rasmussen, S., White, K., Hackett, E., Gaffney, M., & Bick, P. A. (1990). Results of a double-blind controlled trial of sertraline in the treatment of OCD. *Psychopharmacology Bulletin, 26,* 279–284; Clomipramine Collaborative Study Group. (1991). Clomipramine in the treatment of patients with obsessive-compulsive disorder. *Archives of General Psychiatry, 48,* 730–738.

P. 184, *fluvoxamine (Luvox):* McDougle, C. J., Goodman, W. K., Leckman, J. F., Barr, L. C., Heninger, G. R., & Price, L. H. (1993). The efficacy of fluvoxamine in OCD. *Journal of Clinical Psychopharmacology, 13,* 354–358.

P. 184, *beneficial antipanic effects with desipramine:* Lydiard, R. B., Roy-Byrne, P., & Ballenger, J. C. (1988). Recent advances in the psychopharmacological treatment of anxiety disorders. *Hospital and Community Psychiatry, 39,* 1157–1165.

P. 184, *a study that has compared . . . maprotiline to . . . fluvoxamine:* Westenberg, H., & den Boer, J. A. (1989). Serotonin-influencing drugs in the treatment of panic disorder. *Psychopathology, 22,* 69–77; den Boer, J. A., & Westenberg, H. (1984). Effect of serotonin and noradrenaline uptake inhibitor in panic disorders: A double-blind comparative study with fluvoxamine and maprotiline. *International Clinical Psychopharmacology, 3,* 59–74.

P. 187, *other tricyclics have also been shown to be effective:* Gentil, V., Lotufo-Neto, F., Andrade, L., et al. (1993). Clomipramine, a better reference drug for panic/agoraphobia. *Journal of Psychopharmacology, 7*(4), 316–324.

P. 187, *a placebo-controlled dose-ranging study:* Mavissakalian, M., & Perel, J. M. (1995). Imipramine treatment of panic disorder with agoraphobia: Dose ranging and plasma level-response relationships. *American Journal of Psychiatry, 152*(5), 673–682.

P. 187, *Another study has suggested:* Gentil, V., Lotufo-Neto, F., Andrade, L., Cordás, T., Bernik, M., Ramos, R., Marciel, L., Miyakawa, E., & Gorenstein, C. (1993). Clomipramine, a better reference drug for panic/agoraphobia. *Journal of Psychopharmacology, 7,* 316–324.

P. 189, *Monoamine oxidase inhibitors (MAOI's):* Silver, J. M., Hales, R. E., & Yudofsky, S. C. (1994). Biological therapies for mental disorders. In A. Stoudemire (Ed.), *Clinical psychiatry for medical students* (p. 520). Philadelphia: Lippincott.

P. 189, *most widely studied antidepressants:* Liebowitz, M. R., Schneier, F., Campeas, R., Hollander, E., Hatterer, J., Fyer, A., Gorman, J., Papp, L., Davies, S., Gully, R., & Klein, D. F. (1992). Phenelzine vs. atenolol in social phobia. *Archives of General Psychiatry, 49,* 290–300.

P. 189, *One study indicates:* Vallejo, J., Marcos, T., Bulbena, A., & Menchón, J. M. (1992). Clomipramine vs. phenelzine in OCD: A controlled trial. *British Journal of Psychiatry, 161,* 665–670.

P. 192, *marked by a chronic, fluctuating course:* Frank, E., Prien, R. F., Jarrett, R. B., Keller, M. B., Kupfer, D. J., Lavori, P. W., Rush, A. J., & Weissman, M. M. (1991). Conceptualization and rationale for consensus definitions of terms in major depressive disorder. *Archives of General Psychiatry, 48,* 851–855.

P. 194, *Two prospective studies:* Mavissakalian, M., & Perel, J. M. (1992). Protective effects of imipramine maintenance treatment in panic disorder with agoraphobia. *American Journal of Psychiatry, 149,* 1053–1057. Pato, M. T., Hill, J. L., & Murphy, D. L. (1990). A clomipramine dosage reduction in the course of long-term treatment of obsessive-compulsive disorder patients. *Psychopharmacological Bulletin, 26,* 211–214.

P. 195, *higher relapse rates after medication treatment:* Clark, D. M., Salkovskis, P. M., Hackmann, A., Middleton, H., Anastasiades, P., & Gelder, M. (1994). A comparison of cognitive therapy, applied relaxation and imipramine in the treatment of panic disorder. *British Journal of Psychiatry, 164,* 759–769.

P. 196, *duration of treatment may make a difference:* Mavissakalian, M. R., & Perel, J. M. (1992). Clinical experiments in maintenance and discontinuation of imipramine in panic disorder with agoraphobia. *Archives of General Psychiatry, 49,* 318–323.

P. 196, *The preponderance of those studies:* Mavissakalian, M. R. (1993). Combined behavioral and pharmacological treatment of anxiety disorders. In J. M. Oldham, Riba, M. B., & Tasman, A. (Eds.), *American Psychiatric Press Review of Psychiatry* (Vol. 12, Chapter 20). Washington, DC: American Psychiatric Press.

P. 198, *Indeed, psychological techniques aimed at anxiety management:* Bruce, T. J., Spiegel, D. A., Gregg, S. F., et al. (1995). Predictors of alprazolam discontinuation with and without cognitive behavior therapy in panic disorder. *American Journal of Psychiatry, 152*(8), 1156–1160.

P. 198, *Our approach is to minimize sensitization and to foster habituation:* Mavissakalian, M. R. (1993). Combined behavioral and pharmacological treatment of anxiety disorders. In J. M. Oldham, Riba, M. B., & Tasman, A. (Eds.), *American Psychiatric Press Review of Psychiatry* (Vol. 12, Chapter 20). Washington, DC: American Psychiatric Press.

P. 199, *In a second paradigm, the two treatments . . . act independently:* Marks, I. M., Swinson, R. P., Basoglu, M., Kuch, K., Noshirvani, H., O'Sullivan, G., Lelliot, P. T., Kirby, M., McNamee, G., Segun, S., & Wickwire, K. (1993). Alprazolam and exposure alone and combined in panic disorder with agoraphobia: A controlled study in London and Toronto. *British Journal of Psychiatry, 162,* 776–787.

8

A COGNITIVE-BEHAVIORAL TREATMENT PACKAGE FOR PANIC DISORDER WITH AGORAPHOBIA

Frank Wilhelm and Jürgen Margraf

Much of the treatment package that we describe in this chapter is derived from a relatively new model. Earlier psychological formulations neglected panic attacks, concentrating on the agoraphobia of some of these clients in a behavioral analysis of the stimulus-response-reinforcement contingencies of their fear. Later researchers such as Donald Klein and David Sheehan adopted a medical model that emphasized the panic attacks as being the symptom of an unknown biological abnormality transmitted genetically and treatable with specific pharmacological agents. But much of the evidence for panic disorder being a biological rather than a psychological disorder was and is not well supported empirically.

The new model is an alternative to the strictly medical model but acknowledges the importance of panic attacks. We call it the "psychophysiological model" since it emphasizes the interaction of psychological and physiological factors in producing panic attacks. Our formulation of this model is very similar to the formulations of other authors; all of these models can be considered variants of the same theme.

Unlike some biological models, the psychophysiological model postulates that there is just one kind of anxiety, which

assumes different forms according to four important distinguishing characteristics:

- Whether triggering events are internal or external
- Whether anxiety is experienced mainly somatically or
  psychically
- Whether the onset is sudden or gradual
- Whether the feared consequences are immediate or
  longer term

The psychophysiological model does not consider panic
attacks as ever being truly spontaneous: they are the result of a
positive feedback loop between bodily sensations and fearful cognitions. Figure 8.1 illustrates this model.

The feedback loop is formed by the arrows touching the
boxes in the center of the figure. The steps are as follows: after
various triggers such as physical activity or emotion start the
loop going, these changes are perceived and give rise to thoughts
of danger. Through rapid feedback, this in turn gives rise to
more anxiety until slower inhibitory mechanisms can come into
play. Other variables have a modulating effect, as shown outside
the central loop in Figure 8.1.

TREATMENT STRATEGIES

The case of Clara outlined below was treated by a combination
of therapeutic techniques chosen for her particular problems.
Since agoraphobia and panic present in various ways, the choice
of techniques differs from client to client. Figure 8.2 presents a
decision tree listing some of the options.

When there are both agoraphobic behavior and panic attacks,
exposure to phobic situations is essential for treating the agoraphobia and can also diminish panic attacks. In the absence of
external triggers, treatment must focus on the panic attacks

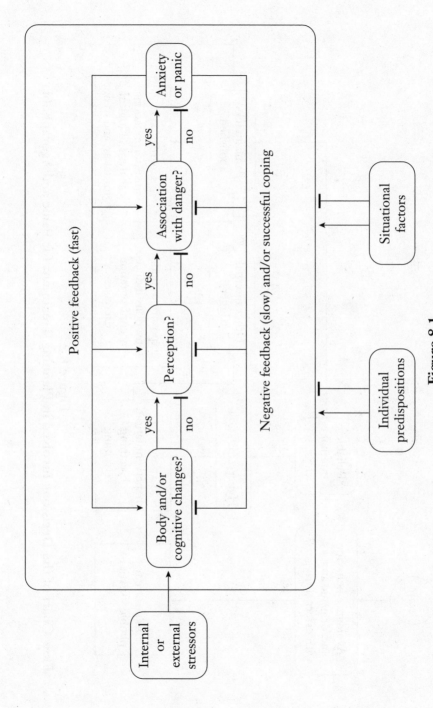

Figure 8.1

Schematic Representation of the Psychophysiological Model of Panic Attacks

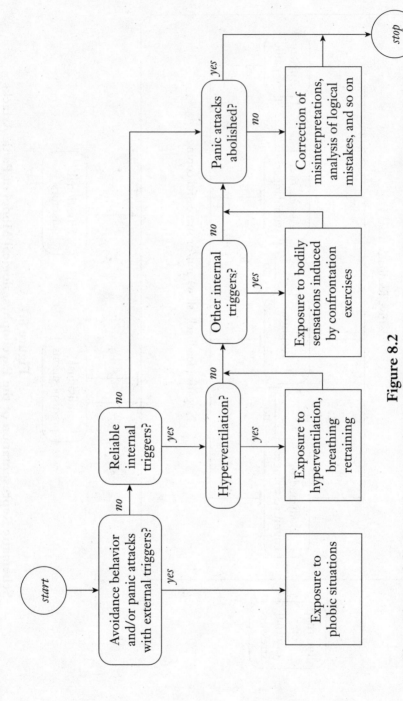

Figure 8.2

Flow Chart of the Decisions Involved in Planning Treatment for Panic and Agoraphobia

themselves. A search for internal triggers may lead to discovering a fear of the somatic sensations of hyperventilation, control of which by changes in breathing can be an avenue toward cure. Other frightening sensations may be provoked in the therapy and controlled by methods other than changes in breathing patterns (for example, relaxation). Exposure to these sensations is the cornerstone of overcoming the fear of fear.

Figure 8.2 implies that agoraphobia and panic attacks can be treated by situational exposure alone, but in most cases treatment directed toward panic attacks speeds recovery and reduces the frequency of relapse. Our therapy program, like most others, applies a combination of various methods without always being sure of the relative contribution of individual components.

CLARA

Clara is not a real person but a composite of several of our clients. We have created a composite case both to protect the identity of our clients and to be able to illustrate a variety of treatment difficulties. In a sense Clara is typical; but like a real individual, she has her specific history and problems. The therapist *I* or *me* below is either Frank or Jürgen; we have not written *we* in the therapy context since the therapy involves a single therapist. Clara sought our help because of increasing distress and disability from panic attacks and agoraphobia. She was thirty years old, a secretary, and not married, but in a stable relationship with her boyfriend.

Four years before coming to us, Clara had had several long-lasting bouts of flu during the winter and was somewhat depressed about the small apartment she and her boyfriend shared. One evening she drank a cup of coffee to overcome her exhaustion and went with him to a crowded restaurant. While waiting to be seated, she became very nervous. All of a sudden she felt her heart racing tremendously. She had trouble breathing, felt unsteady, and thought she was going to die right there. Her boyfriend called an ambulance; the doctor in the hospital told her after a series of tests that her health was perfectly OK. However, a few weeks later she had another strong attack while shopping. She became very afraid of having the next attack. Since her apartment seemed to be the only place she was safe, Clara began to avoid going out.

She eventually gave up her job and asked her boyfriend and mother to take turns doing the shopping for her. After about a year, she got up the courage to start working again, but she still carefully avoided anything that in her opinion might trigger another attack, such as using elevators or public transportation. Her family physician was the only person she had seen for treatment of her anxiety problems.

After a brief telephone contact, she was sent a package of questionnaires and screening forms. About one week later she came for an initial clinical interview based on the Anxiety Disorders Interview Schedule-Revised or ADIS-R, in which she met *DSM-III-R* criteria for panic disorder with agoraphobia. When asked to describe a usual panic attack, she gave the following account:

> All of a sudden I have funny feelings in my body, my heart races, and I get very nervous. I feel like I can't get enough air even though I start to breathe heavily. I feel unsteady and things around me don't look the way they should, like they were far away. Then I get afraid that I might lose control totally, that I might just slip away. I think, "I'm going to die," "I can't breathe," and "I'm never going to make it." Sometimes I'm afraid that I'm going crazy. I've had to go to the emergency room because I haven't been able to control it. If I'm with someone I know, someone I trust, it goes away faster.

A physical examination revealed no signs of organic illness. There had been no particular life stress preceding the onset of the anxiety problems other than some minor trouble at work involving a new boss and recurrent flu. About half a year before her first panic attack, an aunt had died of a heart attack. Clara described her childhood and family background as "average" and her relationship with her boyfriend as "good."

After the initial assessment session, she was instructed to fill out a diary for self-monitoring of her panic attacks for a week until the next appointment. (The diary form is illustrated in Exhibit 1.1 in Chapter One.) Clara was instructed to always carry the diary with her and to fill it out immediately after a panic attack occurred, and again in the evening before bedtime.

THE TREATMENT PACKAGE

The treatment package Clara embarked on is described below. As you see, it is structured, directive, and more confrontational than traditional psychotherapy. The package originated as a treatment manual for therapists in a research project in Germany and has been described in greater detail elsewhere. It is somewhat similar to a treatment package developed by David Barlow and Jerome Cerny. The rationales of some of the therapeutic elements are given in the form of a short monologue, which is different from the dialogues that actually occur. When we present information in the session, we always encourage the client to interrupt and ask questions, and we often interject questions to the client. We do not deny, however, that our approach is mainly one of teaching clients about their anxiety and giving them explanations that we have found effective when tailored to their specific history.

Session 1: The Rationale of Therapy: The Vicious Circle and Stress Model

Clara arrived for the first treatment session with her boyfriend, and I asked him to come back in forty-five minutes. She seemed quite anxious and had a lot of questions about what was going to happen. We first talked about how long the treatment would take; I said that our cognitive-behavioral treatment would last for fifteen sessions spread over ten weeks. A session is about fifty minutes; it is recorded on audiotape so that she can listen to it at home as part of the homework assignment.

I first tried to get an impression of Clara's present anxiety problems without going into much detail. We looked at the anxiety diary that Clara had been filling out since the initial diagnostic assessment. She had recorded the situations in which her panic attacks occurred, and how frequent and intense they were. I emphasized the importance of the diary for the therapy, since it would provide much of the material we would work with.

To give Clara a general framework that would help her understand her anxiety better, I explained to her that anxiety is a normal feeling that every person is familiar with and is associated with physical changes. It is normal when it prepares the body for action, but it can be out of proportion to the actual threat. It may be experienced as painful or as a burden, and it may impose restrictions on daily life. In such cases, the anxiety alarm system has become overly sensitive—triggered by small and harmless changes in the environment or in the body. Then professional help can be useful. This treatment, I said, will help her understand her panic attacks and decrease their frequency and intensity.

Clara and I looked again at the anxiety diary, this time in more detail. We discussed her individual anxiety symptoms and what situations provoked them. This necessitated careful inquiry and perseverance. Some clients can easily identify anxiety-eliciting factors, while others have difficulties with that. They may feel that their anxiety can appear almost anytime and that there is no relationship between situational factors, stressors, physical symptoms, or thoughts and the occurrence of anxiety. During the conversation I introduced the term *internal cues* and emphasized their role in producing anxiety. Internal cues may be physical sensations or symptoms, negative verbal cognitions, or catastrophic images. As you will see later, it is important for the therapy to identify the individual internal cues of the client.

Developing the Idea of the Vicious Circle. I went back to Clara's description of an outstanding panic attack and asked questions to find out how her bodily sensations and cognitions led to an escalation of anxiety, culminating in panic. The vicious circle of anxiety is an essential part of the physiological theory of panic; it is outlined in Figure 8.3.

I asked questions that were useful in elucidating more intermediate steps between calmness and panic in Clara's vicious circle. The idea of a positive feedback loop needed to be made clear: how fearful cognitions amplify somatic symptoms and how somatic symptoms then turn around and amplify cognitive

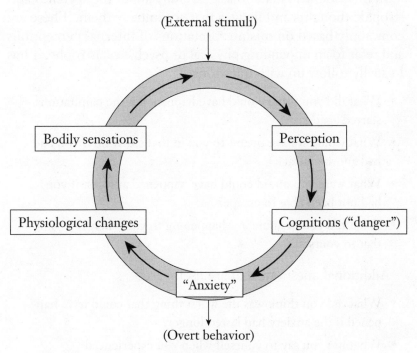

Figure 8.3
The "Vicious Circle" of Panic

Note: This diagram is used in explaining the treatment rationale to clients.

threat. First I asked what physical symptoms Clara had noticed. I wanted to understand the course of symptoms during her panic attack. Then I explored what verbal thoughts (self-talk, inner dialogue) and images (mental pictures) Clara had during her panic attack. Some of these processes are automatic and pass unnoticed if no specific attention is paid to them, so clients commonly come up with vague and nonspecific answers, such as:

- I'm afraid the palpitations could start again.
- I'm worried about having another attack.
- I could only think: "Get out of here!"
- My God, what's happening to me?

In this case, you need to ask carefully about the specific catastrophic thoughts and images that accompany them. These are commonly based on misinterpretations of internal perceptions and refer to an impending physical or psychic catastrophe. Thus I usually follow up with questions:

- What did you think would have happened if the palpitations started again?
- What would it have meant to you in that situation if you had had another attack?
- What were you afraid could have happened at worst if you had not been able to escape?
- What did you imagine *was* happening to you when you said that to yourself?

Additional questions that are useful are:

- What did you think was the worst thing that could have happened if the anxiety had lasted longer?
- What did you say to yourself when you experienced symptom X?
- When these symptoms were at their worst, what did you think they might mean?

As with the exploration of physical symptoms, I focused on changes in thoughts and images over the course of Clara's panic attack. It turned out that she started with a few specific misinterpretations of bodily sensations, followed by more and more catastrophic thoughts and additional misinterpretations.

Finally, after identifying critical cognitions and physical symptoms, I tried to track down specific connections between them. These are some typical connections between physical symptoms and their associated thoughts or interpretations:

- Palpitations, racing heart, chest pain or pressure, sweating, difficulty breathing: "I'll have a heart attack."

- Dizziness, faintness, weakness, visual distortions, trembling, paleness: "I'll faint." "I have a brain tumor." "I'll have a stroke."

- Difficulty breathing, smothering sensations, tightness in the throat: "I'm suffocating." "I'll stop breathing and die."

- Tingling sensations in extremities: "I'm becoming paralyzed."

- Feelings of unreality, being detached from oneself, difficulty concentrating, racing thoughts: "I'm losing control over myself." "I'll go crazy." "I'll end up in a psychiatric ward."

- Intense anxiety symptoms in general: "This anxiety will kill me."

Communicating the Vicious Circle of Anxiety. Now I brought all the gathered information together by drawing a picture. I started out by portraying the prototypical vicious circle and then added to it the thoughts and symptoms Clara had mentioned, one after another, explaining each step. Since sometimes a lot of detailed information has to be integrated, it is easy to lose the client during this intervention. To avoid this mistake, encourage questions and ask for any additional information that might be pertinent. Ideally, the conversation is experienced by your client as a "directed discovery," rather than as a lecture by the therapist. In other words, the client feels that she is discovering new connections. It is especially important at this point that your client articulate doubts and questions. This will help in understanding and absorbing the vicious circle model better.

Two objections often come up.

1.   "Sometimes I have a panic attack when I try to relax." Relaxation-induced panic attacks are a frequent phenomenon. If that happens, the therapist needs to work out (1) what happens in the client's body, (2) how the client's attention shifts, and (3) whether the client is threatened by a feeling of loss of control during relaxation. Since during relaxation we initially direct more attention to our body than to the environment, bodily sensations are noticed more easily. The anxiety resulting from these thoughts feeds into the vicious circle.

2.   "Sometimes my panic attacks happen so quickly that I don't have time to think." Danger appraisals can be very fast, at times automatic, since they evolved out of survival reflexes. Furthermore, some clients forget their catastrophic thoughts after the panic attack. In these cases the therapist emphasizes in the homework assignment that the client should pay particular attention to thoughts occurring during attacks, and to note them in the anxiety diary.

At this point I introduced the stress model, which is complementary to the vicious circle model since various stressors can have an impact on the initial triggering of the vicious circle. I introduce the client to Figure 8.4 and explain how rising stress levels can exceed the threshold for a panic attack. Stressors include waiting for an important telephone call, worrying about when the next panic attack will hit, or emergencies in the family or at the office.

After the vicious circle and the stress model were introduced, I told Clara how the treatment used these models and what she could expect from it. I emphasized that therapy was not easy and would take hard work on her part.

Summary, Homework Assignments, and Clinical Notes. At the end of the session, I summarized for Clara the most important

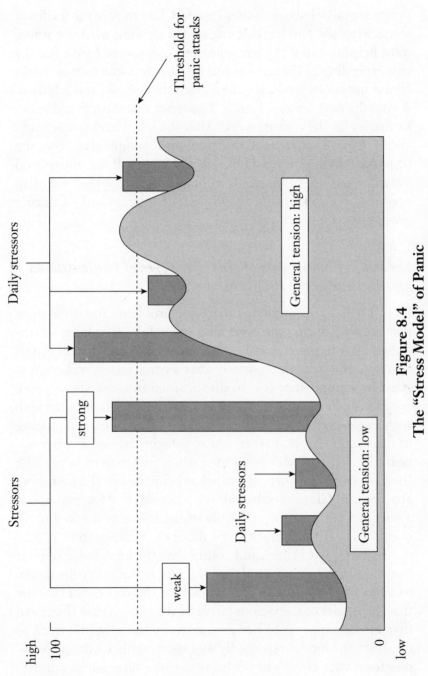

Figure 8.4
The "Stress Model" of Panic

Note: This diagram is used in explaining the treatment rationale to clients.

things we talked about. Then I asked Clara to give me feedback about what she had learned during the session, what she found most helpful, and if she had additional questions. I gave her the tape recording of the session and told her to listen to it at home. If new questions arose, she should jot them down and ask them during the next session. Finally, I gave her new anxiety and activity diaries for the coming week. After she left, I made some notes about Clara's current condition and prognosis, how she responded to the material offered, and how well she understood the information. (This is the general format for the end of all sessions; in descriptions of subsequent sessions only differing procedures are mentioned.)

Session 2: Components of Anxiety, Types of Panic Attacks, and Outline of the Program

First, I had a look at Clara's diary for problems and difficulties that came up during the preceding week. I discussed them without going into much detail at this time. Clara sometimes forgot to fill out the diary immediately after a panic attack, so I emphasized how important it is to do so, since the severity of panic attacks is often overestimated in retrospect. Then I checked, with a role-play, to see if Clara understood the escalating nature of the vicious circle. I asked her to imagine having a conversation with a friend who came to visit her in her apartment. The friend is curious to hear about what happened in the first therapy session. Clara should tell her what she had learned about anxiety so far. I took on the role of the friend and asked naïve questions to test her knowledge about the vicious circle.

Another way to check and consolidate the knowledge of your client about the vicious circle is to let him or her apply the model to a recent panic attack. It is crucial for the success of therapy that the model of the vicious circle be plausible to the client and that she can apply it to her own anxiety. Initially, you need to illustrate the model repeatedly and thoroughly by using examples from your client's life. This is to make sure that she understands the rationale of the therapy and is able to apply it.

Communicating the Three-Component Model of Anxiety. By breaking anxiety down into three distinct components, Clara gained a new understanding of her anxiety. She learned that her symptoms, worries, and behaviors are a common accompaniment of anxiety and are all interrelated. I explained to her that anxiety has three components: a physical one, a cognitive one, and a behavioral one.

Overview and Description of the Therapy Program. After previous explanations of the psychophysiological model of panic and after she had raised questions and articulated doubts, it was apparent to Clara that the basis for her panic attacks was her interpreting certain body sensations as dangerous. I explained the whole therapy program to Clara. I emphasized that her individual life history and learning experiences were decisive in how she developed panic disorder. This is important since it is the basis for acceptance and the effectiveness of the treatment. The session ended with a summary and my giving Clara new diaries and the recorded tape. She was also given a twelve-page brochure with information about causes of anxiety and panic attacks; I asked her to read it several times and become familiar with its content. The brochure contains a detailed description of topics introduced in the first two sessions, graphs, and some new material, such as a description of the physiological processes involved in sweating and breathing.

Session 3: Etiological Model

We began with a look at Clara's diary and discussed ways to improve her keeping track of her panic attacks, since she had forgotten to list all of her symptoms. After going over the agenda for today's session, we rehearsed the psychophysiological model of panic by applying it to one of Clara's latest panic attacks: "In the last session we talked about the three components of anxiety. Now, with your last panic attack, how were these components present? Could you also see how the anxiety escalated?"

Working out an Etiological Model.   Clara, like most clients, was very interested in the question "Why do I have these attacks?" We went back to her first panic attack four years ago. We explored how the stage was set for entering the vicious circle for the first time and how this experience influenced the pattern of following attacks. After asking her questions about the timing and location of the attack, the presence of stressors, and her reactions to the attack, I came to this formulation:

> When you came home from work on the day of your first panic attack, you were tired because you still were having some cold symptoms. You went to a restaurant with your boyfriend, where you got more stressed because it was very crowded. You told me that you often feel anxious in situations where you think people are watching you. Normally you don't pay too much attention to your heart in such situations, but this time your heart was pounding stronger than usual because you were so exhausted, and you had drunk a cup of coffee before. You started to worry about your heart. This may be related to experiences with your aunt. Since she was always worried about having heart disease, she noticed every time her heart did something funny and talked a lot about it. You learned that it could be dangerous if the heart skips a beat or pounds. So in the restaurant you became more anxious and paid even more attention to your heart, which was then beating faster and faster.
>
> That was how the vicious circle began. Your panic got so intense that your partner thought you were having a heart attack. He called an ambulance and you were brought to the hospital. The doctor couldn't find anything wrong with you. After that you started to worry more and more about your health, since you knew something had happened to you in the restaurant. So your general stress level was high, and you observed your body more closely than usual. This brought you to your second panic attack a few weeks later in the shopping mall, where you had to wait in line and felt observed and nervous. Is that plausible to you? What do you think?

As usual, you should encourage your client to articulate any doubts. The reasons for these doubts are important for you to know since the etiological model that you base your therapy on has to be plausible to your client and not just to yourself. In general, don't fall into the role of always having to specify exactly what caused a given panic attack, since this is rarely possible. When you communicate an etiological model, your client needs to understand that probably a combination of several factors led to the first panic attack, and that the crucial factor was a misinterpretation of bodily sensations.

Application of Coping Strategies in the Early Phase of a Panic Attack. At this point, I asked Clara to describe one of her typical panic attacks. We worked out that in the beginning there is always a phase of a relatively slow increase in anxiety. I used the graph depicted in Figure 8.5 to illustrate that this early phase would be the time for certain techniques that she would learn in following sessions to be applied most effectively. Clara's homework assignment was to pay special attention to the first cues of increasing anxiety, and to always note the time it took from this point to the peak of her anxiety. In addition she was given a one-page information sheet about the course of panic attacks (comprising Figure 8.5 and a short explanation).

Session 4: Hyperventilation Test and Dysfunctional Cognitions

We began by briefly discussing Clara's new diary entries with a focus on the early cues of panic. She had had three attacks during the last week and early on observed a slight feeling of shortness of breath quite consistently before the anxiety intensified. She also noticed that she tended to sigh and later experienced some chest pain. A detailed diary is essential, so I reinforced her excellent diary keeping. Then I asked her about stressful events and her mood during the last week to get an impression of her overall condition.

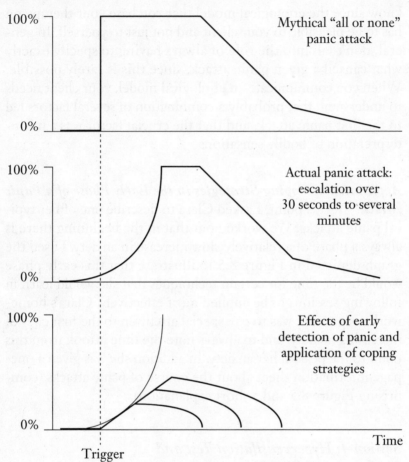

Trigger

Time

Figure 8.5
The Course of Onset of Panic Attacks

Note: This diagram is used in explaining the application of coping strategies to the client.

Hyperventilation Test. The main part of this session was to have Clara hyperventilate and compare the resulting symptoms with her panic symptoms. If there are similarities, hyperventilation can provide her with an additional reason for her physical sensations during panic attacks. Hyperventilation often occurs during panic attacks and often without the client's realizing it. (The hyperventilation test is described in Chapter One.) After the test, I asked her to compare the hyperventilation experience with her symptoms during a panic attack. Clara found them moderately similar, indicating that hyperventilation played at least a moderate role in her panic attacks. But she also emphasized major differences, such as the fact that she didn't have palpitations and only mild anxiety.

After we discussed the most important differences between what Clara experienced during the test and her usual panic attacks, I helped her to see that she may have produced some of the symptoms she feared by hyperventilating.

Breathing Retraining. Some clients not only hyperventilate during panic attacks but also breathe too deeply and/or fast in general, which often can be observed by the therapist during therapy sessions. This so-called chronic hyperventilation can be addressed by instruction in respiratory control. Here, the client learns to regularly practice slow diaphragmatic breathing to reverse the inappropriate breathing habits. The new breathing pattern can also be used as a coping strategy that prevents or interrupts acute hyperventilation and the ensuing anxiety-provoking symptoms.

The client is first told to lie on her stomach. In this position, abdominal breathing occurs automatically. The client concentrates on the breathing movements of the stomach and learns to perceive abdominal breathing. Subsequently, the same is done while lying on the back, sitting, and, eventually, standing.

Once the client has mastered diaphragmatic breathing, she is instructed to imagine anxiety-provoking situations or sensations and to use correct breathing as a way to cope with them. Tape recordings may be useful for teaching breathing exercises at home. A respiration rate of eight to twelve cycles per minute is optimal for most people. An important caveat in this kind of breathing training is that the client must learn not to breathe too deeply when she slows down her breathing, or she can end up hyperventilating anyway.

Additional Ways of Provoking Anxiety Symptoms. For some clients, hyperventilation plays only a minor role in their panic attacks. In that case, you need to try one or more of the following tests to see if they produce the main symptoms your client experiences. The client is instructed to always record the type of exercise, its duration, her anxiety level (0–10), and symptoms in a so-called progress report form.

1. PHYSICAL EXERCISE

Palpitations are the most frequent symptom of panic attacks. Consequently many clients are afraid they have a cardiac disease. In the past, extreme cases of this fear were labeled "cardiac neurosis." Exposure to cardiac sensations can be arranged by using physical exercises such as climbing stairs, knee bends, push-ups, or running in place for one or two minutes. Even mild degrees of exercise lead to increases in heart rate and stroke volume that are much larger than those that usually accompany panic attacks. A comparison of the symptoms accompanying physical exercise and panic attacks facilitates reappraisal of such sensations as palpitations, dizziness, hot flushes, and sweating, which were previously interpreted catastrophically.

2. FAST HEAD MOVEMENT

Dizziness and nausea can be provoked by any of these maneuvers: shaking the head from side to side for a thirty-second period; sitting and bending the head between the legs for thirty seconds and then suddenly sitting upright again; or sitting on a swivel chair, spinning around several times, and then suddenly stopping.

3. RESTRICTED BREATHING

Feeling of suffocation can be provoked by having the client breathe in and out through a straw in the mouth (the large type used in fast-food restaurants) for two minutes. Holding the breath for thirty seconds or as long as possible can produce the same symptoms.

4. VISUAL DISTORTIONS

Some clients complain of unusual visual phenomena during panic attacks (seeing colors, shadows, dancing lines, or objects that suddenly get bigger). This is often taken as an indication of a serious illness, such as a brain tumor. These symptoms may result from worried interpretations of optical illusions. One way to induce visual distortions is to show pictures with close parallel line patterns that start to "flicker" after a while (escalators and moving sidewalks at airports can also produce this effect). Both the therapist and the client should look at such a picture together and compare their impressions. Both will experience visual illusions, but only the client is likely to be made anxious by it, which is an example of how anxious cognitions can cause misinterpretations. Staring at a spot on the wall or into one's own mirror image for two minutes are other ways to induce visual illusions.

5. OTHERS

Other methods that can be applied during a therapy session are: producing numbness and tingling by stopping the blood flow into the arm with a tight rubber band around the upper arm for two minutes; producing feelings of derealization by staring into a moving "starfield simulation" (often part of screen savers on PCs); producing the feeling that the room is suddenly closing in by sitting in a swivel chair and being suddenly moved towards the wall; making voices distant as in depersonalization by wearing ear plugs during a conversation; replicating a perceptual distortion that sometimes occurs during panic by hearing one's own voice amplified over headphones while talking; or producing lightheadedness by lying on the floor and suddenly getting up.

Some methods can only be done as homework: producing tingling or numbness by taking a very hot or cold shower; producing breathlessness or feelings of suffocation by sitting in a sauna; or producing feelings of unsteadiness by rowing a boat or riding a roller coaster or other amusement park attraction.

One or two of the above tests should be conducted. With Clara, I conducted the spinning chair exercise because dizziness often occurred with her panic attacks but was not produced by the hyperventilation test.

Dysfunctional Cognitions. For didactic reasons, this method is presented separately, although it is useful to combine it with the anxiety provocations since they are likely to trigger dysfunctional thoughts. At the end of each exercise, you can ask your client "What is going through your mind right now?" and note the thoughts for use in later sessions (see Correction of Misinterpretations below).

FIRST STEP: THE RATIONALE FOR
DYSFUNCTIONAL COGNITIONS
We begin by explaining that thoughts play a role in anxiety.

> We've already talked about the importance of recognizing early cues of anxiety. Now you'll practice observing your thinking early in the course of a panic attack in order to identify inappropriate thoughts. They may be hard to spot, since they're often automatic in that they're outside of our awareness and appear and disappear in an instant. Let me give you an example. You suddenly feel dizzy at work and think, "There's something wrong in my brain!" But then you're immediately distracted by something else, so you don't register the thought in your memory.

SECOND STEP: IDENTIFYING DYSFUNCTIONAL COGNITIONS
Some clients have a hard time remembering thoughts they had during a panic attack. The anxiety diary is one measure to bring

these thoughts to their attention. As mentioned above, any activities that can produce symptoms and provoke anxiety are useful. In addition, it can be helpful to have the client imagine a situation as if it were happening at the moment. You can take the part of the other person if interactions are involved. Going through certain sequences of a "movie" of an anxiety-provoking situation in slow motion, stopping at points, and asking "What are you thinking now?" often elicits automatic thoughts. Or if you notice an increase in your client's anxiety at any point during a session, you can ask: "What's going through your mind right now?"

THIRD STEP: CONVICTION RATING

The client gives ratings for each of the identified dysfunctional thoughts and images (for example, "I'll suffocate") on a scale of 0–100 percent to specify how convinced she is that the prediction will actually come true. Zero percent means "sure that it will definitely not come true," and 100 percent means "sure that it will definitely come true." This rating is given for two time points for each thought: first, how conviction would be rated during the panic attack, and second, how it would be rated when the client was not anxious. Usually there is a discrepancy between the two time points because conviction is greater during anxiety.

Clara's homework assignment was again to pay special attention to the first signs of increasing anxiety, with particular focus on her thoughts. She was asked to jot down all the dysfunctional thoughts she noticed during the day as soon as they occurred. For that I gave her a sheet of paper with four columns, for (1) the situation that led to anxiety, (2) automatic thoughts in that situation, (3) conviction rating of each thought from 0–100 percent, and (4) an anxiety rating from 0 to 10. Clara was reminded to practice the spinning chair exercise and the hyperventilation exercise once daily. Hyperventilation exercises should not be performed more than twice in a row because of potential side effects such as headache.

Session 5: Confrontation Exercises, Correction of Misinterpretations, and Analysis of Logical Mistakes

Clara had filled out the diary very accurately. We noticed a decrease in the intensity of her panic attacks, and I asked her for an explanation. She attributed the decrease to a feeling that she understood panic much better so that it didn't scare her so much anymore. Clara had had some problems in performing the exercises on her own. She felt that she couldn't continue the hyperventilation long enough because the symptoms were so uncomfortable, and she only did it on three days. I praised her effort in trying and emphasized that although she did not reach the goal of doing them seven times, doing them three times was a relative success. Then we looked at her diary of dysfunctional thoughts. Clara had identified only two thoughts and said she had problems finding dysfunctional thoughts in general. Thus, as an example we worked out together some of the thoughts she had had during a recent panic attack.

Confrontation Exercise. Clara performed the exercise from the last session that was most anxiety-provoking for her, hyperventilation. I helped her to pace her speed of breathing and extended the duration by about half a minute. Compared to the last session, she was less anxious, although the symptoms were the same and their duration was longer. She realized that the reduced anxiety was a success in managing her anxiety. Then she performed the hyperventilation on her own while I was waiting outside the room. She could do it, although she felt more anxious, and was confident now that she could practice it once a day at home.

Correction of Misinterpretations. This procedure can follow confrontation exercises, since they are likely to evoke misinterpretations of bodily symptoms that the client can work on. Other sources for misinterpretations are the diaries and thoughts that were identified during one of the last sessions. In this and the following session, all important misinterpretations need to be corrected, starting with the most anxiety-provoking. After we choose a misinterpretation to work on, the client rates her conviction about it and explores evidence about it pro and con. For example, Clara defended her idea that rapid heartbeat means heart disease with "I have no other explanation for the palpitations. . . . I read in a newspaper that heart diseases are a common cause of death and that palpitations are a symptom of heart disease. . . . Another symptom is chest pain, which I sometimes have. . . . My aunt died from heart disease and I may have inherited it." Against were the following: "None of my EKGs showed anything wrong. . . . The chest pain doesn't get worse with physical exercise. . . . When I'm distracted or someone's with me, the palpitations go away. . . . The main risk factor for heart disease is hypertension and my aunt had high blood pressure, but I don't."

I asked Clara (again in Socratic style) what else could explain why her heart was racing. Could there have been other causes for the palpitations, such as physical or mental stress, exhaustion, or standing up quickly? Were there thoughts that might have triggered anxiety and made the heart beat faster? How about hyperventilation?

Analysis of Logical Mistakes. We can teach clients to correct the dysfunctional thoughts that occur in stress and anxiety situations, including misinterpretations of bodily symptoms. Analysis of logical mistakes is especially useful for clients who tend to make many such mistakes, which is often the case for people with excessive anxiety.

Our method for changing logical mistakes is the four-column technique. The first column lists the circumstances under which an anxiety-provoking thought occurred, the second column describes the thought (which is commonly an unrealistic interpretation of the situation) with a conviction rating between zero and 100 percent, the third column outlines the type(s) of logical mistake(s) out of which this thought arose, and the fourth column describes other possible, more rational thoughts in response to the situation, or alternatively how an objective observer would interpret the same situation. This step teaches clients to develop alternative thoughts that are more helpful in coping with anxiety. For each alternative thought, a conviction rating is given.

1. DRAWING CONCLUSIONS BASED ON INSUFFICIENT EVIDENCE

This is the most important type of logical mistake for individuals with panic disorder, since it is the underlying principle for most misinterpretations of bodily symptoms. This procedure teaches clients to approach their habitual assumptions and catastrophic thoughts as a scientist would approach them. An anxiety-provoking thought is not taken as a fact but as a hypothesis that needs to be confirmed or disproved. The client should learn to ask the following questions by herself: "How do I know that this is the case?" "What is the evidence that this happened (or will take place)?" "What are other possible explanations?" "How likely is that?"

2. ABSOLUTISTIC THINKING

This type of logical mistake is also quite common and can be involved in misinterpretations of bodily symptoms, for example, "I always get afraid when I feel my heartbeat." Absolutistic thinking can easily be recognized by words such as *always, never, every, only, have to, need to, must, mustn't,* or *can't.* It can be challenged with such questions as "Really always?" "Was there ever a time when you felt your heartbeat and didn't get anxious?" "What would happen if you didn't do that?" Absolutistic words can often simply be replaced by relative words, such as *often, sometimes,* or *want to.*

At the end of the session I discussed with Clara some modifications of her confrontation exercises (performing the hyperventilation longer and at least twice outside her home) and gave her a sheet of paper with four columns so that she could apply the newly learned technique to at least five anxiety-provoking thoughts.

Session 6: Confrontation Exercises, Focusing Attention, Correction of Misinterpretations, and Logical Mistakes

First Clara and I looked at her diaries and discussed the confrontation exercises. She had made a lot of progress because she had done them daily and experienced a significant reduction in anxiety. The hyperventilation exercise she did in a department store was very frightening. We also went over her listing of thoughts and their logical mistakes; since some were not quite accurately analyzed, we spent a little more time on their analysis.

Confrontation Exercise. Clara twice performed another exercise, running in place, and recorded in the progress report form her anxiety level, symptoms she experienced, and how long she ran. I asked her to engage in activities that involve physical exercise, such as climbing stairs or walking faster than usual. This would eventually lead to a decrease in her anxiety level.

Focusing Attention. To demonstrate that enhanced attention to internal cues can increase anxiety, I asked Clara to perform another experiment. First she rated her current anxiety level on a scale from 0 to 10 and then concentrated on her heartbeat (I selected this sensation since it was very anxiety-provoking for Clara). I asked her to pay attention to slight changes in her heartbeat and to any other unusual heart feelings. Since she had difficulty in feeling her heartbeat at first, I asked her to lie down, which made it easier for her. Then she rated her anxiety level again; it had increased from 4 to 6. If there is no indication that the client used distraction as an avoidance strategy, then less anxiety may be a sign that progress has already been made.

Correction of Misinterpretations. With the procedure introduced in the last session, we corrected several of Clara's other misinterpretations of bodily symptoms. This needs to be continued until all salient misinterpretations are corrected, which should also be reflected in a decrease in the frequency and severity of panic attacks.

Analysis of Logical Mistakes. Since Clara had progressed well, I introduced new types of logical mistakes and worked with them in the way described in the last session. But as mentioned above, this should only be done if the client has done well with the other techniques.

1. CERTAIN VERSUS POSSIBLE

The assumption that a negative event is sure to happen is quite common when someone is anxious. This type of logical mistake overestimates the likelihood that a certain event will cause another event, for example, "If I don't control my thoughts, I'll go crazy" or "No one will help me if I faint." These unrealistic estimations can be challenged by the client with such questions as "What is the real chance of that?" "Are you distinguishing between certain and possible effects?" "Are you overestimating the probability that that will happen?"

2. ALL-OR-NONE

A common mistake is to perceive the world in extreme categories—good versus bad, all versus none, black versus white—instead of seeing all the gradations between. Panic attacks are often perceived as an all-or-none phenomenon, as with being in either a good mood or a bad mood.

3. OVERGENERALIZATION FROM FEW EXAMPLES

An example of this logical mistake is the client who started to worry about having a heart disease after he heard that someone his age had died of a heart attack. Or the client who stopped driving over bridges after he had a panic attack once while crossing a bridge. Persistent test anxiety after one failed exam is another example. Clients need to learn to recognize when they make excessively negative predictions about their ability to cope with a certain situation and to ask such questions as "Does this one example mean that this will always be the case?" "Have I only had bad experiences with that, or have I also had some good experiences?"

Session 7: Confrontation Exercises, Correction of Misinterpretations, and Self-Instruction Training

Clara and I went over the last entries in her diary and noticed that her panic attacks had decreased even more. I asked her why, and we agreed that the change was related to corrected misinterpretations and to the confrontation exercises. If the client has shown little improvement by session seven, you might say something like this: "We thought last week that you had gotten better at managing panic attacks. I wonder why it's been more difficult than we thought?" This helps you find out to what degree your client has internalized the vicious circle, the stress model, and the correction of misinterpretations, and you can work some more on any deficiencies if necessary.

Confrontation Exercise. Clara performed further exercises to see how much they could still induce anxiety. Usually, the exercises should be continued during the following sessions until the anxiety they produce is consistently low.

Reading a List of Symptoms and Associated Catastrophic Thoughts. This experiment demonstrates that thoughts can induce anxiety or even a panic attack. I asked Clara first to rate her current anxiety level and then to read aloud a list of pairs of words. The first word was a symptom and the second a common catastrophic misinterpretation, for example,

breathlessness   suffocation

Each pair was repeated several times. I ended this experiment when Clara showed clear signs of discomfort; I then asked her to rate her anxiety again, and to observe what was going on in her mind and body for one or two minutes. We discussed what she experienced and I asked her questions to lead her to an understanding of the role of cognitions in the vicious circle: "What do you do with the fact that merely reading words can frighten you? Do you think this experience has given you an explanation for what happens during a panic attack? How does this fit into the vicious circle?"

Correction of Misinterpretations. Often this reading experiment triggers additional misinterpretations that can be corrected, or material from the diaries and previous sessions can be used. Clara reported that in particular the pair

unreal   going crazy

stuck in her mind and made her nervous, so we worked on the underlying misinterpretation.

Self-Instruction Training. This procedure is an extension of the analysis of logical mistakes and the correction of misinterpretations. It focuses on developing concise self-instructions that can be used to prevent an escalation of anxiety. Examples are "My palpitations aren't dangerous, since I know that my heart is healthy," "I've never fainted so why should it happen now?" and "I don't need to criticize myself like that since others can do that for me." Alternative thoughts that were worked out with the four-column technique can provide the material for formulations the client likes. They can be written on little cards to be referred to in anxiety situations or learned by heart. In any case they should be said aloud in the critical situation.

The homework assignment for Clara was to do the new exercises daily, to practice the self-instructions developed in the session, and to come up with at least three new ones.

Session 8: Decatastrophizing

Clara had had one intense panic attack during the past week, during a stressful situation at work. We discussed that incident in light of the stress model. She said that in the situation she was too anxious to use self-instructions, so we worked out what kinds of early signs of anxiety she could have paid attention to.

I explored with Clara the catastrophic images she had when she thought of fainting and how to put them into perspective. So far, the focus of therapy had been to check if certain thoughts that frequently occurred to her in anxiety situations were realistic and to replace them with more appropriate thoughts. With the decatastrophizing procedure, the client learns to think about consequences: what would happen if the misinterpretation or catastrophic prediction came true?

I told Clara that we would do an exercise that would expose her to her catastrophic thoughts about fainting. To make the script more realistic and detailed, I explored the exact circumstances: "Where would it happen? Who would be watching? People you know? Would they talk about you? Where exactly would you faint? How? Which changes in your body would you notice first? And then?" After that I summarized what she had told me, checked with her as to whether the scenario matched what she imagined, and made some modifications. Then I asked Clara to make herself comfortable in the chair, to close her eyes, and to imagine that she was going to a supermarket. I went on to describe the scenery and what she was doing. I observed her reactions to what I said, her facial expression and breathing, and asked from time to time if she had a clear image of what was going on. Then I described the catastrophic events. It is very important to include physical reactions, for example, "Now you're approaching the cash register and you see a long line in front of the counter. You feel the floor under your feet and your legs become weak. Your heart starts to pound and you notice your hands getting soaked. You think 'not an attack again, please. . . .'"

After the imagination exercise, I asked Clara to check if her fantasy actually was as unbearable as she had thought it would be: "Did everyone really look at you? Did your heart stop beating?" etc. Her anxiety decreased after the initial increase, and Clara became more aware of how irrational the catastrophic scenario was. Clara's homework assignment was to practice decatastrophizing by imagining daily a scenario for catastrophic thoughts around her fear of heart disease.

Session 9: Exposure to Feared Situations

Clara had successfully applied the new technique of the catastrophic scenario. We discussed her experiences with that, the confrontation exercises, and the self-instructions. I reminded her of the importance of praising herself for doing the exercises.

Modifying Avoidance Behavior. So far the focus of therapy had been exposure to internal stimuli and the correction of misinterpretations. If the client no longer reacts to bodily symptoms with intense anxiety, the next focus should be exposure to external stimuli ("situational exposure"). Most clients with panic disorder have at least moderate agoraphobia. Working on avoidance behavior helps to generalize the changed cognitions to fearful situations and will consolidate the success. From the diagnostic interview, I had some information about activities and situations that Clara avoided, such as elevators, movie theaters, and physical activity. I now explored in detail factors that could increase or decrease Clara's anxiety in these situations, such as the size of the elevator and how many people were in it, the duration of the physical activity, and the presence of someone known. Using Figure 8.6 and Clara's fear of elevators as an instance, I explained how her avoidance led to increased anxiety in the long run and what she needed to do to overcome this fear of elevators. My tactics were like those described in Chapter Two.

Since I had the impression that Clara understood the rationale of exposure therapy and was motivated to apply it, we talked about specific situations for the homework assignment. We agreed on elevators for the coming week, followed by movie theaters the next week; we planned the exposure exercises in detail. Clara's task was to go to a twenty-story high-rise apartment building in her hometown (she had access to it because a friend lived there), and to ride up and down in the elevator for a while until her anxiety level decreased noticeably. Only after that subsidence should she leave the elevator for a few minutes' rest. She should ride repeatedly for at least one hour and do this exercise

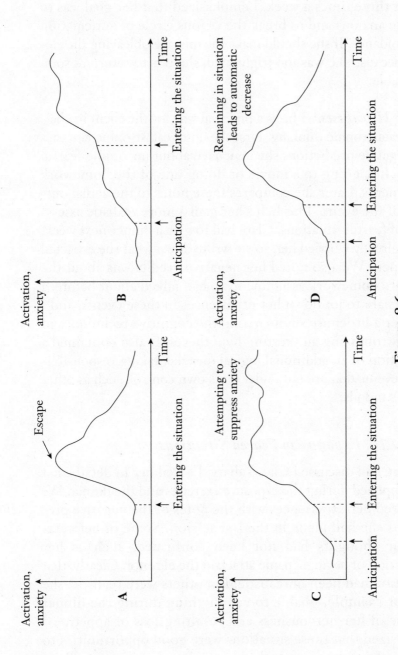

Figure 8.6

The Course of Anxiety and Somatic Activation During Exposure to Anxiety-Provoking Stimuli under Four Different Circumstances

Note: A shows the effects of an escape response, *B* the additional anxiety caused by anticipation, and *C* the effects of attempts to suppress anxiety. *D* shows that anxiety and arousal will decrease automatically (habituate) if the client remains in the situation.

at least three times a week. I emphasized that her goal was to become anxious and to break the vicious circle of anticipation and avoidance. If she should make the mistake of leaving the elevator because she was too frightened, she was to return as soon as possible.

Testing Hypotheses.   This is a practical way for the client to challenge catastrophic thinking. First she notes catastrophic fantasies and negative predictions she may have about upcoming fearful events, like going to a movie or doing one of the homework assignments. Later she compares these notes to the actual outcome of the event. This helps her gain a more realistic assessment of fearful situations. Clara had to give a dinner next week, which already worried her, so we wrote down what she expected to happen. We also noted her negative predictions about the exposure homework assignment we had talked about before. I asked Clara to jot down her experiences in these events, and I gave her a brochure summarizing the cognitive techniques of decatastrophizing and testing hypotheses. It also contained a description of an additional logical mistake: taking responsibility for events that are not under one's own control, such as other people's moods.

Session 10: Exposure to Feared Situations

After we had discussed Clara's diary, I asked her in detail what had happened during the exposure exercises and the dinner. We compared her experiences with the notes of the negative predictions she had made in the last session. Some of her catastrophic thoughts had not been confirmed, such as her expectation of having a panic attack in the elevator. Clearly, that prediction had been unrealistic. But others were realistic: she was, for example, unable to eat anything during the dinner because of her nervousness and resulting loss of appetite. I emphasized that these situations were good opportunities to practice the techniques she had learned, and we discussed how she could have applied them in those situations. I also asked her "what would happen if" questions to help her see that the events were not as catastrophic as she assumed. Since exposure to the elevator had not led to intense anxiety, we tried to find out if we had forgotten to include something important. We decided that Clara needed to do the exercise in a smaller elevator with other people in it and for a longer time in order to really get anxious.

We then discussed an additional exposure exercise for the coming week: going to movies at least three times, something Clara had avoided for two years because she felt too confined there and had several panic attacks. I emphasized that the exercises created a win-win situation. If she didn't get very anxious, she would know that there had been no reason to avoid the situation. If she did get very anxious, she would be able to apply the new techniques and become progressively less anxious. We went over some of the material from the last sessions and saw how Clara was putting what she had learned into practice. I reviewed her successes during the course of the treatment and compared her current condition with her condition before treatment. This was a very encouraging experience for Clara. I emphasized that she now needed to apply the techniques to any situation where she was anxious (more is said about this in session 13).

Session 11: Problem-Solving Training

Clara had successfully applied the exposure exercises and experienced the expected decrease of anxiety on repetition. She hadn't had a panic attack for the last three weeks, so I decided to shift the focus of therapy to teaching her general ways to improve coping with stress, which is linked to panic attacks in the stress model. "Problem solving training" is a very useful approach; here we only outline it briefly since it is a standard behavioral technique. It consists of seven steps:

1. Definition of the problem
2. Definition of the goal

3. Brainstorming about ways to achieve the goal
   (problem-solving strategies)

4. Pros and cons of these strategies

5. Choosing the most suitable strategy

6. Finding ways to put the strategy into
   practice

7. Evaluating its effectiveness

Clara practiced the application of this procedure with two examples of stressful situations at work and at home by filling out a sheet of paper with a column for each of the steps. Her homework assignment was to apply the procedure to several other problems, to continue to use self-instructions in anxious situations, and to perform further exposure exercises.

Session 12: Social-Skills Training

Toward the end of therapy, it can be useful to integrate elements from other therapeutic approaches in order to increase treatment efficacy, especially in clients with obvious social-skills deficits or with personality disorders. Since Clara had anxiety in social situations and some problems in her relationship with her boyfriend, I conducted social-skills training as an adjunct. The main component of the training is to prepare the client for difficult social interactions by conducting role plays and by teaching certain principles of effective communication. Many of my clients have problems in social contexts, partly because of their long agoraphobia and a resultant restricted lifestyle. Some schools of family therapy contend that successful exposure treatment has an adverse effect on close relationships. However, this appears to be the exception rather than the rule. In most couples, marital satisfaction increases after successful agoraphobia treatment, although an initially bad marriage predicts poor treatment outcome in some cases.

Session 13: Generalization

Clara and I discussed her experiences with putting the role plays into practice. Then we conducted some new role plays and applied the problem-solving approach to some of Clara's recent problems. I summarized the successes she had made during the treatment and emphasized the importance of applying the learned techniques to any anxious situation so as to make sure that her improvements will be solidly anchored in all the contexts of her life. Clara and I thought about situations that were likely to occur in the next week to which she had not yet applied her new techniques. I was careful to suggest situations that were not too different from ones successfully overcome in the past, to ensure that Clara would not fail. I also asked her to think of some more situations and to practice the techniques in all these situations.

Session 14: Relapse Prevention

After reviewing some difficulties Clara had had with the new situations, we talked about possible problems that could arise after the end of the treatment and how to prevent them. The psychophysiological model assumes that the risk of relapse is highly determined by remaining misinterpretations of bodily symptoms. They need to be discovered and worked out at the end of the therapy.

Often clients who are completely panic-free at the end of treatment worry about having new attacks. They have vivid images of the times when they had a lot of panic and the resulting limitations and unhappiness. They want to avoid any recurrence of panic, even in a milder form than before. Some clients experience a spontaneous remission and then panic creeps back into their lives.

To check for these kinds of worries, you can ask, "Let's assume you had an unexpected panic attack tomorrow; what would you think?" Clients who don't have irrational fears of relapse say that they wouldn't worry much because they will apply the techniques they have learned. If clients are worried because they have experienced longer periods with little anxiety but then the anxiety has gradually come back, you can ask, "Are there differences between the current and the past relief in anxiety?" The clients need to remember that they now have effective coping strategies that were missing in the past. In general, you should predict fluctuations in the degree of anxiety.

After Clara and I discussed her predictions about relapses and how she would handle them, as a last homework assignment I asked her to write down all the things she had learned that were important for managing her anxiety. I also asked her to apply her coping techniques in as many situations as possible.

Therapists should realize that complete remission without treatment is probably rare if panic disorder symptoms have continued for as long as a year. At the end of treatment, most clients do have a remission of symptoms; that is the time to inoculate them against the possibility of future relapse. Here are some suggestions:

1. Clients must realize that the treatment has taught them ways of overcoming their dual problems of anxiety and avoidance, and that they no longer need to have a therapist around to help them apply these skills when anxiety rears its head, which may occur in a previous setting or in a new one. Improvement can be generalized to new situations if clients take the initiative to make it happen.

2. The therapist must never reassure clients at the end of treatment that their problems are over; quite the contrary. The therapist should predict recurrences of panic and fluctuating background anxiety, but convey that such events are not catastrophes. One panic attack does not render the whole treatment worthless; relapse is not an all-or-none phenomenon. When stressors are present, anxiety tends to increase, which is a reason to keep resolving problems at home and at work as early as possible.

3. Anxiety is not the only human problem. Other problems such as marital distress can contribute to anxiety, but it must be addressed with techniques different from those in this treatment package. Sometimes at the end of therapy, other problems emerge from the background.

4. When feasible, a booster session should be scheduled for some months after therapy ends. The client should know that she can contact the therapist for booster sessions if she is unable to maintain and extend the gains on her own.

Session 15: Review of the Course of Treatment

Clara and I began by discussing in detail remaining problems in applying the coping strategies. We then went over a written list of what she had learned from the program. It is especially important to check for gaps in understanding the vicious circle model. Clara had gained an accurate understanding of her panic attacks, the vicious circle, and the roles of stress and her thoughts. She could explain to me the techniques she would use and in which situations they should be applied. I made a general summary of the progress that Clara had made during the therapy and highlighted some of the main changes that had occurred, for example, that Clara had been panic free for the last seven weeks. We discussed all remaining questions in detail, and I instructed Clara to continue to apply the techniques and skills she had learned. I reminded her about relapse prevention and scheduled a booster session in four months. I encouraged her to always look for challenging new tasks and situations, and I reminded her that the best protection against panic attacks is frequent practice of coping skills.

NOTES

P. 205, *Later researchers such as Donald Klein and David Sheehan adopted a medical model:* Klein, D. F. (1980). Anxiety reconceptualized. *Comprehensive Psy-*

chiatry, *21*, 411–427; Sheehan, D. V. (1982). Panic attacks and phobias. *New England Journal of Medicine*, *307*, 156–158.

P. 205, *But much of the evidence:* Margraf, J., & Ehlers, A. (1990). Biological models of panic disorder and agoraphobia: Theory and evidence. In G. D. Burrows, M. Roth, and R. Noyes (Eds.), *Handbook of anxiety: Vol. 3. The neurobiology of anxiety*. Amsterdam: Elsevier.

P. 205, *all of these models can be considered variants of the same theme:* Barlow, D. H. (1986). Behavioral conception and treatment of panic. *Psychopharmacology Bulletin*, *22*, 803–806; Beck, A. T., Emery, G., & Greenberg, R. L. (1985). *Anxiety disorders and phobias: A cognitive perspective*. New York: Basic Books; Clark, D. M. (1986). A cognitive approach to panic. *Behaviour Research and Therapy*, *24*, 461–470; Goldstein, A. J., & Chambless, D. L. (1978). A reanalysis of agoraphobia. *Behavior Therapy*, *9*, 47–59; Ley, A. R. (1985). Agoraphobia, the panic attack, and the hyperventilation syndrome. *Behaviour Research and Therapy*, *23*, 79–81.

P. 210, *based on the Anxiety Disorders Interview Schedule-Revised or ADIS-R:* DiNardo, P., & Barlow, D. H. (1988). *Anxiety disorders interview schedule-revised (ADIS-R)*. Albany, NY: Graywind Publications.

P. 211, *The package originated as a treatment manual for therapists:* Margraf, J., & Schneider, S. (1989). *Panik: Angstanfälle und ihre Behandlung [Panic: Anxiety attacks and their treatment]*. Berlin: Springer.

P. 211, *a treatment package developed by David Barlow and Jerome Cerny:* Barlow, D. H., & Cerny, J. A. (1988). *Psychological treatment of panic*. New York: Guilford Press.

P. 239 *"Problem solving training":* Falloon, I. R., Boyd, J. L., & McGill, C. W. (1984). *Family care of schizophrenia*. New York: Guilford Press.

9

A COGNITIVE-BEHAVIORAL TREATMENT PACKAGE FOR SOCIAL ANXIETY

Karin Gruber and Richard G. Heimberg

Social phobia is one of the most debilitating of the phobic anxiety disorders. Unlike other phobic disorders, social phobia directly impacts the way we interact with others. If severe enough, it can prevent the development of peer or intimate relationships, hinder career success and advancement, interfere with developing and maintaining social support networks, and contribute to general loneliness and isolation. It is the most common anxiety disorder and the third most common psychiatric disorder, ranking in lifetime prevalence after major depressive disorder and alcohol dependence. In addition to being a major psychological disorder, social phobia also represents a risk factor for both alcoholism and depression.

Social phobia is a fear of social situations in which the individual is afraid that he or she might do something inappropriate. *DSM-IV* defines social phobia as "a marked and persistent fear of one or more social or performance situations in which the person is exposed to unfamiliar people or to possible scrutiny by others. The individual fears that he or she will act in a way (or show anxiety symptoms) that will be humiliating or embarrassing." In contrast to the transient, easily dismissed feelings of embarrassment that come up in everybody's life and thus are not anticipated or dwelt upon, social phobics are individuals with a marked and persistent fear of embarrassment.

Individuals who suffer from social phobia generally either fear one or a few social situations or they fear most or all social situations. According to *DSM-IV,* those who fear most social situations are diagnosed as having *generalized social phobia;* those who fear one or more (but not most) social situations are diagnosed as *nongeneralized social phobia.* Among the most commonly feared social situations are public speaking, dating, parties, meetings, and interactions with authority or with the opposite sex. Less common situations are writing in front of others, using public restrooms, and eating in public.

THE VICIOUS CIRCLE IN SOCIAL PHOBIA

Vicious circles provide us with an explanation of why social phobia, once established, tends to continue at the same intensity or to become even worse. A vicious circle explains how anxiety is amplified, how self-confidence is undermined, and why the sufferer avoids social situations provoking anxiety. The nature of a vicious circle is to repeat and to spiral upwards, the anxiety becoming more intense and the loop harder to break out of. We describe below three important components of the vicious circle: fearful anticipation, avoidance, and negative self-attributions.

Fearful Anticipation

Social phobics anticipate and dwell upon upcoming social situations that could lead to embarrassing moments. They are highly concerned about becoming conspicuous, appearing ridiculous, or manifesting visible signs of anxiety and thus being disapproved of or judged negatively. This expectation is often expressed by thoughts such as "I'm going to make a fool of myself," "They'll see my incompetence and ignorance," "She's not going to like me," and "What if my voice shakes?" Attempts to hide and cover up only makes things worse. When social phobics become preoccupied with the quality of their performance and with their anxiety symptoms, they become less focused on the task at hand and thus more likely to actually perform poorly and in fact be visibly anxious. In addition, social phobics tend to think that if something embarrassing happens, it will inevitably lead to negative consequences such as disapproval, rejection, or failure. They tend to view the consequences of embarrassment as severe, unbearable, and unmanageable.

Avoidance

The second main component of the vicious circle of social phobia is avoidance. Avoidance can begin at any point. Some social phobics are so highly avoidant that they don't approach feared situations at all—either cognitively or behaviorally. Most social phobics we have treated, however, do attempt to enter feared situations to some extent, either by thinking very hard about participating in a social interaction or by actually participating. For them, avoidance begins when the thought or event becomes too anxiety-provoking. They then stop intending to participate or alter their participation in a way that relieves anxiety, for example, by becoming very quiet in a group. Although avoidance reduces anxiety temporarily and thus is rewarding, it ultimately reduces the social phobics' quality of life, restricting day-to-day activities and accomplishments more and more, in both private and professional spheres.

Negative Self-Attributions

Negative thinking and avoidance affect social phobics' opinions of their future ability to cope in social situations. Their negative view of themselves as social beings retards them in recovering their social confidence after embarrassments. Feeling like a failure or innately flawed, social phobics stop thinking that they can cope with awkward moments. The more negatively social phobics feel about their social skills, the less inclined they are to tackle new or challenging situations, thus increasing their socially avoidant behavior. Not having successes to draw upon feeds into their negative self-perception by seeming to confirm that they are incompetent, no good, and unable to master their fear. The result is loss of self-confidence.

A Case Description

The case example of Tina, which we describe below, illustrates how debilitating social phobia can be. Her name has been changed to protect her anonymity, but the rest of the information about her and what she is quoted as saying is accurately reported. She came to the first author, Karin, to find a way out of her anxiety spiral. Karin offered her cognitive-behavioral therapy for social phobia as part of her Ph.D. research project at the Stanford University School of Medicine. Karin's treatment approach is based on the treatment manual by Richard, the second author. He calls his treatment Cognitive Behavioral Group Treatment (CBGT) for social phobia. Karin was trained in Richard's laboratory and was supervised by him and Dr. Harlan Juster. CBGT has been demonstrated in controlled studies to be an effective psychological treatment for social phobia with improvement maintained at a 4.5- to 6.25-year follow-up. The goal of CBGT is to help social phobics overcome their incapacitating anxieties in a fast, efficient, and cost-effective manner. The interested reader can find descriptions of additional cases treated with CBGT referenced at the end of the chapter.

TINA

Tina, a forty-two-year-old successful business manager at a well-known company, came to Karin to keep her New Year's resolution:

to deal with her anxiety in a healthier way. She sought help in being able to speak up and express her opinions in managers' meetings. On their first meeting, Tina impressed Karin as a very poised, strong woman. However, during the first interview a different picture emerged. With great pain she revealed her anxieties, which she had kept secret for twenty-four years.

Tina's main fear is being the center of attention and having to express her opinions. As a high-level business manager, she happens to work only with men. She feels she must struggle for respect and to maintain her position when interacting with her colleagues in meetings. Consequently, she is constantly aware of how she verbally presents herself, trying to portray herself in a "professional manner." Tina does not avoid speaking up; however, anxiety accompanies her in all her efforts. She feels she expends a tremendous amount of energy when participating in managers' meetings: "It's with me all the time. It is like wanting to climb a mountain and having to carry a big rock with me. So whatever I do, I have to work twice as hard."

In order to manage these situations and to protect herself, she often detaches mentally from her feelings. The dissociation allows her to avoid feeling anxious, as evidenced by her statement "I'm nonemotional when I'm doing it." Therefore, according to Tina, whenever she speaks up she comes across as "not nervous at all," and as "very determined and eloquent." In spite of that, she is unable to enjoy what she is doing or experience satisfaction or pleasure since the anxiety is only postponed. Afterwards the anxiety hits and she starts ruminating: "Oh, what did they think? I talked too much! They don't like me, I shouldn't have spoken up." "I feel like a babbling idiot who lost control during that meeting"—which left her "drained" and "tired."

Tina suffered from social phobia. Her anxieties had disrupted her life in many ways. She received therapy to help her overcome her fears. We now explain CBGT treatment in more detail, using examples of what Tina did and said. Most of what follows is from the CBGT manual.

BEFORE TREATMENT CAN START

Before treatment can start, careful preparation and organization is required. For the group treatment to be successful and helpful, therapists need to adhere to specific inclusion and exclusion criteria. The following criteria are basic guidelines to consider.

The Structured Interview

The first step is a clinical evaluation to establish the nature and extent of the client's anxiety. Our clients are given the Anxiety Disorder Interview Schedule for *DSM-IV* (ADIS-IV Lifetime). However, failure to meet criteria for social phobia does not necessarily disqualify potential clients, nor does meeting criteria necessarily qualify them. Overly needy, aggressive, loud, or verbose clients can be disruptive for group activities and can impede group cohesion. Similarly, extremely avoidant group members stall the group process and may be better suited for individual treatment. On rare occasions, a social phobic cannot be treated in a group because the group itself is perceived as an overwhelming threat.

Social phobics with concurrent anxiety disorders or mood disorders more severe than the social phobia are inappropriate for a treatment that focuses mainly on social phobia. In such cases, the more severe disorder has to be taken care of first. On the other hand, social phobics who are depressed over their social dysfunction but are not suicidal or psychomotorically retarded are appropriate candidates.

In general, social phobics on psychoactive medications should be advised to see their physician about tapering off medication before treatment starts. One problem with medication is that clients tend to attribute any improvement to the drug rather than to their own efforts, thus undermining the cognitive-behavioral rationale for therapy. If clients or their physicians do not agree to taper off medication before therapy, however, or if clients have found tapering too difficult in the recent past, psychological treatment can still be offered as the best chance for improvement. The possibility of tapering can be raised again at a later point in therapy.

The Second Interview as Preparation for the Treatment

Once selected, the client is asked to come in for a second interview, which mainly serves for planning the individualized "fear and avoidance hierarchy." The hierarchy is a rank-ordered list of the client's feared social situations; it serves as a guide for the therapist in developing a contract with the client regarding the goals of treatment and in selecting target situations for attention during group sessions. Its use in that context is described under the heading Exposure Simulations later in this chapter. Finally, the cognitive-behavioral treatment approach is introduced in a way that encourages the expression of clients' questions and doubts.

The individualized fear and avoidance hierarchy is established from the client's descriptions of his or her anxiety-provoking situations. The ten most relevant feared situations are ranked-ordered by increasing severity of fear. These situations are often interrelated, in that they are variations of the same social situation. For example, an individual with fear of public speaking imagines her worst scenario as standing in front of authority figures and having to give a prepared talk without any interruptions. A less anxiety-provoking situation would be either sitting down or having the audience interrupt her, momentarily taking away the spotlight. With regard to our clinical example, for Tina the worst fear was speaking up in a managers' meeting.

In order to be able to create the hierarchy, it is necessary that therapist and client have an emotional intensity scale in common. Therefore, the Subjective Units of Discomfort Scale (SUDS) is introduced, a subjective scale for measuring the client's anxiety from 0 to 100 with defined anchors. 0 is defined as no anxiety: the client feels very relaxed, on the verge of sleep. One hundred is the worst or greatest anxiety the client has ever experienced or could ever imagine when confronting a feared situation. Fifty is the anxiety level that is high enough to start interfering with the task at hand. A rating of 75 means that the anxiety level is so severe that the client becomes preoccupied with it, and he or she has thoughts of escaping from it.

The amount of anxiety elicited by possible anxiety-provoking situations is rank-ordered by asking the clients for their SUDS rating. Therapists briefly describe an anxiety-provoking situation and then ask "What would your SUDS be in that situation?" Clients learn to respond quickly with a number between 0 and 100. The SUDS is a way to define anxiety in numbers, resulting in a very precise and concise communication between therapist and client.

Hierarchy planning also includes a verbal contract or treatment goal. The contract represents an agreement between therapist and client to work on one central anxiety-provoking social situation and its variations. Setting a treatment goal gives clients clarity, structure, and orientation during the course of treatment. It is especially helpful for clients with more generalized social phobia to understand that it is not possible to tackle every single social situation, given the short duration of treatment. Furthermore, social phobics who are afraid of a variety of social situations (including dating, group interactions, and public speaking) may want to concentrate on a single problem. Tina agreed to work on her fear of becoming the center of attention by speaking up.

The remaining interview time is used for the therapist to describe details of the treatment and respond to specific questions and uncertainties, and for organizational preparation such as deciding the location and time of therapy. During the treatment description, the cognitive-behavioral approach is explained in understandable terms with individualized examples, emphasizing that confronting one's own fears is the best way to overcome them.

OVERVIEW OF COGNITIVE-BEHAVIORAL GROUP TREATMENT

Our CBGT groups took place in twelve weekly sessions, each lasting two and a half hours. Other time arrangements may be just as effective, but the efficacy of alternatives is still uncertain. One of the authors, Richard, is currently doing research on the optimal length of CBGT. The three main components of therapy are

1. Cognitive restructuring
2. Exposure simulations
3. Homework assignments

We first give you a short overview of these components and then discuss them in greater detail in separate sections.

The *cognitive restructuring* process entails the disputing (challenging, refutation) of "automatic thoughts" and the development of "rational responses." The term *automatic thought* (AT) was first coined by Aaron T. Beck. Automatic thoughts are defined as "illogical, negative thoughts about oneself, other people, the future, or the world in general." Dispute of these automatic thoughts focuses on their illogical nature. This means that group members are trained to adopt a questioning attitude toward their automatic thoughts to examine whether they are rational or not. If the disputing is conducted reasonably, the answers derived will lead to a rational response, which is a short summary statement that counteracts group members' illogical ideas.

Exposure simulations are role plays of the group members' feared real-life situations. The group members' task during the an exposure simulation is to perform experiments that test the validity of their automatic thoughts. In addition to testing out thoughts and beliefs, such simulations help group members confront their fears and situations and to learn new coping skills.

The third component of therapy is *homework assignments*, which are carried out between sessions. Homework assignments foster cognitive restructuring skills and let group members practice these skills by confronting their feared situations in the real world. Homework assignments are the link between therapy and real life.

Advantages of Group Treatment

As the term indicates, CBGT is a group, not an individual, treatment. Although group treatment might seem too harrowing for social phobics, it has the considerable advantage of getting social phobics to confront their social fears in a social context from the very first session. By talking about their own fears, group members reveal something that often has been kept secret for a long time. They get multiple chances to test whether these reactions are as negative as they thought. Moreover, by talking in front of others about fear of speaking or of being the center of attention, the social phobic confronts the fear itself.

The group serves as a powerful corrective experience by showing members that they are not the only ones with social anxiety. Moreover, social phobics tend to cover up their problem as much as possible, thinking that this kind of anxiety is an indication of being flawed, abnormal, or mentally ill.

The group gives an opportunity for vicarious learning that can be powerful in promoting progress. It saves time because many group members learn from a therapist's intervention directed to another member. Also, group members may serve as better coping models than a therapist, since in the group members' eyes therapists are often perceived as fearless and confident—unlike themselves.

The group also affords an immediate opportunity to test phobics' distorted beliefs about their own behavior and how other people perceive them. For example, group members may erroneously think that they show visible signs of anxiety in feared situations; this misperception can be corrected by feedback from other group members.

Setting up the Group

Ideally, group treatment is conducted by two cotherapists, a man and a woman. Having therapists of both sexes provides a greater variety of interactions with members. Six members seem to be an ideal group size since that is small enough to give each person individualized attention but big enough to establish group interaction. It's also preferable to have a mixed-sex group, with at least two members of each sex. In addition, clients with different fears can be mixed in the same group with the benefit that all members do not have the same sensitivities and distorted beliefs; this makes it easier for members to help each other be more objective and reasonable.

The setting should be a room with comfortable chairs and enough personal space for each member, since social phobics often have an exaggerated need for their own space. An important piece of equipment is the easel and paper pad, which is used in every session. The easel is used to document the elements of the cognitive restructuring process, specifically to write down automatic thoughts and rational responses so that they can easily be referred to by the group during the disputing phase and also later during the cognitive debriefing phase.

THE TREATMENT SESSIONS

The first two sessions are distinctly different from the following ten sessions in that they are highly didactic. The idea of cognitive restructuring and its important concepts and steps are presented to the group members before they are asked to apply this technique to personal anxiety-provoking situations.

Session 1

The first session begins by outlining the cognitive-behavioral model for social phobia. The concept of social phobia as a learned response, a habit, is introduced. Social phobia consists of three components: physiological, cognitive, and behavioral. The description of the components is followed by a thorough explanation of the three components of treatment, which deal with all the different aspects of the anxiety. The first treatment component, cognitive restructuring, addresses the cognitive part of the anxiety; the second treatment component, exposure simulation, works on both physiological and behavioral components; and the third treatment component, homework assignments, helps unlearn the anxiety response and foster a new habit. It helps the clients generalize their new skills to their natural environment.

A main topic during the first session is the concept of automatic thoughts. Clients learn that thoughts drive emotions, which shape our attitudes and behavior toward social situations. This concept is illustrated by a personal example of a feared situation that one of the cotherapists experienced. Afterwards we elicit automatic thoughts associated with fears of the group members about coming to the first session, and the illogical nature of these thoughts is critically examined. Homework for the next session is for group members to collect examples of their automatic thoughts around stressful situations.

We often observe two difficulties explaining automatic thoughts. The first is that group members have trouble identifying their automatic thoughts. For instance, one group member said: "I'm not aware of negative automatic thoughts. I can't find any; I'm just anxious." In such cases, therapists need to be supportive and encouraging by emphasizing that it can take time to become aware of these thoughts and that that is the reason they are called automatic. The second difficulty is that group members may be aware of their automatic thoughts but have difficulty seeing that their view of social situations might be illogical or distorted. One group member said, "This is my reality. How do you know that this is illogical if it seems real to me?" Therapists must strive to convey that their intention is not to "convince" the client of a different "reality" but to help them consider a different view from the one they presently hold.

Our main concern is with automatic thoughts that are negative, illogical, and maladaptive. When clients ask us whether automatic thoughts can be positive, we say yes. However, such thoughts can also be distorted and illogical. Examples include statements like "I'm going to make a great impression," "I'll get the job," or "I'm going to have fun at the party." We point out that an unrealistically positive thinking style—Pollyanna thinking—must also be rejected. Our intention is not to sell the "power of positive thinking" but to see the situation and its components as rationally and objectively as possible. From a realistic viewpoint, most social threats never lead to overwhelming catastrophic events; but on the other hand, dangers like the possibility of being fired from a job can be real and should not be blindly ignored.

Session 2

The second session focuses on the entire cognitive restructuring process, which includes demonstration of the cognitive distortions, the disputational approach, and the development of rational responses. We review the cognitive restructuring procedures of later sessions, with examples from Tina, in the sections under the heading Cognitive Restructuring.

Other elements include homework review, description of cognitive distortions, how automatic thoughts are detected and disputed, and homework assignments. First, after reviewing the group members' homework, a list of typical categories of cognitive distortions is handed out and explained. Although not crucial for the disputing phase, the list of distortions makes it easier to understand the illogical and misleading nature of automatic thoughts. Second, once the types of cognitive distortions have been explained and discussed, we go on to how these distortions can be challenged. Third, we then practice identifying and disputing automatic thoughts with both a fictional example and with group members' own material derived from the homework review. The results of the disputations are summarized in more reasonable and objective statements, the rational responses.

The largest part of the second session is explanation of cognitive distortions. Covering all the categories of cognitive distortions used in therapy is beyond the scope of this chapter, so we limit ourselves to those most frequently encountered.

All-or-Nothing Thinking. The all-or-nothing thinking style describes a world view that lumps things into dichotomous categories. The world is seen in black and white: people are good or bad, ugly or beautiful, stupid or intelligent. Examples of all-or-nothing thinking are thoughts such as "Everybody hates me," "I will never get a date," "I always get anxious," and "I will make a bad impression." Furthermore, social phobics tend to construe reality in such a way that they end up in the negative realm, since the "black" or negative category is much bigger and closer than their "white," positive one.

Jumping to Conclusions: The Mind-Reading or Fortune-Teller Error. "She doesn't like me" is a statement that is highly reasonable to social phobics. They treat such a thought as a proven fact without any evidence that it is correct. If you ask social phobics for some evidence, they will respond, "I know it! Look at how beautiful she is; she doesn't want to talk to a loser like me." So you ask the client, "How do you know that? Did she tell you that?" And the social phobic responds, "I don't have to ask her, it's too obvious. Besides, she wouldn't give me an answer anyway." This is called mind-reading, acting on assumptions about other people's states of mind as if one had magical access to other people's thoughts. An example of fortune telling is "I will mess up when I give my presentation." The client claims to know what will happen in the future.

Magnification or Minimization. This kind of thinking applies different standards to the same behavior. The importance of one's own achievement is minimized while the same achievement by someone else is exaggerated. Conversely, the importance of one's own mistakes is blown out of proportion while the same mistake by someone else is forgiven and forgotten. This cognitive distortion is also called the "binocular trick."

Disqualifying the Positive. Disqualifying the positive is a biased view of an action. Social phobics are quick to take responsibility for negative outcomes. In addition, they attribute positive outcomes to impersonal forces beyond their control or to other people. For example, a social phobic disqualifies a successful simulated exposure experience by saying that it was not a real-life situation. By discounting the exposure simulation, he ignores the fact that he accomplished the task, for example, that he gave a speech or talked to a stranger.

Should Statements. *Should* statements are the hallmark of perfectionistic thinking. It is not a distortion to have high standards, but the social phobics we have treated seem to hold exceedingly high standards, such as not allowing themselves to stumble over a word or to feel momentarily perplexed and puzzled. These perfectionistic standards are almost impossible to meet. The bottom-line belief is often a version of "I have to be perfect in every single situation." We must add that not all researchers have found this to be true for all social phobics. In some studies, social phobics espouse lower standards—perhaps for protective reasons.

Labeling. Labeling occurs when social phobics observe a behavior, judge it negatively, and then assert that it is a general, characteristic deficit of the individual rather than a single *faux pas*. For example, difficulty conversing on a date is automatically interpreted by a social phobic as meaning that she is inadequate, boring, and incapable of dating at all. The problem with this particular cognitive distortion is that it erases the distinction between correctable errors and stable personality traits.

In summary, cognitive distortions end up increasing the individual's irrational and debilitating anxiety. By viewing and labeling social situations as horrible, awful, or terrible, and oneself as stupid, dumb, or a loser, social phobics set themselves up for emotional pain, social failure, and isolation.

Sessions 3 to 11

After the first two didactic sessions, sessions concentrate on cognitive restructuring, exposure simulations, and homework discussions. These are explained later in the chapter.

Homework Assignments and Review

The success of this model of therapy depends to a great degree on the completion of homework assignments. Sitting in a group once a week for two and a half hours is not enough by itself to achieve significant improvement. Together with clients, therapists need to come up with assignments with specific and measurable behavioral goals for review in the next session. The therapist and client try to find assignments that challenge but do not overwhelm.

Homework assignments can involve all sorts of tasks, depending only on clients' and therapists' creativity. For instance, opportunities for a public-speaking phobic to practice could include church activities, giving toasts at family dinners, short speeches at work, reading stories out loud to friends, or joining Toastmasters International. The therapist should not impose an assignment on the client but work with him or her collaboratively. Once group members understand what homework assignments are about, they often come up with their own ideas and opportunities. A proper "homework attitude" is the desire to actively seek out ways to confront anxieties.

Having assignments with specific and behavioral goals is not sufficient in itself. It is crucial for the transfer of anxiety management skills that group members prepare themselves cognitively for their homework. Before entering the feared situation, they should imagine the specific situation in detail, record the automatic thoughts, identify any cognitive distortions in these thoughts, and dispute them (as described later). The disputing process should then end in a rational response.

Finishing the task does not complete the homework. Group members need to review what happened. They need to recall their cognitive preparation, check whether their goal was completed, determine if anticipated or unanticipated automatic thoughts occurred, and identify the extent to which they used their coping skills. Finally, they are encouraged to give themselves a reward for their efforts.

Since the cognitive steps around the behavioral assignments are very detailed and require a lot of study, we distribute a sheet called "Summary of Homework Procedures" in the third session. It summarizes the steps necessary for cognitive preparation and debriefing. Clients should be aware that cognitive preparation is the main factor in whether behavioral assignments are successfully completed.

The beginning of each session is devoted to review of homework assignments. This is the time where group members have a chance to bring their own life experiences into the sessions. It also provides the therapists with individualized intervention opportunities. In addition, homework reviews can inspire exposure simulations and further treatment planning. It is important to remember, however, that therapists cannot cover every single detail during homework review.

It happens to even the most skilled therapists that group members come to a session only to report that they could not complete their homework assignments. Then it is important for the therapists to find out why. In cases of procrastination or avoidance, it is crucial to determine the underlying automatic thoughts and to challenge them during homework review. If the assignment involved a situation that was too anxiety-provoking, the next week's homework assignment has to be adjusted accordingly. Too much anxiety is not the group member's failure, but rather the result of the therapist's miscalculating how frightening the situation would be.

Therapists can facilitate homework compliance, but ultimately it is up to the client to choose his or her own homework pace. Karin is currently doing research on how to improve the homework attitude. A part of this research is to examine the usefulness of a hand-held computer as an adjunct to CBGT. Group members are taught to use the computer in conjunction with homework assignments. The computer program, based on CBGT principles, is written to give clients systematic guidance in their efforts to cope with social phobia. In addition, the computer keeps a record of what social situations group members actually entered, and of how anxious they felt; this provides feedback to the therapist of client progress.

The Last Session

Because the last session is the end of the therapy, it is special. In this session, after having completed a homework review and one or two exposure simulations, the therapists devote the rest of the time to an open discussion of what has happened. Therapists need to focus on group members' remaining anxieties and suggest specific strategies to overcome them in the future. We stress that the members now know the tools of anxiety management that will help them cope with upcoming anxiety-provoking situations.

During the final discussion, some group members may express disappointment that they did not manage to eliminate their social anxiety. This gives the therapists an opportunity to reiterate that anxiety is a normal human feeling that cannot be completely done away with. But with cognitive behavioral management they can cope such that they no longer feel victimized by their anxiety. Anxiety management reduces the distress and interference caused by anxiety without completely eliminating the anxiety itself. In fact, well-managed anxiety provides us with energy that can help us perform efficiently.

Last but not least, as with every skill that one wants to maintain and keep well tuned, what was learned in the group needs continuing practice. Group members are encouraged to think of therapy as a one-year treatment even though the sessions only last three months. The homework attitude needs to be maintained indefinitely.

Booster Sessions

Booster sessions are one-on-one sessions offered to the clients once the treatment is completed. There is no established policy on how many booster sessions therapists give, but we ordinarily offer one individual booster session to each group member at the end of treatment. Booster sessions can be helpful in providing former group members with the knowledge that they will have somewhere to go for competent advice when having to face unusual difficulties.

COGNITIVE RESTRUCTURING

Automatic thoughts lack logic. Staying logical and reasonable during the cognitive restructuring process eventually leads to rational responses. In essence, the process of cognitive restructuring involves four important steps.

Eliciting Automatic Thoughts (ATs)

The therapists can start uncovering automatic thoughts by having the group member imagine the feared situation he or she will be working on. Instructions like "Play a movie in your head" or "Visualize the situation as vividly as you can and focus on what is going on in your mind" can be helpful in eliciting automatic thoughts. Additional questions like "If worse comes to worst, what do you think might happen?" or "What are you afraid of?" can help the group member identify these thoughts. Another approach is to say: "Think about your last experience. What actually happened? Why do you think you have to avoid these situations?"

Some clients may be too embarrassed to share their automatic thoughts in front of the whole group. In those cases, questions that do not directly refer to anxiety or fear can help identify their automatic thoughts. "What are you worried about?" or "What are you concerned about?" may be less threatening to the client because the words *worry* and *concern* sound less pathological than *anxiety*. After the therapists have some success in getting clients to acknowledge automatic thoughts, clients usually pick up the ball and identify these thoughts themselves.

The initially elicited automatic thoughts have to be examined further to get to the bottom line: the core belief that most pointedly expresses the source of unreasonable anxiety. In the beginning of treatment the therapists should elucidate the sequence of thoughts leading to the core belief. This excerpt, which emerged in an early stage of Tina's therapy, illustrates our approach:

Tina: I'll get very anxious and then I'll lose my train of thought. And that's horrible.

Karin: Two automatic thoughts are right there: "I'll get very anxious" and "I'll lose my train of thought." OK, let's go a step further. Why is it so horrible for you to lose your train of thought?

Tina: (fidgety) Because I won't be able to get back on track and I'll get more and more nervous, which is awful.

Karin: Bear with me, Tina. It's painful if anxiety spirals up like that. . . . Let's look at your ATs for a moment. They are "I won't be able to get back" and "I'll get more anxious." Now, say you're losing your train of thought and you are getting more and more anxious. What do you think might happen next?

Tina: (blurts out) I'm standing there, sort of mouth-dead and shaky. Everybody is staring at me, everybody can feel me getting more and more anxious and they are all noticing my weakness.

Karin: Here we go! There are a bunch of automatic thoughts: "I will be mouth-dead," "Everybody is staring at me," "Everybody can see my anxiety, can see me getting very anxious," and "Everybody will notice my weakness." And then?

Tina: This is my worst fear, I couldn't bear it; in such a moment I wish I would die.

Karin: What do you think you might really do in such a moment?

Tina: I think I would run out of the room.

Karin: OK, it seems like your automatic thought "I'll have to run out of the room" is the bottom line. It seems to me your biggest fear is exposing your anxiety to everybody, feeling awfully embarrassed and humiliated, and consequently wanting to die, and having to leave the room (in order to survive).

Tina: Yes, you're right. I've never thought this through.

On the other hand, group members may state the core issue of their anxiety at the outset, and then the therapists need to elucidate the chain of beliefs that starts in the periphery and leads to the core belief. These beliefs should be formulated as behaviorally and specifically as possible.

Identifying Cognitive Distortions

The second step of cognitive restructuring uses the list of cognitive distortions that is distributed in the second session. Questions such as "In what sense do you think this thought is distorted?" or "What kind of cognitive distortions can you find in this thought?" are answered by members of the group. Especially in the initial phase of therapy, it is helpful to ask group members to elaborate how a specific cognitive distortion has been expressed in a specific thought.

Sometimes, group members label an automatic thought as exemplifying a cognitive distortion that does not seem to apply. If that happens, the therapist should ask for clarification. You may be amazed what kind of explanations group members come up with, although from their perspective the label fits. Furthermore, the same aspect of one automatic thought can entail several distortions since cognitive distortions are not mutually exclusive categories.

Challenging the Automatic Thoughts

A third exercise is to challenge the automatic thoughts. Challenging can be difficult for therapists, especially in the beginning of their training. It is advisable to focus on one line of reasoning and not get side-tracked. Challenging is done with the help of "dispute handles," a list of which is distributed in session 2. This list of questions helps group members adopt a questioning attitude, thus guiding themselves toward more reasonable thinking. Examples of dispute handles are:

- How certain are you that your thought or a certain feared outcome will come true? (This question challenges group members' views about the imagined threat of social situations. As illustrated in the first section, it exposes the pattern of exaggerating the chances that a negative event will occur.)

- What is the worst that could happen? (This question highlights the illogical aspect of exaggerating the consequences of a perceived negative event. It challenges the clients' belief that they could not survive the feared outcome or its consequences. Systematically answering this question leads to the realization that the outcome is indeed not as consequential as initially assumed.)

Examples of other questions that promote insight into phobic thinking about feared situations are:

- Could there be any other explanations for that?
- Does being anxious or slow mean that you are stupid, dumb, and worthless?
- Are there other ways to view the situation?
- What would you say to a friend who had the same problem?
- How would a confident person react in that embarrassing moment?
- Ten years from now, how would you evaluate this situation? Was this event really so important that your entire future depended on it?

It is important during the challenging process to keep focused and specific. Successful disputing asks for the specific meaning of terms, such as *boring*, *witty*, or *humorous*. Having the word defined in behavioral terms makes it possible to attack underlying perfectionistic assumptions. Logical questioning serves the purpose of breaking amorphous and vague thinking into concrete and precise steps that can be challenged.

As an example of the process of disputing, here is an excerpt from Tina's cognitive restructuring:

> *Tina:* If I allow myself to experience the anxiety, then I know I will blank. For me blanking is the beginning of the vicious cycle, because if I don't recover then my anxiety spirals upwards and gets out of control . . . and if I'm that nervous I won't be able to go on. And then I think, "that's it." That's the end of the speech. That means, I failed.
>
> *Karin:* OK, let's take the automatic thought "I'll blank" because, as you said, that's the start of the whole chain. Do you know for certain that you will blank in that meeting? (dispute handle)
>
> *Tina:* Well, no, not in every circumstance, but I'm pretty sure I will.

Karin: OK, let's try this one. (Karin decided to drop this approach because she sensed that Tina might hang tightly to that belief.) Does going blank have to equal your failing?

Tina: Yes, in their mind I'm pretty sure, because what they'll do is they'll laugh at me and won't take me seriously, and then I will feel ridiculed.

Karin: How likely is it that they will laugh at you? (dispute handle)

Tina: There's a few people in that meeting who are really going to get their kicks by laughing at other people.

Karin: OK, a few people. How many out of the whole meeting?

Tina: We are ten in the meeting. And there are three or four people, I'm pretty sure, that will laugh and ridicule me.

Karin: OK, 30 or 40 percent of the people in that meeting might laugh at you or ridicule you. Let's leave that for a moment, because I'd like to ask you something else. How would you react if somebody's mind went blank and you were sitting in the audience? (The question is aimed at trying to elicit different perspectives on the situation.)

Tina: I'd feel sympathy for that person, because I know what he or she is going through. Also, for me as part of the audience, I think sometimes pauses are good; they give me some time to reflect on what the speaker said.

Karin: So, you, as part of the audience, view blanking as a welcomed pause, as something positive. Let's go a step further. How would you feel if you as part of the audience would see somebody else making fun of the person who is trying to give a speech? (a question that might trigger another possible perspective)

Tina: I would feel compassion for that person; I would think "Why are they picking on that person?"

Karin: What would you say to that person who was attacked?

Tina: I would say "You are doing your best! You are hanging in there, despite these jerks."

Karin: These are wonderful answers. Do you think you could say it to yourself: "I am doing my best" and "I am hanging in there"?

Tina: I've never said this to myself, but actually, the more I visualize the scene from that point of view, the more I like these replies.

Karin: So let's take these rational responses as yours, OK? Now, going back to the three or four people in that meeting who might ridicule you. After all we said, what would you say about them?

Tina: Actually, I think these people are not very secure themselves, and on top of that, they are jerks.

Karin: Yes, that might very well be. Do you think you could give your talk even if people in the audience ridicule you? (This question is aimed at preparing her for the worst outcome. See the section Exposure Simulations.)

Tina: Yes, I think I could, because after all the talking we did in here, I think normal people wouldn't do this. It'll hardly ever happen, and if it does it just means I'm in the wrong group.

Karin: I'm impressed by your answer. Despite feeling afraid of being ridiculed, you are doing it, you are hanging in there. These are excellent rational responses: "I'm doing my best" and "I am hanging in there, even if I feel anxious."

Developing a Rational Response That Addresses the Automatic Thought

As in Tina's example above, a rational response is a summary statement of the foregoing disputing process. It represents a more realistic and rational thought or statement that helps group members adopt an approach rather than an avoidance attitude. A rational response is task-focused rather than anxiety-focused, and it helps group members stay with the feared situation. Group members should be discouraged from using thoughts like "I may have a fantastic time at the party." Instead they should create rational responses oriented towards an objective goal or task rather than towards a positive mood or state that may be outside their control. As clients change their thinking habits, alternative and more reasonable thoughts begin to seem less foreign and more natural; they may eventually become second nature.

A challenging, questioning approach is the engine of every cognitive-behavioral therapy. This concrete four-step program of (1) eliciting automatic thoughts, (2) identifying cognitive distortions, (3) challenging the automatic thoughts, and (4) developing a rational response offers group members the opportunity to become their own cognitive restructuring therapists.

Goal Setting. After client and therapist agree on a rational response, they discuss in detail how the simulation will be conducted. Then they set a goal for the simulation. An acceptable goal is attainable, measurable, specific, and under the group member's control. Vague and perfectionistic goals based on feelings have to be avoided. Lowered anxiety is reasonable for a long-term goal, but it has to be translated into behaviorally defined steps if it is to be manageable and achievable. A good goal is one for which everybody in the room can see whether or not it has been met; anxiety and calmness can be hard to observe. Also, a good goal is under the client's control, so its focus has to be on his or her own behavior rather than on other people's since the latter can be difficult to control. For instance, the goal of giving a presentation should not be to capture the attention of every listener but to present the required information.

> *Karin:* What's your goal for the exposure simulation?
> *Tina:* That I can maintain my focus and my calmness and not go blank.
> *Karin:* That's a pretty vague goal and hard to measure,

which makes it hard to achieve. How about a more measurable, specific goal which is under your control?

Tina: I can bring myself back to my focus, if I get unfocused or distracted.

Karin: That's almost OK. The only thing is how can you do that? What could be a measurable sign to see that you are task-focused? We all would like to see whether you've met your goal. What's your job in that meeting?

Tina: My task is to offer opinions.

Karin: Good. Could your goal be to offer, say, two opinions?

Tina: Yes, I think I could offer two opinions.

Karin: Great! Let's go with that.

EXPOSURE SIMULATIONS

Exposure simulations are role plays of real-life situations. They are designed to reproduce the client's feared real-life situation as closely as possible. Exposure simulations have several advantages over real-life situations. First, they are available when needed so that you can do them when you choose. Second, they are under therapist control to the extent that group members can be instructed to act in ways that lead the target member to experience feared outcomes under controlled conditions. Third, targeted group members can be monitored and observed by therapists, making immediate interventions possible. Fourth, honest feedback and exchange of ideas can be provided afterwards. And finally, exposure simulations can be tailored to the group members' anxiety, exposing them to challenging yet manageable anxiety levels.

One rationale for exposures is to provide tangible proof that feared consequences are not as likely to occur as the member assumed. And if feared consequences do occur, they are most likely to turn out to be a "normal" and natural part of human life, not as horrible as anticipated.

Guidelines and Rules for Exposure Simulations

The CBGT manual suggests having three exposures in each session; this permits four or five exposures per client in a twelve-session treatment with a six-member group. Simulations should reflect the client's ultimate therapy goal as targeted in the second interview—for example, dating or speaking in public. The hierarchies created in that interview are used for planning the sequence of exposure simulations, which begin in session 3. Since hierarchies of ten situations were created, there is time in the therapy only to work on half of them. They should be done in order of increasing difficulty. A rule of thumb is to begin with a situation estimated to provoke a SUDS level of 50 or 60. The worst fear on each member's hierarchy is saved until later. Of course, all situations, regardless of whether they were chosen for exposure simulations, need to be practiced as homework.

Each exposure simulation has to be carefully planned. It is important to make exposure simulations realistic, even if role players of the appropriate age and sex need to be brought in from outside the group. Also, the simulation needs to elicit group members' specific worries. For social phobics, embarrassing moments and feared outcomes need to be incorporated into the exposure simulations or else the effectiveness of the exposure suffers. Role players can be instructed to be aloof, quiet, challenging, abrupt, distant, or overly friendly and warm, features which may add or subtract from the client's anxiety.

Pointing out anxiety symptoms to group members by saying such things as "Hey, I noticed your forehead is sweating. Is it hot in here?" sounds inhuman or cruel at first. However, not saying anything only repeats what they ordinarily experience in life, while putting their worst fear into words is therapeutic because it forces the group member to find ways to cope with that fear. Responding to the challenge means learning to cope.

Interrupting the exposure whenever the SUDS level jumps up in order to "rescue" a group member is a mistake. Fluctuations in anxiety can be a response to situational variables that make some moments more anxiety-provoking than others. Anxiety usually begins to abate after several minutes; in some cases, however, anxiety shoots up and stays up. If anxiety spirals upwards and interferes with the exposure simulation by producing spurious behaviors such as joking, fits of coughing, or obvious psychological withdrawal, the simulation has to be interrupted for a moment. This is a good time to inquire about automatic thoughts and what rational responses can be substituted before continuing.

SUDS Ratings and Rational Responses During the Exposure Simulation

As mentioned above, during the ten-minute exposure simulations target group members are interrupted every minute to state aloud their anxiety level. The purpose behind this is threefold: first, it provides therapists with exact feedback about what is most anxiety-provoking. Second, it gets group members to be aware of fluctuations in their anxiety, since anxiety-provoking situations are often regarded as global and amorphous. Third, being prompted for SUDS ratings is a cue for the target group member to read his or her rational response out loud from the easel. The repetitive interruption for SUDS rating and the reading of the rational response helps clients learn to shift their focus from the feeling of anxiety (SUDS rating) to the task at hand in the outside environment and ways to cope with it (rational response).

Cognitive Debriefing

Cognitive debriefing is the time to review and summarize SUDS ratings, automatic thoughts, coping strategies, goal achievement, and learning experiences. Questions such as "Did you meet your goal?" "What happened at that point when your SUDS level shot up to an 85?" and "How did you get down?" can lead into fruitful discussions about coping. It is useful to ask group members directly what they learned from an exposure simulation. Here is an example:

> *Karin:* Tina, did you meet your goal?
>
> *Tina:* Yes I did.
>
> *Karin:* Congratulations! You expressed your opinions, so you did meet your goal. Actually, I think you exceeded it, because you supported your opinions with arguments. Tina, did you feel out of control? (one of her ATs)
>
> *Tina:* No, but there were some times where I thought, "Gee, I could have said that a little better, but it wasn't so bad."
>
> *Karin:* I think there's an automatic thought: "I could have expressed it in a better way." Or "I should have expressed myself in a better way."
>
> *Bill (another group member):* And also disqualifying the positive— she said it and she said it well.
>
> *Karin:* Yes, Bill spotted it right away. All we could hear were good statements, Tina. And they *were* good. We could not see or hear the standards that were going through your mind.
>
> *Tina:* Hmm . . . you are right, it's all up in my head.

LIMITATIONS OF CBGT

Although powerful, CBGT has its limitations. As with many therapies, clients who are verbally expressive, self-reflective, and motivated seem to fare better than those without these features. In our experience, clients with an active mind and an inquisitive nature, who enjoy exploring new territory, tend to benefit most quickly from the cognitive-behavioral approach. This does not mean that people without these characteristics cannot benefit from CBGT, but only that their pace of improvement may be slower. Two other factors associated with poor treatment outcome are homework noncompliance and depression, although depression has not been a negative predictor in every study. Both factors work against maintaining a motivated attitude and impede progress, even when the therapist is highly skilled.

Certain social phobias are hard to handle with CBGT. Sexual issues can be difficult to work on. Even if the problem of freely discussing sexual issues could be solved, finding practice situations can be difficult. How to intervene during an exposure simulation when the client's worst fears of failure seem to be realized is another challenging problem. In general, when the individual has special needs, individual sessions of cognitive-behavioral therapy may be better, since the therapist has to balance the needs and concerns of individual clients with those of the rest of the group.

Final Comments

Cognitive-behavioral therapy for social phobics is conceptualized as short-term therapy with a clearly stated treatment goal. The goal and length of therapy are established before treatment starts and define the framework and course of therapy. Within this framework, clients and therapists operate in the here and now; interpretations of unconscious factors are not made. The focus is neither on the past nor on personality change, but on the reduction of current life stressors. Therapists and clients form a problem-solving collaboration to improve the client's present life. CBGT prescribes an active and directive role for therapists, who invite clients into a structured dialogue and guide them into more reasonable thinking. The ultimate goal is to direct clients into corrective emotional experiences and behavioral change.

Although the focus of cognitive-behavioral therapy is on the here and now, group members are not forbidden to share past experiences with the group, as exemplified in Tina's insightful comments:

Tina: I had an amazing experience last Friday. On Friday I had our women's group, where I expressed my opinion.

My number 10 fear, my most intense fear, was speaking up and expressing an opinion in a group of people.

Karin: That's a big step towards your therapy goal.

Tina: Yes, and all these automatic thoughts went through my head—"This might be simplistic," "This might sound stupid"—but I spoke my opinion anyway. And afterwards the group were telling me they were glad that I said something. They said every time I contributed it has been very thoughtful.

Karin: So in other words, your automatic thoughts turned out to be wrong!

Tina: Yeah! I was standing there and I was so overwhelmed by their feedback and by the fact that I said something. Also, I have to tell you this. As I was driving away from the group meeting, all these thoughts started coming out and I knew why I have this problem. When I was growing up I was very inquisitive and real curious, and every time I asked a question the response of my parents would be "That's a stupid question" or "That's really childish, why did you ask that?" And here is my worst fear, my worst intense fear of speaking up and expressing an opinion.

Karin: These are powerful insights. And your awareness of them means you can change and challenge them. In other words, you don't have to respond automatically anymore.

Tina: Yeah! And then—I really have to tell you this—when I had my manager's meeting on Wednesday, I expressed an opinion. But what was even more important is that for the first time I could allow myself to feel the anxiety. For the first time, I felt connected!

NOTES

P. 245, *If severe enough:* Schneier, F. R, Heckelman, L. R., Garfinkel, R., Campeas, R., Fallon, B. A., Gitow, A., Street, L., Bene, D. D., & Liebowitz,

M. R. (1994). Functional impairment in social phobia. *Journal of Clinical Psychiatry, 55,* 322–331.

P. 245, *It is the most common anxiety disorder:* Kessler, R. C., McGonagle, K. A., Zhao, S., Nelson, C. B., Hughes, M., Eshleman, S., Wittchen, H. U., & Kendler, K. S. (1994). Lifetime and 12-month prevalence of DSM-III-R psychiatric disorders in the United States. *Archives of General Psychiatry, 51,* 8–19.

P. 245, *social phobia also represents a risk factor for both alcoholism and depression:* Schneier, F. R., Johnson, J., Hornig, C. D., Liebowitz, M. R., & Weissman, M. M. (1992). Social phobia: Comorbidity and morbidity in an epidemiologic sample. *Archives of General Psychiatry, 49,* 282–288; Chambless, D. L., Cherney, J., Caputo, G. C., & Rheinstein, B. J. G. (1987). Anxiety disorders and alcoholism: A study with inpatient alcoholics. *Journal of Anxiety Disorders, 1,* 29–40.

P. 245, *The individual fears:* American Psychiatric Association. (1994). *Diagnostic and statistical manual of mental disorders* (4th ed., p. 416). Washington, DC: Author.

P. 246, *Vicious circles provide us with an explanation:* Clark, D. M., & Wells, A. (1995). A cognitive model of social phobia. In R. Heimberg, M. Liebowitz, D. Hope, & F. Schneier (Eds.), *Social phobia: Diagnosis, assessment, and treatment* (pp. 69–94). New York: Guilford Press; Heimberg, R. G., Juster, H. R., Hope, D. A., & Mattia, J. I. (1995). *Cognitive behavioral group treatment for social phobia: Description, case presentation, and empirical support.* In M. B. Stein (Ed.), *Social phobia: Clinical and research perspectives* (pp. 293–321). Washington, DC: American Psychiatric Press.

P. 246, *Attempts to hide and cover up:* Barlow, D. H. (1988). *Anxiety and its disorders.* New York: Guilford Press.

P. 248, *Cognitive Behavioral Group Treatment (CBGT):* Heimberg, R. G. (1991). *A manual for conducting cognitive-behavioral group therapy for social phobia* (2nd ed.). Unpublished manuscript, State University of New York at Albany, Center for Stress and Anxiety Disorders, Albany.

P. 248, *CBGT has been demonstrated:* Heimberg, R. G., Dodge, C. S., Hope, D. A., Kennedy, C. R., Zollo, L., & Becker, R. E. (1990). Cognitive behavioral group treatment of social phobia: Comparison to a credible placebo control. *Cognitive Therapy and Research, 14,* 1–23.

P. 248, *maintained at a 4.5- to 6.25-year follow-up:* Heimberg, R. G., Salzman, D., Holt, C. S., & Blendell, K. (1993). Cognitive behavioral group treatment of social phobia: Effectiveness at 5-year follow-up. *Cognitive Therapy and Research, 27,* 325–339; Heimberg, R. G., Juster, H. R., Brown, E. J., Holle, C., Makris, G. S., & Leung, A. W. (1994, November 10–13). *Cognitive-behavioral versus pharmacological treatment of social phobia: Posttreat-*

ment and follow-up effects. Poster presented at the annual meeting of the Association for Advancement of Behavior Therapy, San Diego.

P. 248, *The interested reader can find descriptions:* Hope, D. A., & Heimberg, R. G. (1990). Dating anxiety. In H. Leitenberg (Ed.), *Handbook of social and evaluative anxiety* (pp. 217–246). New York: Plenum; Hope, D. A., & Heimberg, R. G. (1993). Social phobia and social anxiety. In D. H. Barlow (Ed.), *Clinical handbook of psychological disorders: A step-by-step treatment manual* (2nd ed., pp. 99–136). New York: Guilford Press; Hope, D. A., & Heimberg, R. G. (1994). Social phobia. In C. Last & M. Hersen (Eds.), *Adult behavior therapy casebook* (pp. 125–138). New York: Plenum Press; Heimberg, R. G., Juster, H. R., Hope, D. A., & Mattia, J. I. (1995). Cognitive behavioral group treatment for social phobia: Description, case presentation and empirical support. In M. B. Stein (Ed.), *Social phobia: Clinical and research perspectives* (pp. 293–321). Washington, DC: American Psychiatric Press.

P. 250, *(ADIS-IV Lifetime):* Di Nardo, P. A., Brown, T. A., & Barlow, D. H. (1994). *Anxiety disorders interview schedule for DSM-IV lifetime.* New York: Graywind Publications.

P. 251, *Subjective Units of Discomfort Scale (SUDS):* Wolpe, J., & Lazarus, A. A. (1966). *Behavior therapy techniques.* New York: Pergamon Press.

P. 253, *first coined by Aaron T. Beck:* Beck, A. T. (1967). *Depression: Clinical, experimental, and theoretical aspects.* New York: Harper & Row. Republished (1970) as *Depression: Causes and treatment.* Philadelphia: University of Pennsylvania Press.

P. 253, *Automatic thoughts are defined:* Heimberg, R. G. (1991). *A manual for conducting cognitive-behavioral group therapy for social phobia* (2nd ed.). Unpublished manuscript, State University of New York at Albany, Center for Stress and Anxiety Disorders, Albany.

P. 257, *Our main concern:* Persons, J. B. (1989). *Cognitive therapy in practice: A case formulation approach.* New York: Norton.

P. 257, *First, after reviewing the group members' homework:* Burns, D. D. (1980). *Feeling good: The new mood therapy.* New York: Morrow; Persons, J. B. (1989). *Cognitive therapy in practice: A case formulation approach.* New York: Norton.

P. 259, *the "binocular trick":* Burns, D. D. (1980). *Feeling good: The new mood therapy.* New York: Morrow.

P. 259, *It is not a distortion to have high standards:* Juster, H. R., Heimberg, R. G., Frost, R. O., Holt, C. S., Mattia, J. I., & Faccenda, K. (in press). Social phobia and perfectionism. *Personality and Individual Differences.*

P. 259, *In some studies, social phobics espouse lower standards, perhaps for protective reasons:* Alden, L. E., Bieling, P. J., & Wallace, S. T. (1994). Perfectionism in an interpersonal context: A self-regulation analysis of dysphoria and social anxiety. *Cognitive Therapy and Research, 18,* 297–316.

P. 259, *Labeling occurs:* Persons, J. B. (1989). *Cognitive therapy in practice: A case formulation approach.* New York: Norton.

P. 261, *Then it is important for the therapists to find out why:* Leung, A. W., & Heimberg, R. G. (in press). Homework compliance, perceptions of control, and outcome of cognitive-behavioral treatment of social phobia. *Behaviour Research and Therapy.*

P. 266, *Challenging is done with the help of "dispute handles":* Sank, L. I., & Shaffer, C. S. (1984). *A therapist's manual for cognitive-behavior therapy in groups.* New York: Plenum.

P. 274, *Two other factors associated with poor treatment outcome:* Klosko, J. S., Heimberg, R. G., Becker, R. E., Dodge, C. S., & Kennedy, C. R. (1984, November 1–4). *Depression, anxiety, and the outcome of treatment for social phobia.* Paper presented at the annual meeting of the Association for Advancement of Behavior Therapy, Philadelphia; Holt, C. S., Heimberg, R. G., & Hope, D. A. (1990, November 1–4). *Success from the outset: Predictors of cognitive-behavioral therapy outcome among social phobics.* Paper presented at the annual meeting of the Association for Advancement of Behavior Therapy, San Francisco.

ABOUT THE AUTHORS

Richard Almond, M.D., is a psychiatrist and psychoanalyst in private practice in Palo Alto, California. He is a clinical professor of psychiatry at the Stanford Medical School, and a member of the faculty of the San Francisco Psychoanalytic Institute. Dr. Almond went to Harvard College and received his medical and psychiatric training at Yale Medical School. He is the author of *The Healing Community: Dynamics of the Therapeutic Milieu* (1974) and (with Barbara Almond) *The Therapeutic Narrative: Fictional Relationships and Therapeutic Process* (1996), as well as professional articles in psychiatry and psychoanalysis.

Richard Carr, Psy.D., is a clinical psychologist and assistant professor of clinical psychiatry at the University of Medicine and Dentistry of New Jersey—Robert Wood Johnson Medical School in Piscataway, New Jersey, where he has been studying behavioral and psychophysiological factors in panic disorder and asthma. He has published the results of several studies on the relationship between these two disorders.

Patricia Marten DiBartolo, Ph.D., received her doctoral degree at the State University of New York, University at Albany. Her research interests include assessment and treatment of anxiety disorders in children and adults. She is currently an assistant professor at Smith College, Northhampton, Massachusetts.

Wolfgang Fiegenbaum, Ph.D., is president of the Christoph Dornier Foundation for Clinical Psychology, which has research and therapy centers in Münster and at the universities of Braunschweig, Dresden, and Marburg. He is a professor of clinical psychology at the University of Marburg, Germany. Dr. Fiegenbaum's primary research interests are cognitive behavior therapy, anxiety disorders, affective disorders, and sexual dysfunction. He has written a number of articles on panic disorder and agoraphobia.

Karin Gruber, Dipl. Psych., was educated at Syracuse University in New York and Philipps University, Marburg/Lahn, Germany, obtaining her diploma in clinical psychology in 1991. After working as a clinical psychologist treating anxiety disorders, in 1993 she came to the Stanford University School of Medicine, where she conducted her Ph.D. research project on the adjunctive use of computers in the treatment of social phobia. She is currently working as a research associate with Walton T. Roth, M.D., in the Department of Psychiatry and Behavioral Sciences and at the Veterans Affairs Palo Alto Health Care System. She has received special training in cognitive-behavioral therapy in Germany and the United States.

Richard G. Heimberg, Ph.D., received his doctoral degree in clinical psychology in 1977 from Florida State University. After completing his internship at West Virginia University Medical School Consortium and a postdoctoral year at Florida State, he joined the faculty of the clinical psychology training program at the State University of New York, Albany, where he was a professor and director of the social phobia program of the University's Center for Stress and Anxiety Disorders. Dr. Heimberg recently moved to Philadelphia where he is a professor of psychology at Temple University. He has published two books and over 120 articles and chapters, mostly on the topics of social phobia, information processing biases in the anxiety disorders, and cognitive-behavioral assessment and treatment. He currently serves as associate editor for the journal *Cognitive and Therapy Research* and sits on the editorial boards of five other scientific journals.

Stefan G. Hofmann, Ph.D., is a research scientist at the Center for Stress and Anxiety Disorders, Phobia and Anxiety Disorders Clinic in Albany, New York. Dr. Hofmann was formerly a visiting scholar at Stanford University School of Medicine and the Veterans Affairs Palo Alto Health Care System and assistant professor (wissenschaftlicher Angestellter) at the University of Dresden, Germany. Among his primary research interests are the psychopathology and treatment of social phobia, specific phobia, and panic disorder.

Paul Lehrer, Ph.D., is a clinical psychologist and professor of psychiatry at The University of Medicine and Dentistry of New Jersey—Robert Wood Johnson Medical School in Piscataway, New Jersey, where he heads the Center for Stress Management and Behavioral Medicine. He studied progressive relaxation under the tutelage of Edmund Jacobson and has been a major contributor to the research literature on progressive relaxation and on specific effects of various self-regulation therapies. He has received several federal grants to study respiratory factors in stress and relaxation and is coeditor of the widely acclaimed text *Principles and Practice of Stress Management*, now in its second edition.

Joseph W. Lenz, Ph.D., received his doctoral degree in clinical psychology from the University of British Columbia in Vancouver, where he continues to work as a research associate. Ongoing research projects include evaluation of effectiveness of brief crisis-oriented inpatient psychiatric programs and the development of a brief psychological treatment for essential hypertension. He has conducted research on nonclinical panic attacks and has worked as a therapist in hospital-based programs treating panic disorder, generalized anxiety disorder, obsessive-compulsive disorder, depression, headache, and irritable bowel syndrome.

Wolfgang Linden, Ph.D., is professor of clinical psychology at the University of British Columbia in Vancouver. He was born in Germany and received his initial education in psychology at the University of Münster; he obtained his Ph.D. from McGill University in 1981 and has been at the University of British

Columbia since then. He maintains an active research program on psychological factors in cardiovascular disorders and has published a number of chapters, a major review paper, and *Autogenic Training: A Clinical Guide* (1990).

Jürgen Margraf, Ph.D., has been professor of clinical psychology and psychotherapy at the Technical University of Dresden in Germany since 1993. He obtained his doctoral degree in clinical psychology from the University of Tübingen on the basis of work done at Stanford University from 1983 to 1986. Subsequently he was assistant professor in Marburg from 1986 to 1991 and professor of clinical psychology at the Free University in Berlin from 1992 to 1993. His primary research interests are cognitive-behavioral therapy of anxiety disorders, diagnostic assessment of mental disorders, and public health. Dr. Margraf is currently chairman of the Department of Psychology in Dresden. He is author or coauthor of over 200 publications and is on the editorial board of several scientific journals.

Matig R. Mavissakalian, M.D., is professor of psychiatry at Ohio State University in Columbus. Since 1986 he has directed the Phobia and Anxiety Disorders Clinic at the Medical Center. He received his M.D. degree from the American University, Beirut, Lebanon; after psychiatric training in the United States he began a highly productive academic and research career. A major focus of his research has been to test the efficacy of combined pharmacological and behavioral treatment of panic attacks and agoraphobia. He is author of over thirty research publications and reviews.

Walton T. Roth, M.D., is chief of the Psychiatric Consultation Service of the Veterans Affairs Palo Alto Health Care System and professor of psychiatry and behavioral sciences at the Stanford University School of Medicine. After completing his medical education at the New York University School of Medicine, he came to Stanford for his psychiatric residency, where he has remained most of the time since. He is author of more than 125 articles on the psychophysiology of psychiatric disorders. Recently, he and his students have been measuring the physiological reactions of phobics when confronting their feared situations: flying phobics in an airplane, driving phobics driving on a freeway, agoraphobics walking in a shopping mall, social phobics giving an impromptu speech, and self-conscious blushers singing a silly song.

Martina Ruhmland, Dipl. Psych., is a doctoral candidate at the Christoph Dornier Foundation for Clinical Psychology at the University of Dresden, Germany, where she is engaged in the treatment of anxiety disorders in adults. Her primary research topics are cognitive and psychophysiological mechanisms in the development of anxiety disorders in children of anxiety patients.

Martin T. Ryan, M.D., is a Phi Beta Kappa graduate of Ohio Wesleyan University with majors in philosophy, pre-theology, and pre-medicine. He earned his M.D. degree at Ohio State University, where he is a fourth-year resident and clinical instructor in the Department of Psychiatry. He lives in Delaware, Ohio.

Silvia Schneider, Ph.D., is director of the Christoph Dornier Foundation for Clinical Psychology at the University of Dresden, Germany. She is a behavior therapist and a supervisor of behavior therapy. Before taking her current position, Dr. Schneider was assistant professor of psychology at the Universities of Marburg and Berlin. Her primary research interests are cognitive behavior therapy for anxiety disorders, familial transmission of anxiety disorders, and the use of structured interviews for diagnosing mental disorders.

Brunna Tuschen, Ph.D., is a researcher and lecturer in the Department of Clinical Psychology, University of Marburg. Among her primary research interests are cognitive and behavioral therapy with patients suffering from anxiety disorders, eating disorders, and infertility. She has developed a method for treating patients with bulimia nervosa in outpatient and inpatient settings and is presently conducting research to evaluate its effectiveness. In addition, Dr. Tuschen is carrying out research on the mechanisms of psychological disorders.

Frank Wilhelm, Ph.D., received his doctoral degree in clinical psychology in 1996 from the Philipps University, Marburg/Lahn, Germany on the basis of work he did at Stanford University from 1992 to 1996. At Stanford, he investigated autonomic and respiratory abnormalities in panic disorder, generalized anxiety disorder, and flying phobia in laboratory and ambulatory settings. His postdoctoral research at the Harvard School of Public Health will focus on psychophysiological mechanisms that increase risk for cardiovascular disease in anxiety disorders.

INDEX